The Postconventional Personality

SUNY series in Transpersonal and Humanistic Psychology

Richard D. Mann, editor

The Postconventional Personality

Assessing, Researching, and
Theorizing Higher Development

Edited by
Angela H. Pfaffenberger
Paul W. Marko
and
Allan Combs

Published by State University of New York Press, Albany

© 2011 State University of New York

For information, contact State University of New York Press, Albany, NY
www.sunypress.edu

Production by Diane Ganeles
Marketing by Anne M. Valentine

Library of Congress Cataloging-in-Publication Data

The postconventional personality : assessing, researching, and
    theorizing higher development / edited by Angela H. Pfaffenberger,
    Paul W. Marko, and Allan Combs.
        p. cm. — (SUNY series in transpersonal and humanistic psychology)
    Includes bibliographical references and index.
    ISBN 978-1-4384-3465-0 (hardcover : alk. paper)
    ISBN 978-1-4384-3464-3 (pbk. : alk. paper)
    1. Transpersonal psychology. I. Pfaffenberger, Angela H., 1957–
II. Marko, Paul W., 1945– III. Combs, Allan, 1942–

BF204.7.P67 2011
155.2'5—dc22   2010025991

10 9 8 7 6 5 4 3 2 1

Contents

PART III:
THEORIES OF ADVANCED DEVELOPMENT

Tables

Introduction

Exceptional Maturity of Personality

An Emerging Field

Angela H. Pfaffenberger
Paul W. Marko

In the third stage, the super-logical, the mind seeks to return to immediacy, to solve the dualism and oppositions inherent in the practical life of thought and action. One or another of the great ideals arises and becomes the place of retreat; and the universal categories of thought, the absolute forms of value, and the various panaceas of feeling erect their claims to final authority. [And so in the grand scheme] the leading motives of development [are seen passing] from perception and memory, through the various phases of the reasoning processes, and finding their consummation in the highest and most subtle of the super-logical, rational, and mystic states of mind.

—Baldwin (1930, p. 13)

This volume, although rooted in Jane Loevinger's work, goes beyond it in significant ways and presents a comprehensive examination of optimal adult development coming out of positive, developmental, and humanistic psychology. The introduction supplies the background and structure for a theory of the maturation of consciousness and introduces the reader to a rudimentary understanding of Loevinger's (1976) model for ego development. It represents the path that most chapters in this text are either explicitly based on or the underpinning from which their work is derived. Additionally, this chapter presents a background into what

1

is known and theorized about how consciousness changes as it expands from one stage to another, and how this expansion appears as lived experience. It ends with an overview of the studies that appear in this volume and the book's overall significance for future research.

Developmental views in philosophy are at least as old as Friedrich Hegel's 1807 publication of *The Phenomenology of the Spirit*. James Mark Baldwin (1861–1934), one of American psychology's founding fathers was keenly aware of the importance of development for the human mind, but did not articulate a systematic theory of it. Since the mid-20th century, however, there has been a growing interest in individual maturation, or what many of the present authors term personal evolution. Especially in the second half of the 20th century, such developmental theorists such as Jean Piaget (1952), Laurence Kohlberg (1969), and Ken Wilber (1986, 1995, 2006) have catalyzed both academic and popular interest in developmental studies. Although Maslow (1954/1970) introduced the concept of *self-actualization and optimal development* into American psychology half a century ago, systematic, empirical research did not begin to emerge until recently under the term *postconventional personality development* (Hewlett, 2004; Miller & Cook-Greuter, 1994; Torbert, 2004). Only in recent years, however, has serious academic attention been turned toward the examination of the most advanced stages of personality growth and development. Contemporary developmental theorists for the first time are chronicling growth paths from birth to advanced stages of maturation (Hy & Loevinger, 1996; Kegan, 1982; Loevinger, 1976; Wade, 1996; Wilber, 1986).

Until a few decades ago it was common to conceive of personal development as beginning at birth and proceeding in an orderly fashion through a sequence of developmental stages culminating in conventional adult functioning. The pioneering work of Jean Piaget (e.g., 1952, 1977b) had led to a model of epigenetic, or structural, levels of growth, a stage theory, according to which cognitive development progresses through an invariant sequence of hierarchically arranged stages that form qualitatively distinct units of development. Conceiving of development in this fashion puts an emphasis on the dynamic aspects of state transitions and allows us as well to conceptualize stages of growth that are empirically rarely seen. Work by Lawrence Kohlberg (1969) and Loevinger (1976) offered the most innovative and influential of the early neo-Piagetian theories, applying stage theory to the domains of moral reasoning and ego development, respectively.

Loevinger (1976) defined an ego stage as a frame of reference or a filter that the individual uses to interpret life experiences. It implies a level of character development, cognitive complexity, an interpersonal style, and a set of conscious preoccupations. Loevinger developed a projective assessment instrument for measuring the level of ego development titled the Washington University Sentence Completion Test (SCT). The SCT translates qualitative observations about personality into quantitative data. Using this test, Loevinger laid the empirical foundation for hundreds of later investigations of adult development.

Loevinger conceptualized nine stages of personality development. The way the stages are named and numbered has changed over time, so the reader is cautioned that the same number may describe different stages in various research reports, and different names may describe the same stage. In this introduction we follow the latest version of the scoring manual (Hy & Loevinger, 1996). The reader is referred to Table I.1, showing names and numbering systems used by different authors in this volume. We can describe the first three, *Symbiotic*, Stage 1; *Impulsive*, Stage 2; and *Self-protective*, Stage 3, as *preconventional*. These stages represent normal developmental stages in childhood, but also are maladaptive strategies in adulthood that can be associated with psychopathologies such as borderline disorders. Individuals at this level fail to understand another's point of view, thus they are devoid of compassion and tend to lead lives narrowly focused on their own personal gain and advantage. Miller and Cook-Greuter (1994) estimate that about 10% of the adult population function at this level.

The following three stages are termed *conventional*. They describe about 80% of all adults in our culture. The fourth stage, *Conformist*, describes individuals who are identified with the values and norms of the social group to which they belong. They strive to express this through appearance and behavior, and are concerned about their reputation and possible disapproval from the group. In the eyes of the Conformist,

Table I.1. Correspondence of Ego Development Models

Stage	Hy and Loevinger 1996		Cook-Greuter 1999	Torbert 2004	Joiner 2007
2	Impulsive	E 2	Impulsive	Impulsive	Enthusiast
3	Self-protective	E 3	Self-protective	Opportunist	Operator
4	Conformist	E 4	Conformist	Diplomat	Conformer
5	Self-aware	E 5	Self-aware	Expert	Expert
6	Conscientious	E 6	Conscientious	Achiever	Achiever
7	Individualist	E 7	Individualist	Individualist	Catalyst
8	Autonomous	E 8	Autonomous	Strategist	Co-Creator
9	Integrated	E 9	Construct Aware	Alchemist	Synergist
10			Unitive	Ironist	

good is what the group approves of. There is strong emphasis on outer, material aspects of life. A rigid black-and-white worldview in regard to what is acceptable in terms of gender roles and opinions predominates. Loevinger emphasized that members of nonconforming groups within the general culture, such as "hippies" or "punks," often show and expect conforming behavior within their own groups.

The fifth level, *Self-aware,* is the modal stage of the majority of adults in the contemporary Western culture (Cohn, 1998). Moving to this stage, adults gain more independence in terms of their ability to reflect on group norms, and there is a growing awareness of an inner life. A person can consider different possibilities and alternatives as well as exceptions to the rules. Cognition and affect, however, remain within established categories and are rather undifferentiated. The *Conscientious* stage, Stage 6, presents a significant step toward further internalization and differentiation. Individuals have established personal standards and values. Moral considerations and responsibilities toward others are now important, as are long-term goals. The Conscientious person strives to understand motivation and individual differences. Situations as well as problems can be seen within specific contexts, and the perspectives of other people are appreciated. In short, the outer direction of the Conformist, Stage 4, has now been fully replaced by an internal orientation that encompasses self-chosen values and standards to which the person strives to achieve.

Stage 7, the *Individualistic* stage, represents the first of several *postconventional* stages. To grow beyond Conscientious, Stage 6, a person must become more inner-directed and more tolerant of themselves and others. The self-established standards of the previous stage must become more contextualized and flexible. Persons at the Individualistic stage become aware of contradictions, such as the conflict between their need for autonomy and their need for emotional connection. They are willing to live with emotional and cognitive complexities that may not be resolvable, and they become more psychologically minded.

The *Autonomous* Stage, Stage 8, and the subsequent Stage 9, *Integrated,* describe about 10% of the U.S. adult population. Autonomous individuals are able to accept conflict as part of the human condition. They tolerate contradictions and ambiguities well and demonstrate cognitive sophistication. The Autonomous person respects the autonomy of others and values close personal relationships. Self-fulfillment and self-expression gain increasing importance in this person's life. High social ideals of justice are also typical of this stage. Unfortunately, Loevinger found it difficult to arrive at a definitive description of Stage 9 because the sample pool of observable subjects at this stage was so small.

Significant work in regard to the higher stages has been completed by Cook-Greuter (1999), who evaluated more than 14,000 SCTs in an effort to understand the complexities of advanced development. She emphasized a cognitive shift that takes place at the Autonomous level, Stage 8, describing it as the embracing of systemic and dialectical modes of reasoning. Such individuals can hold multiple viewpoints and are interested in how knowledge is arrived at. In the language of the post-Piagetians such as Richards and Commons (1990) this constitutes a postformal way of reasoning. Individuals are aware of subjectivity in the construction of reality, accepting interpretation as the basis for the creation of meaning. Cook-Greuter constructed two *postautonomous* stages to replace Loevinger's final Stage 9, and suggested that about 1% of the population reach this level of development. The ninth stage in her system is called *Construct-aware*. At this level, individuals become conscious of how language shapes the perception of reality. Language is experienced as a form of cultural conditioning that people usually remain unaware of throughout their lives.

According to Cook-Greuter (1999) individuals can subsequently progress to an understanding that their egos are actually constructed from memory and maintained through an ongoing internal dialogue. As their self-awareness increases, they become interested in alternative ways of knowing. Transpersonal episodes, such as peak experiences, become increasingly common and people become drawn to meditation, alternate ways of knowing, and the witnessing of the internal process. At this stage, the individual experiences conflict between ordinary consensual reality and transpersonal awareness. This may be evident in the ego's ownership and evaluation of transpersonal episodes, or in seeming paradoxes such as attachment to nonattachment. Only at Stage 10, the *Unitive* stage, can individuals sustain an ongoing openness to experience that is fluid and without struggle. They are now able to make use of transpersonal experiences free from ego clinging. Individuals have been tested who are found to be functioning at the Unitive stage, ranging upward from 26 years of age (S. Cook-Greuter, personal communication, December 3, 2003).

It is important to note that ego development, as conceptualized by Loevinger, is but one conceptualization of maturity; one that places emphasis on cognitive complexity and a mature conceptualization of the individual's position in the social environment. Hy and Loevinger (1996) point out that ego development cannot be seen as an indicator of social adjustment, nor does it suggest mental health and subjective well-being (see also Helson & Srivastava, 2001; Pfaffenberger, 2007).

According to structural developmental theory, all stages must be negotiated in consecutive order. And the level currently experienced sets the stage for the dilemmas that must be resolved before progressing to the next higher stage. Individuals who occupy the higher stages of development must, at some point during their lives, have experienced the earlier stages of development. Virtually all models of higher development maintain that each individual begins at the lowest possible stage and progresses onward through the developmental levels in sequence. Thus, people understand the thinking and worldviews of lower developmental stages, but their comprehension of or empathy toward worldviews at higher levels is limited. When they encounter worldviews that do not fit their existing paradigm, they tend to see them with selective attention, screening out perceptions they do not understand or agree with. This phenomenon can lead to awkwardness between a person who has recently moved to a higher stage of growth and his or her previous cohort members. Movement from one stage of development to another creates moral, philosophical, and behavioral changes. If development proceeds into the highest range it can cause a psychological dissonance with the ambient society that exists in the midrange. Consequently, we can assume that individuals who function at high levels of development have experienced, perhaps on several occasions, alienation from those around them due to changes in worldview. These events may have occurred periodically throughout life and perhaps even began in childhood.

Why rapid development occurs for some and not at all for others remains a mystery. If, as is true in most cases, postconventional individuals were exposed to the same rigors of ordinary life as their cohorts, and subjected to the same growth limiting norms, what has provided the impetus for their extraordinary growth? The following pages address this and other enigmas of postformal personality development as they have begun to be illuminated by contemporary psychological research.

Part I

Assessing Advanced Personality Development

The accelerating interest in postconventional and postautonomous stages of human development has given birth to a number of different forms of inquiry. This volume combines many of these, including longitudinal studies, qualitative inquiry, and theoretical explorations. To set this emerging field on a sound foundation, the accurate assessment of high stage development needs to be an ongoing concern. The first part of the present volume is devoted to this subject.

1

Assessing Postconventional Personality

How Valid and Reliable is the Sentence Completion Test?

Angela H. Pfaffenberger

Jane Loevinger's (1976) theory of ego development evolved simultaneously with the associated instrument, the Washington University Sentence Completion Test (SCT). The theory and the test were entirely data driven. This chapter briefly reviews the psychometric properties of the SCT (Hy & Loevinger, 1996; Loevinger, 1998b), with a special emphasis on the use of the test for measuring advanced development accurately.

Loevinger's (1976) SCT is unlike any other instrument available; it measures the normal range of personality functioning expressed as a developmental variable. The SCT consists of 36 sentence stems. Examples are "Raising a family" and "When a child will not join in group activities." Test-takers are asked to complete the sentence stems. In accordance with the projective hypothesis, it is assumed that participants project their own thoughts and frame of reference onto the completions. A trained rater, using a match-based manual, scores each individual item. Attempts at having the SCT scored by a computer have failed (Loevinger, 1998b). The manual has gone through several revisions with the latest edition being published in 1996 (Hy & Loevinger, 1996). The final ego stage score, called the Total Protocol Rating (TPR), is based on an algorithm of the individual stem ratings. The test translates qualitative data into quantitative developmental categories, thereby allowing for

9

a clear operationalization and assessment of any developmental stage. The modal stages of adult development, the conventional tier of development, are usually considered to consist of Stages 4 to 6. Advanced development, also called the *postconventional* tier, starts with Stage 7, *Individualistic*, and progresses to Stage 8, *Autonomous,* and Stage 9, *Integrated.* Few adults achieve these levels of development and multiple studies (Miller & Cook-Greuter, 1994; Torbert, 2004) have convincingly demonstrated the benefits of such development.

Validity and Reliability of the SCT

This part of the chapter presents the most pertinent and recent findings about the SCT. Technical details about the test can be found in Loevinger (1998b). The available literature that criticizes or supports the construct of ego development theory and its measurement is extensive. The *face validity* of the instrument is demonstrated by the sheer fact that it has been used in more than 300 research studies. These research studies include such diverse topics as parenting behaviors, managerial effectiveness, and effects of meditation on recidivism rates. Compared with structured tests, the psychometric properties of projective instruments are hard to assess, which is further compounded by the fact that the SCT does not intend to predict behavior, measure social adjustment, or evaluate psychopathology. Instead, it is designed to assess a soft construct, the maturity of personality expressed as a developmental variable. Structural-development theories aim to describe an underlying concept that is unique and can be difficult to define. Not only Loevinger (1976) but also Kohlberg (1969) struggled with the fact that a development stage is not clearly expressed in any particular behavior. However, Loevinger (1998b) cogently argued that correlation with real-life data is important, because a test that does not correlate with anything but another test may be of limited value.

Loevinger (1998b) cited good evidence for the sequentiality of the stages as demonstrated through longitudinal data. Kroger (2008) used Rasch scaling to show sequentiality and also demonstrated correlations with Kegan's (1982) assessment tool called the Subject/Object Interview. SCT scores in several studies correlated, as predicted, with interview data and behavioral observations in regard to cognitive complexity and the understanding of psychological mindedness. Manners and Durkin (2001) reviewed evidence for the construct validity of the SCT and concluded that those studies support the construct related evidence for the SCT. Novy and Frances (1992) administered the SCT and a battery of structured personality tests that addressed positive, inner orientations. All correlations were low, usually around .2. Novy (personal communication, May 16, 2005) attributed the low correlations to the fact that ego development is a more abstract concept than any of the other measures used.

Novy and Frances (1992) completed an extensive reliability study of the current form of the SCT. The reliability for the test is good, and it exceeds that of other projective instruments. Internal consistency as evaluated by Cronbach's coefficient α, which establishes the lowest estimate of reliability, is .91. The interrater agreement of the TPR is .94. The SCT has 36 items. Administering the first and second half of the test separately, these authors found a coefficient α of .84 and .81, respectively for each half. The correlation between the two halves was .79. Shorter tests usually are less reliable than longer tests, meaning they contain more error. The extent of the error in the correlation between two tests can be estimated and compensated for through the use of a statistical formula, called *correction of attenuation*. After applying this procedure, the correlation between the two halves of the test rose to .96. Novy and Frances suggested that the two test halves are usable as equivalent forms, although Loevinger (1998b) emphasized that only the complete 36-item form allows for optimal results and should therefore be preferred.

One of the recurring issues for projective tests is standardization of test administration. Loevinger (1998b) specified the number of sentence stems per page because the available space may signal the test taker how much is expected in terms of the completion. The SCT is usually administered as a paper-and-pencil measure to a group with the written instruction of "Complete the following sentences." Loevinger (1998b) pointed out that all tests show inconsistent results if the instructions change, which is not something specific to the SCT. She strongly urged researchers to use the standardized instructions because that would allow a comparison of the results across studies.

Several researchers have experimented with modified instructions (Blumentritt, Novy, Gaa, & Liberman, 1996; Drewes & Westenberg, 2001; Jurich & Holt, 1987). The consensus seems to be that modified instructions, such as "Be mature" or instructions about the concept of ego development allow participants to achieve higher scores, but the increases are small and consistent across several studies, usually only one stage. The fact that significant changes are not achievable attests to the validity of the theory of epigenetic stage sequencing; individuals cannot understand and intentionally move to a higher stage. Jurich and Holt (1987) and Blumentritt et al. (1996) attributed the modest increases to a reduction in the ambiguity of the stimulus. Under conditions of more specific instructional sets, participants become more engaged and achieve their higher scores through better motivation when taking this test. However, Drewes and Westenberg (2001) argued that a person cannot be seen as being at a fixed stage. Instead individuals express a developmental range, with a *functional level* that is evidenced under standardized instruction conditions, and an *optimal level* that is evidenced by more specific instructions. In any given test protocol a person usually gives responses at a variety of levels. The SCT assumes that if a high enough answer is given often enough that this is the modal level of functioning for that person.

A newer concern about test administration deals with computer-based administration. If the test is sent to a research participant as an e-mail attachment, the administration is no longer standardized. As a Word document, the test-taker can change the spaces provided for the answers, and we do not know for sure if the test was actually taken by that person in one session. Only one unpublished study (W. Johnson, personal communication, December 1, 2004) has investigated the issue of computer administration. The results showed that in computer-based testing situations, subjects had a significantly higher word count but ego levels remained unchanged.

Issues concerning the *discriminant* and *convergent* validity of the SCT have probably received the most attention recently. Discriminant or divergent evidence is concerned with the uniqueness of a test and its concept from other psychological constructs. Convergent validity is evidenced by high correlations with other factors or test results. Convergent validity or lack of discriminant validity may present a threat to validity because we may not be measuring what we intend; we may just be measuring an established variable and giving it a new name. At the same time, a variable might be conceptually intertwined with another in a meaningful manner, in which case we want to see convergent validity. Loevinger (1998a, 1998b) convincingly argued that in personality testing, correlations are commonly seen, and it may indeed be hard to find out if this presents a distortion or a meaningful relationship.

Loevinger (1998b) pointed out that the SCT correlates with verbosity, which is quantitative production, at about .31. This may not be spurious, because low ego levels are often indicated through short, bland responses, such as "Education—boring" whereas higher rated stem completions need more words to express complexity. An example would be "Education—is more than what you learn in school." The SCT correlates with education, socioeconomic status, and complexity of work, which has been shown to hold true across international samples. This is not surprising because education and social class relate to aspects of impulse control, goal orientation, and conscious preoccupations, which is exactly what the SCT is meant to assess.

The discriminant validity of the SCT regarding intelligence has been widely debated. Lubinski and Humphreys (1997) specifically argued that personality tests, such as the SCT, add very little to assessments of general aptitude and intelligence. Numerous studies have investigated the discriminant validity of the SCT in regard to intelligence. Cohn and Westenberg (2004) identified 42 such studies and performed a meta-analysis. These authors showed the correlation between the SCT and intelligence tests to be .31 across studies. Consequently, they argued that the discriminant validity is good. Loevinger (1998b) herself argued that almost all tests show some correlation with intelligence because it is indeed an aspect of personality functioning and influences professional aspirations and other aspects of development. Cohn and Westenberg also discussed the *incremental validity*, which addresses the question of whether a test allows for useful inferences that we could not arrive at without it. The authors controlled for intelligence and identified 16 studies that addressed this question. They concluded that the incremental validity varied significantly among different variables being assessed. Ninety-four percent of the studies reported significant relations between criterion variables and the SCT after intelligence is controlled for. Based on their research they rejected the claim by Lubinski and Humphreys that the SCT does not add anything significant to our understanding of personality.

Loevinger (1998b) discussed other potential threats to validity as well. First, there is the size of the sample. Although the original sample was based on only a few hundred completed tests, a few years later Loevinger and her associates made an effort to get in touch with all researchers who had used the test and requested the copies of the tests that they had scored. This led to a sample size of well over 1,000 tests. Second, there is the question of how representative the sample is. Loevinger emphasized repeatedly that the test is not based on a normative sample representing the whole population because her project team never had the resources to undertake a project that would allow for randomized sampling. Because many different researchers contributed, diverse social groups were represented. Although the original sample was strongly weighted toward women, later efforts compensated for this and special efforts were made to review the test items and the scoring manual with that concern in mind. Third, there is the issue of whether the sample presents a limited range. Loevinger stated that she made a special effort to include the research of psychologists, who had participants presenting the extremes at either end of the developmental spectrum, because the general population does not indeed fall into the middle range. She therefore included data from Harvard graduates at midlife as well as the prison population. In general, we can say that Loevinger, with the help of other researchers, accumulated impressive evidence for the validity of the SCT.

Assessing Postconventional Development With the SCT

Loevinger noted that postconventional protocols are rare in the general population, which makes it difficult to study those participants as a group. In the current test manual (Hy & Loevinger, 1996), the directions for scoring protocols at the upper stages remain rudimentary. Participants at those stages of development often exhibit creativity and unconventional interests, which makes it hard to design pertinent matches. Especially the difference between Stage 8, Autonomous, and Stage 9, Integrated, is not well explicated in the current manual. At Stage 8, individuals are concerned with realizing their potential, and they readily acknowledge internal conflict. According to Loevinger, Stage 9 is a more nuanced presentation of the Autonomous stage. Because of the difficulties involved in differentiating the highest stages, she suggested that they could be combined. In most samples less than 5% of the participants score at the final two stages. Loevinger (1998b) cautioned that we need to be careful when extrapolating from the general sample to those individuals who were underrepresented, such as individuals at the upper end of development. Consequently, we have to consider that the excellent psychometric properties of the SCT cannot be generalized to the use of the SCT for postconventional development.

Construct-Related Evidence Using Interview Data

Construct-related evidence for assessing postconventional development with the SCT can be derived from several studies that enrolled participants at postconventional stages of development and scored interview data. The earliest of these studies (Sutton & Swenson, 1983) attempted to validate the SCT through interview data based on the Thematic Apperception Test (TAT). The authors assigned codes to interview and TAT materials based on the SCT scoring manual. They assembled a sample spanning all developmental stages and concluded that the SCT shows excellent concurrent validity compared with the interviews and the TAT for the preconventional and conventional stages of development. However, for the postconventional tier of development, the SCT assigned ego-level scores that were consistently too low. This study had a number of weaknesses, such as a small number of postconventional individuals, and low interrater agreement for the highest stages.

Within the last few years, four qualitative dissertations (Hewlett, 2004; Marko, 2006; Page, 2005; Stitz, 2004) used the SCT to find participants at postconventional stages of development. All studies collected interview data from the participants in addition to administering the SCT. The dissertations enrolled a combined sample pool of about 86 participants, who can be seen as a known group or criterion group at higher development. Consequently, these studies combined constitute a valuable source for examining the external validity of the SCT for higher development. The interviews can be used as construct-related evidence for the SCT. The aggregated data is powerful because the conclusions of the authors appear to converge around some important points. The principle findings from those studies suggest that the SCT is usable for the assessment of higher development, but some cautionary notes have to be taken into consideration.

Hewlett (2004) offered the most detailed analysis of SCT validation with interview data. He interviewed 25 individuals who Cook-Greuter had identified with her SCT scoring system as being either at the Autonomous stage, or Cook-Greuter's Construct-aware (Stage 9), or Unitive stage (Stage 10), being the developmentally most advanced sample of any published study. Hewlett rated the interview materials without prior knowledge of the SCT scores. SCT scores concurred with interviews after the data analysis coding 56% of the time, with the number of cases where the SCT score was higher or lower than the interview materials being almost equal. Scoring at Stage 8, Autonomous, was a requirement for participation in his research. None of the participants who scored at the postconventional level in order to enter the study were reclassified as being at the conventional tier of development after the interviews.

Stitz (2004) used SCTs and interview materials from 10 conventional participants and 10 postconventional participants, the latter being at Stage 7, Individualistic, or higher. Of her postconventional participants, 40% evidenced noticeable differences between SCT scores and interview materials, making a definitive stage determination difficult. Page (2004, this volume), who interviewed White renunciates from three different religious traditions, used purposive and convenient sampling. She did not employ the SCT to screen participants for inclusion but made an ego score determination of conventional versus postconventional development an important aspect of her data analysis. In verbal communications

(March 19, 2006) she confirmed that she found discrepancies between SCT scores and interview data, but all participants remained within the respective tier of development. Marko (2006) noted discrepancies between the SCT and the interview data in about 10% of his sample. He noted the following:

> The levels are really ranges. So in your dissertation study a low 7, Individualistic, could interview as a 6, Conscientious, and you would get a non-match. This finding, to me, does not prove that the SCT was wrong, it simply highlights the fact that we are looking at a continuum. (personal communication, March 16, 2006)

I designed an exploratory study to inquire further into the issue of whether the SCT assigns stage scores that are potentially too low. Eight participants, who had received SCT scores in the conventional tier, Stage 6 or below, were chosen out of the pool of almost 100 respondents because their demographics matched those of 20 postconventional participants in the same study. All participants formed an international sample recruited over the Internet. The demographics showed a strong trend for postconventional participants to be older than 40 years of age and to have advanced degrees in the people professions. Approximately half of them were Buddhist or members of alternative spiritual groups. All interviews were scored for ego stage using materials based on Hy and Loevinger (1996), and Marko (2006). Five of the eight participants who had received Stage 6 scores (62.5%) gave interviews that were clearly conventional. There was attention on outer behavioral change prompted by circumstances and on overcoming adversity. Overall complexity and inner-directedness were low. However, three participants (37.5%) included postconventional themes in the interviews. Some of these participants were highly introspective, the growth was intentioned, and there was a distinct quality of lived experience that was openly shared. However, the breadth of subjects, the complexity of worldview evidenced by the other postconventional participants, was not present. The findings from this small sample partially support the observations of Sutton and Swenson (1983). The majority of persons (62.5%) who received SCT scores in the conventional tier were found to express that level of development in an interview. However, the minority found to be low scoring on the SCT and to interview at a postconventional level was rather substantial. A person can obviously produce a Stage 6 protocol on the SCT, and show distinct elements of postconventional awareness. It is important to note that among the participants who had postconventional SCT scores, none received interview scores in the conventional range. These findings are clearly preliminary and need further exploration because these projects enrolled very small samples. However, if the SCT does indeed select a subgroup of postconventional individuals, this would be important to know for research purposes, exactly because our knowledge of postconventional development often is built on the group of participants who are high scoring on the test.

In summary, these studies allow for the conclusion that the SCT appears to be valid for sorting participants into the postconventional or conventional tier of development, but in regard to the exact ego stage an error margin of about 50% may need to be taken into consideration. It is important to keep Marko's suggestion in mind that participants do not necessarily fit neatly into exact development categories; they may evidence behavior and verbal productions from several stages under different circumstances and in regard to different aspects of human functioning. In sum, the SCT is clearly useful for researchers in the field, but an unequivocal endorsement for its use cannot be given at this time because more definitive studies about reliability and validity still need to be completed.

Current Issues and Recent Developments

Cook-Greuter (1999) refined the SCT in order to make it more applicable for the measurement of higher development. She developed new scoring categories for the SCT in order to make the test useful for assessing the postconventional tier of development. Her work was based entirely on reevaluating existing SCT protocols; she enrolled no participants. Cook-Greuter proposed two postautonomous stages, Stage 9, Construct-aware, and Stage 10, Unitive, to replace Loevinger's Stage 9, Integrated. She succeeded in training raters in recognizing the new stages and scoring them correctly. She claimed that her research is an extension of ego development theory, and that it demonstrates that the SCT with her modifications can be used to assess higher development.

A detailed analysis of Cook-Greuter's (1999) work, however, suggests that her claims to validity might be premature. Her research neglects important aspects of ego-development theory, and recently published studies question some of her core assumptions. One of the central issues in ego-development theory is the unitary nature of the ego. The ego, as conceptualized by Loevinger (1976), represents the integration of motivational, emotional, social, and cognitive aspects of personality. Cook-Greuter (1999), however, has given primacy to cognition. She wrote "Since I have chosen the 'perspectives on the self' as the element that develops, it appears that the cognitive aspect drives the others in my approach" (p. 39). Several sources that she relied on for her theory of higher development, such as Basseches (1984) and Kegan (1994), clearly are focused on cognitive complexity.

However, recent publications support the idea that cognition and self-integration are separate lines of development. Researchers who promote this perspective include Skoe and von der Lippe (2002) and G. Rogers (2002). Based on their research Skoe and Lippe convincingly argued that ego development is linked to the ability to "organize and make sense of experience in terms of personal significance" (p. 491), whereas cognition is more related to an abstract relationship to an issue, such as social justice. Rogers reported aspects of a comprehensive longitudinal study by Mentkowski and Associates (2000) that focused on assessing domains of development over a 15-year time span. The authors, using factor analysis, found that "cognition" and "integration of self in context" showed up as distinct factors that remained stable throughout the study period. The SCT consistently loaded onto the second factor. In summary, Cook-Greuter's (1999) conceptualization of advanced development departs from Loevinger's theory significantly, and it is no longer clear if Cook-Greuter is using a similar enough construct. It appears that Cook-Greuter is not necessarily measuring ego development as defined by Loevinger, but advanced cognitive development instead. In that case, her research cannot be seen as establishing validity for a measurement of advanced development in the area of personality.

Cook-Greuter (1999) and Torbert (this volume) currently use the SCT with significant changes, and renamed it the Leadership Development Profile (LDP). The differences between the SCT and the LDP are significant. First, as discussed earlier, the construct of ego development is conceptualized differently. Second, how sentence completions are scored has been changed. Third, the scoring algorithm is different. Fourth, the instructions given to test-takers have been altered. Fifth, instead of the standardized Form 81, about one-fourth of the stems have been changed. In short, Cook-Greuter and Torbert developed a system for assessing personality that is related to but not necessarily identical to the SCT and ego-development theory. Cook-Greuter's influence on the field of advanced personality development has increased in recent years because few other researchers have worked specifically in the area of refining the SCT for higher development, and no other instruments for the assessment of advanced development have emerged. Torbert and Cook-Greuter use the business name Harthill, and currently serve predominately as consultants to the private commercial sector. In their work, the purpose of the test and its function have changed. The first difference is that Loevinger clearly saw the SCT as a research instrument, however, in their consulting work, Cook-Greuter and Torbert use the LPD as a way of giving management executives feedback and encouraging insight. Furthermore, there appears to be a change in the market forces. Loevinger specifically set up the training so that any graduate student or researcher could become a reliable scorer through self-training, thus making the instrument widely available. Because Harthill doesn't cater to the academic sector, they are not motivated by having people become scorers without deriving profits. Consequently, they have set up an expensive training program for so-called *certified* scorers, when it appears questionable that any such training is necessarily or that equivalent proficiency in scoring could not be obtained through diligent self-study.

It seems to be of paramount interest to know how TPR ratings that are based on the LPD compare to TPR ratings based on the latest scoring manual (Hy & Loevinger, 1996) in order to understand if the approaches are comparable in pragmatic terms. This approach would allow us to estimate the reliability of the SCT across the two systems when measuring high stage development. Some published studies of postconventional development relied on the Loevinger system (Helson, Mitchell, & Hart, 1985), whereas others used the Harthill system (Hewlett, 2004; Page, 2005), and we need to know if the participants who were designated as postconventional individuals in one system are indeed also designated as such in the other system.

I designed an exploratory study to investigate this question. Twenty-two SCT protocols that were at or near the postconventional tier, Stage 7, Individualistic, and above, were scored with the Hy and Loevinger system, after I had completed all the training exercises in the manual and achieved satisfactory ratings on the sample tests provided. Then the test protocols were forwarded to a rater trained in the Cook-Greuter system, Dane Hewlett (2004). Half of all participants submitted easy-to-score protocols and had definitive scores, such as solid 8, Autonomous. In those cases, interrater agreement was achieved. However, the other half of all protocols were near a boundary, either barely 7, or at the high end of 7. In these cases, the raters arrived at different conclusions. Detailed analysis showed that the lack of agreement was due to either of two reasons. First, the scoring algorithm, which is based on an exponential function Loevinger (1976) termed the *ogive* rule, differs in the two systems. According to the Cook-Greuter/Torbert (1999) system more answers at the higher stages are needed to receive the higher stage score. For several participants, the Loevinger system assigned higher stages because they met that stage requirement with the number of answers given but they did not meet the criteria in the Cook-Greuter/Torbert system. A second reason for divergent SCT ratings between the raters was that some stems were scored differently because the systems differ in emphasis. For example, offering more elements within any given sentence can lead to a higher rating in the Hy and Loevinger (1996) system, but Cook-Greuter (1999) places more emphasis on content. Without exception the Loevinger system assigned higher stages than the Cook-Greuter system. There was no exception to this observation, however the disagreement between the raters was always within one stage.

It appears from this research that the Hy and Loevinger (1996) system and the Cook-Greuter/Torbert (1999) system are overlapping, but they are not equivalent when scoring protocols at the upper end of development. Loevinger (1998c, p. 9) reports an interrater agreement for the TPR of .90 for a large sample of protocols from all stages of development. Regrettably she does not indicate what statistic was used to calculate it. Hewlett (1999), in the appendix of his dissertation, provides raw data that suggests that he and Cook-Greuter achieved an interrater agreement of 86.9% (N=23) with a Cohen's κ of .79, which is considered excellent. Hewlett and Cook-Greuter both scored the protocols using the system that Cook-Greuter developed. In contrast, in the above discussed study, Hewlett and this author used different systems and achieved an interrater agreement of 59% (N=22) with a κ of .43. This clearly demonstrates that the two systems are not equivalent, and consequently we need to be careful with conclusions drawn across studies. A postconventional sample that is identified with the Cook-Greuter system is not identical to a postconventional sample that was found using the Hy and Loevinger manual. In light of the fact that Cook-Greuter uses more stringent rules for achieving the postconventional stages, we can assume that a sample that was identified with her system is developmentally more advanced than a sample using the Hy and Loevinger system. In summary, this preliminary evidence suggests that reliability estimates of the SCT when using the two different systems are low. Hewlett is the only author reporting data of interrater agreement between two scorers who both trained in the Cook-Greuter system, and those reliability statistics look excellent. An interpretation of these data remains difficult, and probably hinges on future research about what personality development at the highest stages actually means. Cook-Greuter suggested that we place emphasis on cognitive differentiation and insight into the constructed nature of mind and consensual reality. However, Loevinger (1976) placed more emphasis on emotional and motivation aspects of inner differentiation, thus making it difficult to determine if Cook-Greuter's approach stays within the boundaries of how the whole personality was conceptualized in ego development theory. It is hoped that future researchers report what scoring system they are using so that their research can be located in the spectrum when a review is written.

Discussion

Beside the SCT some other instruments for the assessment of optimal development have been published. Maslow encouraged and contributed to the development of the Personal Orientation Inventory (POI; Knapp, 1990/1976; Shostrom, 1963), which became popular following its publication in the 1970s. The psychometric properties, especially the validity of the POI, have remained controversial (Whitson & Olczal, 1991). Critics have noted that it is predominantly based on theory and face validity and the scales do not show good distinction when factor analysis is used (Weiss, 1986, 1991). In the last few decades, the POI and its revised version, the Personal Orientation Dimensions, have not been used much. The POI has spawned a number of shorter instruments, such as the Short Instrument of Self-Actualization (Jones & Crandall, 1986), the Brief Index of Self-Actualization (Sumerlin & Bunderick, 1996), and the Measurement for the Actualization of Potential (Lefancois, Leclerc, Dube, Herbert, & Gaulin, 1997). These tests show similar psychometric properties. None have been validated with a criterion group approach. A correlation study did not show a statistically significant correlation between one of the POI scales, Inner-directedness, and the SCT (Novy & Frances, 1992). However, no attempts have been made to establish convergence of the SCT and the complete POI.

One of the disadvantages of the SCT is that it is time-consuming and expensive to score. It takes about 20 to 40 minutes to score a single protocol; professional fees for scoring range from $30 to more than $200 for a single test. A structured test would clearly offer many advantages and attempting to develop such a test could prove a rewarding and fruitful effort. We would need to establish a criterion group based on interview materials and then find test items that distinguish between that group and a control group that is matched for demographic attributes. Having such an instrument available would certainly facilitate research in optimal adult development because it would make it easier to find participants, especially larger groups that would allow for statistical research designs and quantitative data analysis.

In summary, we can say that currently no accurate, well-validated instrument for the assessment of higher development is available, nor does it appear likely that such an instrument can be found any time soon. This opens the question of how studies of advanced personality development can best be undertaken at this time. Using the SCT despite its limitations appears as the best choice right now because over time this will allow an accumulation of more information about its strengths and weaknesses.

Ideally, a researcher may prefer not to rely exclusively on test scores because qualified participants might be excluded and, in a form of circular reasoning, we may draw conclusions from a small, yet high-scoring group that is not representative of all persons at higher stages of development. These considerations are in part influenced by the research of Colby and Damon (1992), who assembled a group of people who demonstrated exceptional moral commitment in their lives. They studied those people and concluded that the formation of a "moral identity" a deeply internalized commitment, facilitated the expression of moral behavior. When they administered Kohlberg's instrument of moral development, the Moral Judgment Interview (Colby & Kohlberg, 1987), the researchers found much to their surprise that the so-called "moral exemplars" did not necessarily reason at Kohlberg's highest level. Consequently, Colby (2002) cogently argues that moral thought and moral action are separate lines of development that make differential contributions to our society. Colby and Damon (1992) were able to add significantly to our understanding of moral development and offer innovative aspects of the theory, exactly because they did not start with the instrument and did not use it as a criterion for inclusion in the study. Similarly, it is entirely possible that individuals progress to the highest stages of development and show all aspects that Maslow (1954/1970) described as self-actualization, yet they may not be high scoring on a verbal test. Interesting and creative findings await us in the area of postconventional personality development, if we are ready to think outside of the box and design innovative studies.

2

My Brain Made Me Do It

Brain Maturation and Levels
of Self-Development

Fred Travis
Sue Brown

Research at the Center for Brain, Consciousness and Cognition has focused on investigating brain patterns of higher states of consciousness in meditating individuals. These experiences are suggestive of the fourth tier of human development, as defined in Cook-Greuter's (2000) full-spectrum model of development. Her model comprises the three tiers investigated in life-span development and quantified by Loevinger's Sentence Completion Test (SCT)—preconventional, conventional, and postconventional—and a fourth tier that is postrepresentational. Preconventional and conventional tiers include development from infancy to adulthood. At the postconventional tier, individuals question norms and assumptions; they are aware of interpretation as an inevitable aspect of all meaning-making. They consider networks of interacting variables and multiple points of view. Postrepresentational stages are postsymbolic, nondiscursive, and involve ego transcendence. Postrepresentational experiences can be considered to be higher than postconventional in that they (a) are at least as far beyond conceptual or representational thought as symbolic representation is beyond the sensorimotor domain; (b) require major neurophysiological maturation; (c) resolve the fundamental and epistemological constraint that the reflective knower cannot know himself or herself; (d) not only are nonrepresentational but postrepresentational; and (e) are functionally higher—more adaptive and stable, more equilibrated, and characterized by more veridical perception (Alexander et al., 1990).

Although Western culture prizes linear, discursive, rational thought, meditation traditions from the East—the Vedic tradition of India (Maharishi Mahesh Yogi, 1969, hereafter referred to as Maharishi), and the Buddhist traditions of Tibet (Zelazo, Moscovitch, & Thompson, 2007), China (Austin, 2006), and Japan (Shear, 2006)—provide systematic meditation procedures that lead to postrepresentational experiences. For instance, in the Buddhist tradition, a meditative state is described as simple awareness without active focus or discursive thought (Lutz, Dunne, & Davidson, 2007); and in the Vedic tradition, an experience during practice of the Transcendental Meditation (TM) technique occurs that is called pure consciousness—where consciousness is open to itself (Maharishi, 1999). Pure consciousness is beyond the division of subject and object. It is completely differentiated from all active levels of mind, including the individual ego, and is described as the absence of time, space, and body sense with an expanded sense of self-awareness (Maharishi, 1969; Travis & Pearson, 2000). These postsymbolic experiences are direct modes of experience in which knower and known merge, and the personal self-sense is transcended.

This chapter discusses data—brain states, scores on psychological tests, including Loevinger's SCT, and semistructured interviews—recorded in two separate studies with individuals who reported the continual experience of pure consciousness, the inner continuum of self-awareness, during waking, sleeping, and dreaming. This integrated state is the first stable state of enlightenment in the Vedic tradition called Turyātāt Chetana or Cosmic Consciousness (Maharishi, 1999). Maharishi describes this state:

> This is cosmic consciousness, when the mind, completely saturated with the state of pure Being, comes back to live in the world of sensory perception. All things are experienced as before, but not, as before, in ignorance of the inner state of Being. Now the full inner state of Being is lived. It has pervaded the mind. Yet everything in life is being experienced. (Maharishi, 1986, p. 291)

In this quote "Being" refers to pure consciousness, which is one's universal nature. In Cosmic Consciousness you see the world; you act in the world as before. The eyes still see. The ears still hear. The mind still thinks and the intellect decides. However, now the default state, the home base for relating to the world and creating meaning from experiences—their center of gravity (W. James, 1902/1961)—is pure consciousness (Maharishi, 1963). It is as if the ocean, whose center of gravity was an individual wave, now gains awareness of its full extent. The ocean's center of gravity shifts from a single wave to its unbounded status. Both coexist—waves and the vast extent of the ocean; ever-changing experiences on the never-changing state of one's inner Being. Heaton's chapter in this volume discusses pure consciousness and Cosmic Consciousness.

Can physiological functioning give insight into postsymbolic reality? At first, this may sound like reductionism: an attempt to collapse the richness of ego transcendence into increased brain blood flow or patterns of brain electrical activity. On deeper analysis, the brain can be seen to be the interface with our world. The brain transforms sensations of outer objects into perceptions, and perceptions into ideas, plans, and dreams. Thus, brain patterns may serve as proxy variables to measure conscious functioning. You cannot see the mind think, but you can see the brain fire. This gives an objective measure of growing subjectivity.

Brain Patterns During Sleep In Individuals Reporting

Permanent Postrepresentational Experiences

This is the first of two studies that are presented, investigating individuals reporting stabilized postrepresentational experiences. This study examined brain patterns during sleep in individuals reporting a continuum of self-awareness throughout the night, even as the body rests deeply. This is not insomnia, in which the person is attending to outer sounds. Rather, it is inner wakefulness. The senses have closed down, there is no perception of outer stimuli, but inner wakefulness remains. This is called "witnessing sleep" (Maharishi, 1963).

Sleep electroencephalography (EEG), muscle tone, and eye movements were compared in three groups of White participants: 11 individuals reporting witnessing sleep (9 females and 2 males; 39.7±5 years old; 17.8±4.9 years TM), 9 short-term TM practitioners (7 females and 2 males; 27.1±4.8 years old; 1.4±0.8 years TM), and 13 nonmeditating controls (females; 29.5±1.5 years old) (Mason et al., 1997). EEG patterns in the witnessing group during deep sleep (Stages 3 and 4), compared with the other two groups, were characterized by no differences in delta activity, the marker of restoration of sleep, but significantly higher theta–alpha activity, a brain pattern seen during TM practice. Also, compared with the other groups, the witnessing group had reduced muscle tone, indicating deeper physical rest, and increased rapid eye movement (REM) density during REM periods indicating greater wakefulness. These brain patterns during sleep support the description of wakefulness (alpha) during deep sleep (delta).

Physiological and Psychological Measures during Eyes-Open Tasks in Individuals Reporting Permanent Postrepresentational Experiences

This is the second of two studies that are reported, investigating individuals reporting stabilized postrepresentational experiences. This study examined brain patterns, scores on paper-and-pencil tests, and semistructured interviews during eyes-open challenging tasks in another group of participants: 17 nonmeditating participants (10 males, 7 female; 39.7±11.5 years old), 17 short-term TM (10 males, 7 female; 42.5±11.5 years old; 7.8±3.0 years TM) and 17 participants reporting the continuum of pure consciousness throughout waking, sleeping, and dreaming (9 males, 8 female; 46.5±7.0 years old; 24.5±1.2 years TM) (Travis, Tecce, Arenander, & Wallace, 2002).

The Brain Integration Scale. Nine brain measures including inter- and intrahemispheric coherence, absolute and relative power, power ratios, and cortical preparatory responses were derived from EEG recorded during simple and choice reaction-time tasks in three groups of participants. Of these nine brain measures, three were entered in a multiple discriminate analysis of group differences:

1. higher broad-band (α: 8–12 Hz, β: 12.5–20 Hz, and γ: 20.5–50 Hz) frontal (F3–F4) coherence,

2. higher α β power ratios, and

3. better match between task demands and brain preparatory response. (Travis et al., 2002; Travis, Tecce, & Guttman, 2000).

These empirically identified measures were converted to z-scores and combined to form a scale called a Brain Integration Scale (BIS; Travis et al., 2002). This name was chosen because the long-term participants in this research reported the permanent integration of deep meditation experience with waking, sleeping, and dreaming states. Also, the name was chosen because EEG frontal coherence, which is a measure of brain connectivity (Thatcher, Krause, & Hrybyk, 1986), was the first variable entered in the multiple discriminate analysis.

Research to test the construct validity of BIS scores was conducted with world-class Olympic athletes and top-level managers in Norway.

Meditation practice was not a criterion for selection in these studies, only a high level of performance. If BIS scores reflect connection with inner resources, then BIS scores should be higher in individuals who are more successful in life. Research reported higher BIS scores in Norwegian athletes who, for at least three seasons, placed amongst the top 10 in Olympic games, national games or world championships compared with matched professional athletes who did not consistently place (Travis, Harung, & Cook-Greuter, 2009). Higher BIS scores were also seen in top-level Norwegian managers, who were identified by a former CEO of Manpower Europe and Manpower Nordic region, and who were listed in the Norwegian Administrative Research Foundation—the major Norwegian institution for management research. The BIS scores for the world-class athletes were 2.78 and for top-level managers were 2.34. These were above the mean for the short-term TM group (BIS scores, 2.0) and suggest that higher BIS scores have practical benefits for success in different areas of life.

Phenomenological Measures of These Individuals. The same three groups used to construct the BIS were also given a semistructured interview and four standardized personality tests including inner/outer orientation, moral reasoning, anxiety, and emotional stability (Travis, Arenander, & DuBois, 2004). Scores on the psychological tests were factor-analyzed. The first unrotated component of these variables was called a "Consciousness Factor," which accounted for more than 50% of the variance among groups. The Consciousness Factor is analogous to "g," or general intelligence in intelligence research. BIS scores in these participants positively correlated [r (50) = 0.4–0.7] with emotional stability, inner orientation, moral reasoning, and openness to experience—a trait positively correlated with ego stage (McCrae & Cost, 1980)—and negatively correlated with anxiety (Travis et al., 2004).

Analysis of unstructured interviews of these participants revealed fundamentally different descriptions of self-awareness. Some phrases from these 30- to 40-minute interviews are included in Table 2.2. The full content analysis has been reported earlier (Travis et al., 2004). Individuals who described themselves in terms of concrete cognitive and behavioral processes (an Object-referral mode) exhibited lower Consciousness Factor scores and lower BIS scores. In contrast, individuals who described themselves in terms of ego transcendence—an abstract, independent sense-of-self underlying thought, feeling, and action—exhibited higher Consciousness Factor scores and higher BIS scores. Thus, subjective and objective measures can distinguish participants reporting stabilized postrepresentational experiences.

Relation of Brain Development Across the Life Span

Brain patterns are distinct in individuals reporting postrepresentational experiences. However, brain patterns should not only be different in these participants, but also should explain movement through the tiers of development. As presented in Table 2.1, the brain undergoes major developmental transformations in the first 25 years of life. These transformations in brain structure and function follow the sequential emergence of increasingly sophisticated modes of meaning-making.

At birth, babies have all the brain cells that they will have as adults (about 100 billion)—however they are not connected. Through the first 3 years of life, 24 million new connections are created every minute. This is called neural exuberance. With an increasing number of frontal connections, object permanence grows; with an increasing number of motor connections, the child begins to grasp objects. The number of connections remains high until age 10, then connections begin to drop off, which is called "pruning." Pruning is governed by a "use-it-or-lose-it" rule. The brain circuits used in the first 10 years of life survive and are further strengthened. The ones you haven't used drop off (Sowell et al., 2004). Although the number of connections is increasing and decreasing, the quality of the connections matures—the output fibers gain a fatty layer called myelin (Toga, Thompson, & Sowell, 2006). Myelinated fibers move information 20 times faster than unmyelinated fibers.

These transformations in brain connectivity are stage-like rather than continuous. Bursts in rapid brain growth are reported at ages 3, 7, 11–12, and 15 years as evidenced by spurts in head circumference, in peak resting EEG moving from theta (4–8 Hz) to alpha frequencies (8–13 Hz; Epstein, 1986), and in higher cerebral blood flow to supply the energy needed to support spurts in brain weight (Epstein, 1999). Although no work has been done on the relation of brain development and ego development, brain development in humans correlates with the onsets of the main Piagetian stages of reasoning (Epstein, 2001) and cognitive development correlates with ego development (Snarey, 1986).

Table 2.1 presents age, state of brain maturation, Piaget's cognitive stages, Alexander's sequence of predominant processes of knowing, and Loevinger's ego-development stages. Links between the first three columns are strongly supported by research. The links between cognitive stage development and dominant levels of mental processing is theoretically strong. This relation is adapted from Alexander et al. (1990) who argued that the dominant mode of mental processing—body, senses, desire, thinking mind, deciding intellect, individual ego, and uni-

Table 2.1. Comparison Brain Maturation in Piaget's, Alexander's, and Loevinger's Life Stages

Age (Years)	Brain Maturation	Piaget's Cognitive Stages	Alexander's Predominant Process of Knowing	Loevinger's Ego Stages
0–2	Neural exuberance and myelination of sensory and motor areas	Sensorimotor	Behavior senses	*Preconventional* Presocial 1. Symbiotic
2–7	Maximum number of connections	Preoperations	Desire	2. Impulsive
7–11	Corpus callosum myelinates and pruning begins around age 10	Concrete operations	Mind	3. Self-protective
11–18	Prefrontal connections begin to myelinate at age 12, and pruning finishes at age 18	Formal operations	Intellect	*Conventional* 4. Conformist 5. Self-aware 6. Conscientious
18–25	Prefrontal myelination finishes		Feeling and intuition	*Postconventional* 7. Individualistic 8. Autonomous
	Experience continues to shape brain circuits throughout one's life span.	Post-formal operations	Individual ego	9. Integrative (Cook-Greuter's Construct-Aware and Unitive)
25+	Techniques such as meditation practices are needed to promote postsymbolic experiences		Universal ego	Higher states of consciousness

Note: Relation between age, brain maturation, cognitive development, and predominant process of knowing, plus exploratory relations between these variables and ego development. Progress through these levels is affected by life experiences.

versal ego, the "levels of mind" articulated in Maharishi Vedic Science (Maharishi, 1999)—determines our current stage of cognitive, moral, and ego development. The links between stages of ego development and the other four variables are exploratory links. Although preconventional stages of ego development are roughly associated with age (Westenberg & Gjerde, 1999), conventional and postconventional stages are not. As discussed later, the lack of relation between ego development and age, and by inference brain development, may reflect an interaction between natural brain development and ongoing experience. We have graphically presented this situation by leaving out lines between the conventional stages and placing dotted lines between postconventional stages.

As seen in this table, Piaget's sensorimotor period and Loevinger's presocial stages occur during a time of continual increases in number of brain connections and myelination of sensory and motor areas. The infant's world is a confusing, uncontrolled mass of lines, colors, movements, disconnected touch and sounds. The Symbiotic self is "confused and confounded." In the first 2 years, the process of seeing the world organizes ocular dominance columns in visual areas. Now, the child can see stable forms and track them through space. The process of hearing sounds organizes the auditory cortex into a sequence of brain areas that respond to ascending tones. Now, the child can isolate speech sounds. The process of touch organizes multiple body maps in the somatosensory system. Now, the child knows where his or her skin ends and the environment begins. In these first years, the sensory and motor areas of the brain are most developed. Thus, the most salient outputs of brain processing are concrete sensory images. This is Alexander's level of behavior and senses. The center of gravity of the infant's awareness is the senses. The sense-of-self is collapsed to what is currently being seen, heard, or felt. Infants are completely absorbed or identified with what is currently on their senses. If a 6-month-old cries, give him or her a new toy.

The next row in Table 2.1 includes Piaget's Preoperational stage and Loevinger's Impulsive stage. These stages occur when neural exuberance has reached a stable (high) level of cortical connections. At this stage, the young child has the most brain connections that he or she will ever have. This high level of brain connectivity allows the child to begin to initiate action to choose specific experiences. This is Alexander's level of desire. Now, the most salient output of brain processing is individual intention to direct experience. Now the child is not identified with sensory experience, but can choose specific sensory experiences. The Impulsive self can focus on single concrete features of experience. This is one explanation of the terrible 2's and terrible 3's. The child is now completely absorbed or identified with his or her desires or intentions to act. When something unexpected happens, the child's sense-of-self is threatened, and because the child is identified with his or her desires, the child (appears to) over react.

The next row in Table 2.1 contains Piaget's Concrete Operational stage. At this age, the child has had a high stable level of cortical connections for many years, and the corpus callosum, which connects the left and right hemispheres, is myelinating. When myelinated, the corpus callosum is able to integrate specific concrete experiences with the bigger picture. This is Alexander's level of the mind. Now, the most salient outputs of brain processing are symbolic images of outer objects. The child is now completely absorbed or identified with his or her thinking. The child can operate on anything on his or her senses—any concrete experience.

The next row in Table 2.1 contains Piaget's Formal Operations, which emerges as pruning ends and myelination of frontal executive circuits is in full swing. Pruning results in an optimal density of brain connectivity that allows the adolescent to have stable internal symbols. At the same time, frontoparietal circuits are myelinating. When myelinated, these circuits are more efficient in transforming concrete images generated in the back sensory area into ideas in the frontal abstract thinking area, allowing the individual to think about thinking. This is Alexander's level of the intellect. This newly emerged ability, based on brain maturation, is now the dominant mode of processing. Teenagers question just to question. As infants rehearsed their sensorimotor schema, so teenagers—to the consternation of their parents—rehearse their ability to question.

As seen in Table 2.1, natural brain maturation finishes by age 25. If our stream of logic is correct and ego-development stages emerge with brain development and are parallel with the emergence of stages of cognitive development, then, when frontal circuits are fully myelinated, all adults should be functioning at formal operations of cognitive development and at the Conscientious stage of ego development. But this is not seen. Less than half of adults perform at the formal operation level on developmental tests (Alexander et al., 1990; Danner & Day, 1977), and, as Cook-Greuter reports in this volume, a sample of 1,292 adults were spread across the conventional tier: 21.3% were at the Conformist stage, 31.7% at the Self-Aware stage, and 23.5% at the Conscientious stage.

Interaction of Natural Maturation and Ongoing Experience

This spread in distribution of adults across the conventional tier, and the reported lack of relation between age and ego development within the

conventional tier, may reflect the interaction of natural brain maturation with ongoing experience throughout one's life. The brain is a river
and not a rock. The strength of connections between two brain cells
is determined by their use—if two cells fire together, they are wired
together. Experience flowing through the brain leaves its trace in the
structure and function of the brain. For instance, violin players have
larger cortical representations in the primary somatosensory cortex
corresponding to the fingers of their left hand, the hand that forms
the chords, than their right hand, which holds the bow (Elbert, Pantev,
Wienbruch, Rockstroh, & Taub, 1995). London taxi cab drivers with
greater years of navigation experience have higher hippocampal gray
matter volume, an area associated with spatial memory, than do novice
taxi cab drivers (Maguire, Woollett, & Spiers, 2006). The "phantom
limb" experience in amputees results from cortical reorganization following the loss of the limb (Flor et al., 1995).

In the first few years, brain maturation is primary and experience
secondary for determining the dynamics of brain development—neural
exuberance is seen in all newborns in all cultures, socioeconomic status
levels, and psychosocial environments. In the teenage years, experience
becomes primary and natural brain maturation becomes secondary.
For instance, high psychosocial stress causes brain regions involved in
memory and emotions, such as hippocampus, amygdala, and prefrontal
cortex, to undergo structural remodeling with the result that memory
is impaired and anxiety and aggression are increased (McEwen, 1998,
2006). Thus, although natural myelination of frontal circuits occurs
in everyone in teenage years, experience determines the magnitude of
frontal maturation and the final brain circuits.

Experience is a major determinant of ego stage. Language is
considered vital for growth from the sensorimotor level to the conceptual
domain of ordinary adult thought. Cook-Greuter (2000) observes: "When
a child begins to speak, the representational, discursive, personal, or
mental self is born out of the sense-dominated body-self" (p. 238).
Similarly, Alexander et al. (1990) proposes: "Just as language acquisition
frees attention from the control of immediate sensory stimuli, a
mechanism that promotes transcending of representation may be required
to free attention from the habitual domination of symbolic thought" (p.
298). In the absence of a post-language technology, development may
appear to "freeze" in late adolescence or early adulthood (Alexander
& Langer, 1990). Thus, different life experiences may be responsible
for the broad distribution of individuals across the Conventional tier
of development.

Effects of Postrepresentational Experiences on
Ego-Development Scores

Because experience shapes brain connectivity, regular experiences, such as those resulting from TM practice, should enhance growth through the stages of ego development, and individuals reporting sustained postrepresentational experiences should at least be at the highest stages of the third tier of ego development.

The first prediction is supported by a 10-year comparative study (Chandler, Alexander, & Heaton, 2005) of Maharishi University of Management (MUM) students, who practice the TM technique as part of the curriculum, and students at three control universities in the midwest. Students at the four universities had similar ego-development scores at pretest (6.1 for MUM students, and 6, 5.1, and 4.9 for the control universities). However, 10 years after graduation, when the students again completed the SCT, mean scores for the MUM students, who continued to practice TM over the 10 years, increased to 6.8, whereas scores for the three comparison groups remained the same— 5.6, 5.4, and 5.1. Statistical analysis of these pre–post-test differences yielded significant improvements in the MUM students ($p<.0001$), and no significant changes for the three comparison groups. Thus, regular postrepresentational experiences appear to facilitate growth of ego development.

We present new data to test the second prediction. Eleven of the 17 individuals reporting postrepresentational experiences in the second study, presented above, 11 also had completed the standard SCT. These participants also had scores on the BIS and had been interviewed. In this sample, there were six females and five males, average age 48.7 to 5.2 years, range 38.2 to 58.6 years, and average years TM practice of 23.1 to 3.1 years, range 19.3 to 30.1 years. The second author, Sue Brown, analyzed these SCT protocols. She trained with Susanne Cook-Greuter and has scored nearly 400 protocols—300 of these were from participants practicing the TM technique. As there was no second scorer, interrater reliability is not available for these protocols. However, in a previous study, the interrater reliability with Cook-Greuter was acceptable ($r = 0.93$.)

Table 2.2 presents data for these participants including BIS scores, scores on Loevinger's SCT, and phrases from their response to the semistructured interview probe: "Please describe yourself." Some of the excerpts in this table include descriptions of inner wakefulness during sleep.

Table 2.2. Brain Integration Scale (BIS) Scores, Scores on Loevinger's SCT, and Response Phrases

	BIS Score	Ego Score	Segment From Interview
1	3.09	6 Conscientious	Before I started TM, the world was concrete and awareness was abstract. I had my tendencies. I had my likes and dislikes. … After practicing TM for two years, there was a shift—consciousness became dominant; it became the concrete part of life. It was underneath all my thoughts, all my feelings, and all my perceptions of myself. There was this swelling up of something. I just felt fuller inside, I just felt more whole; more something was solid that was not there before. It was not a way of thinking, it wasn't a thought, it wasn't an emotion about anything, it was my awareness itself. I'm more awake. There's something inside of me that's just there, that wasn't there before.
2	3.38	5 Self-Aware	It is very subtle. It is a sort of invincibility that hadn't been there before. It is very subtle and could be overlooked. But it is always there, kind of backing me up.
3	3.71	8 Autonomous	There's a continuum of awareness there, which is always the same. This is so pervasive that I'm quite sure that the "I" is the same "I" as everyone else's "I." Not in terms of what follows right afterward. I am tall, I am short, I am fat, I am this, I am that. But the "I" part; the "I am" part is the same.
4	3.79	7 Individualistic	It's the I am-ness. It's my Being. It's my essence there. There's a channel underneath underlying everything that does not stop where I stop. … By "I," I mean this 5 ft. 2 in. person that moves around here and there.
55	2.26	8 Autonomous	We ordinarily think my self as this age, this color of hair, with these hobbies. My experience is that my Self is a lot larger than that. Actually I'm immeasurably vast on a physical level. When I look out, my experience is I see this beautiful divine Intelligence, you could say in the sky, in the tree, but really being expressed through those things. This is who I am.

66	2.46	5 Self-Aware	Obviously, in the course of living in the world we say me and I and you and all of those things. But I find those to be just figures of speech. I can just as easily debate and I'm as comfortable with the idea that I don't exist at all. . . . The reality is so simple it doesn't have to have identity or nonidentity applied to it. It just is. If there is an "I" that is to arise, its created for the purpose of communication.
7	1.72	6 Conscientious	When I fall asleep, there are first layers of the body settling down and then I notice when the body is asleep and then I would just watch lots of dreams come and go or just fatigue leaving the body, and then afterward, 5-6 hours, the body wakes up again in gradual layers and being aware of the other side. I feel the covers. I hear the birds. At first there is no impulse to attend to it. Then I wake up.
8	3.21	5 Self-Aware	The individuality thinks a certain way. But under that is a knowingness that kind of knows reality more and doesn't think that these little things are the reality. There's more of an underlying connectedness with everything. Everything being in its right position and right time and there's a joyfulness about that, which goes along with experience.
9	0.75	6 Conscientious	There is a continuum there during sleep. It's not like I go away and come back. It's a subtle thing. It's not like I'm awake waiting for the body to wake up or whatever. It's me there. I don't feel lost in the experience. That's what I mean by a continuum. You know, it's like the fizzing on the top of a soda when you've poured it. It's there and becomes active so there's something to identify with. When I'm sleeping it's like the fizzing goes down.
10	2.41	8 Autonomous	During sleep, it's like an engine idling. You're just there. You're not doing it; you're not performing any function; you're just letting everything function in its idle state.
11	1.61	5 Self-Aware	There is silence. Deep inner silence that pervades time. Even right now. I am performing action. But what pervades inner and outer is this palpable physical silence. It sits sometimes, space sits, it's heavy on the shoulders. In that silence is an awareness—the simplest form of awareness. This simplest form of awareness just stirs something in me, stirs to go here or go there, and I act.

Note, these individuals reported the experience of Cosmic Consciousness—the permanent coexistence of pure consciousness with waking, sleeping, and dreaming. Many elements of these descriptions of sense-of-self convey postrepresentational experiences—postsymbolic, and transpersonal. The Ego stages for these individuals range from the middle of the conventional tier, Stage 5 (Self-aware) to the middle of the postconventional tier, Stage 8 (Autonomous).

A Pearson correlation of BIS scores and ego-development scores was positive but very low [$r(10) = .16$]. Correlations are deflated when the range of variables is small, as was the case for both variables. Thus, the correlation is conservative, yet still low. Even though we are dealing with reports from only 11 participants, two points stand out in Table 2.1. First, as the interviews revealed, these individuals reported permanent postrepresentational experiences during waking, sleeping, and dreaming. They recognize the personal structure of their individual self, but are identified more with their transpersonal Self not bounded by body, situation, culture, time, or space. The phrases from the interviews included in this table give a flavor of their inner experiences.

Second, no ego development scores were at postautonomous levels. Three were at the Autonomous stage (8); four scored at the Self-aware stage (5), which is the middle of the conventional tier. From the description of the state of Cosmic Consciousness and these participants' descriptions of sense-of-self in their interviews, one might expect many individuals to score at postautonomous levels.

This paradox brings up the question: Can a language-based paper-and-pencil instrument rooted in discursive, symbolic thought reliably detect postrepresentational stages, which are inherently postsymbolic and nondiscursive? By analogy, could a test of sensorimotor dexterity (preconventional stages) reliably detect the sophistication of symbolic thought (conventional stages)? A superficial answer to this question would be that a language-based, paper-and-pencil instrument cannot fully capture postrepresentational experiences. This conclusion ignores the painstaking efforts of Cook-Greuter to identify language cues for the last stages of the third tier of development in more than 4,000 protocols, and her success in identifying two postautonomous stages—Construct-aware and Unitive stages.

Another answer to this paradox is that at least some of these participants may have responded at a "functionally adequate" level (Cook-Greuter, 1999, p. 25). The individuals may be responding to the sentence stems in a way that completes the task, but doesn't reflect their true inner life. As the sixth participant remarks: "If there is an

'I' that is to arise, it's created for the purpose of communication." At higher levels of development you have the ability to act at lower levels—whatever is called for by the situation at hand.

This is reminiscent of the common experience of walking outside and seeing the sun rise in the morning and saying the sun is rising (sensory perception dominates)—yet, you know it is the earth that is turning (intellectual perception). Both perceptions of reality coexist without interfering with one another. Thus, a sentence-completion test, especially with a minimal amount of space provided for responses, may elicit lower, more conventional responses; especially compared with an interview, involving direct communication with another person.

Another possible answer to this paradox is that ego development and growth to higher states may be parallel processes rather than part of a single hierarchical sequence. Ego development is described as the sequential emergence of deeper more inclusive levels of meaning-making. Meaning-making processes are *processes of knowing* that are argued in this chapter to be constrained by the dominant level of processing the world—the senses, mind, intellect, and ego. In contrast, higher states of consciousness are the emergence of fundamentally different states of the *knower,* who uses those meaning-making processes to deal with the world.

Higher states may not be in a hierarchical sequence that requires the last stage of ego development before higher states can emerge. Rather, experiences of and transformation to higher states could begin even when one is at conventional stages. This suggestion is supported by the experience of pure consciousness during TM practice in 10- and 11-year-olds (Dixon et al., 2005). Theoretically, one's processes of knowing might be centered at the level of the mind, the Self-aware stage, whereas the status of the knower is of the universal self. This was seen in four of the individuals reported here. By analogy, ego development may be sharpening the tools in your workshop; higher states may be moving into a bigger workshop with natural lighting and bringing your tools with you, using them according to the needs of the time.

Conclusion

Cook-Greuter (2000) mused: "as a linguist—I was keenly aware of the irony of trying to capture fine differentiations in the postrepresentational sphere of experience with a brief paper-and-pencil test" (p. 233). She went on to recommend that: "A combination of personality tests, self-assessment . . . as well as physiological and other measures are needed to ascertain whether an individual operates from a stage of consciousness beyond the personal realm" (p. 237).

The combination of interviews, projective tests, and brain measures in this study presents a more detailed picture of postconventional stages and growth to higher states of consciousness. Future research could study additional participants reporting stabilized postrepresentational experiences. This research should cross-reference interview responses with written responses on the SCT and measures of brain functioning to create a more finely calibrated understanding of the subjective and objective reality of postrepresentational experiences.

The SCT may identify the dominant level of knowing through which the knower is creating meaning from daily experience—senses, mind, intellect, feelings, or individual ego. Interviews and patterns of brain function access a parallel dimension of growth—that of the knower himself or herself who is creating the meaning. Combining these measures could better reveal the multidimensional expansion of our inner Being into full enlightenment.

3

Generating and Measuring Practical Differences in Leadership Performance at Postconventional Action-Logics

Developing the Harthill Leadership Development Profile

Elaine Herdman Barker
William R. Torbert

In this chapter, we offer a somewhat informal, narrative introduction to our work and the way in which it relates to research based on Loevinger's Sentence Completion Test (SCT) (Hy & Loevinger, 1996; Loevinger, Wessler, & Redmore, 1976). We write in this way partly in the hope that it offers a more lively, engaging, and contextualized sense of the work. And in part we do so because the postconventional developmental action inquiry (Torbert, 2000a, 2000b) scientific paradigm within which we work (Stage 10 in the common numbering system we are using in this book) invites us to highlight both the distinctions and the interrelations among first-, second-, and third-person developmental research and practice, rather than restricting ourselves only to the discussion of third-person "objective" findings and methods (D. Chandler & Torbert, 2003).

Our story is divided into three sections: first, the historical and ontological basis of our work; second, the evolution from Loevinger's SCT to the Harthill Leadership Development Profile (LDP) and the continuing validity testing of the LDP; and third, new understandings of postconventional leadership based on current studies.

The Historical and Ontological Basis of Our Work

We met only seven years ago, after Elaine had been trained as a scorer for Harthill Consulting Ltd. UK by Susanne Cook-Greuter. Since then, we have repeatedly worked closely together in workshops, served in an ongoing fashion as shadow coaches for one another, and shared the lead in ongoing research on the Harthill LDP. Elaine trained early in ballet, then in business consulting, next in developmental theory, method, and practice during the past decade, and is now Harthill's lead LDP scorer, as well as an executive coach and consultant to major organizations. Elaine will now recount Bill's history of developmental research and practice.

Ten years before Elaine and Bill met, Bill had introduced Susanne to David Rooke and Jackie Keeley, the managing partners of Harthill Consulting, who have sponsored much of the research on the LDP and even more of the client-centered debriefing materials over the past 20 years. Bill had met David and Jackie in the late 1980s, introducing them to developmental action inquiry disciplines, which they began to introduce into their consulting and executive coaching practice, along with a measurement instrument that was evolving from the Loevinger SCT to the Harthill LDP. Through intensive 3-day workshops, they along with Elaine, Bill, and Susanne, until she continued on her own, developed a cadre of some 200 postconventional coach/consultants authorized to debrief the LDP.

Still earlier, in the late 1970s, when Bill became the graduate dean of the Carroll School of Management at Boston College, he and his faculty colleagues were transforming the MBA program from below the top 100 to the top 25 by creating an action-oriented and developmentally transforming curriculum, along with a strong research component to the innovation aimed at discovering whether students' approaches to leadership really did transform. He determined that the most psychometrically valid and demanding measure of whether persons transform their way of interpreting and acting in the world was Loevinger's SCT. With research funding from IBM, he therefore invited all entering and graduating full-time Boston College MBA students to take the test for several years in a row, and contracted with Cook-Greuter, then a Loevinger-trained SCT scorer in the Boston area, to do the scoring. Bill and Susanne continued to work together in a variety of ways for the next 20-plus years.

Bill's interest in translating among different developmental action-logics may go as far back as 1947, when Bill was three and his father was serving in the U.S. Foreign Service. As a result, Bill's first foreign language was Spanish, learned in Madrid. His second foreign language was German, learned in Vienna and Salzburg, starting at 6. His third was French at 8. Later, speaking to himself in the different languages (of which he retained primarily only a child's vocabulary), he realized that they alerted him to different aspects of situations and of his own internal world of thoughts and feelings, thus leading him to act differently than had he been limited to a single language. Sometimes, he would speak to himself in several languages in rapid succession as a way of differently tasting the same situation; and this practice, not surprisingly, led to qualitatively different action. In these ways, he received powerful early imprintings of the ontological/epistemological lesson that "what-we-see," "seeing," "languaging," "feeling," "embodied-self-sensing-and-enacting," and "intentional attending" refer to qualitatively distinguishable yet intimately interwoven territories of experience. Later, the notion that one can speak inquiringly and usefully to oneself (or others) in a variety of different developmental languages as well seemed plausible and natural.

The Ontological Basis of the Developmental Theory

In one of his early books, *Learning from Experience: Toward Consciousness* (Torbert, 1972a), Bill critiqued the map-territory or theory-data model of modernist science and instead named four distinctive territories of experience, first, *the outer world* (as seen and otherwise sensed by a person or measured by an instrument [including others' actions seen from the outside—altogether, what modern science calls "the territory"]); second, *the self-sensing of one's own embodiment*, breathing, and so on; third, *one's own ongoing thinking and feeling* (which in dialogue with others in a scientific community of practice generate what modern science calls "the map"); and fourth, *the intentional attention* (which can be distinguished from the other three territories, can experience all three simultaneously, and can be voluntarily cultivated in adulthood, but rarely is in our culture).

In one of his later books (Torbert, 1991), Bill describes how anyone can confirm for him or herself the reality of each of these four territories through thought and attention experiments, somewhat like

Descartes' doubting procedure to establish the indubitable fact that we think. To highlight this difference between his "theorizing about trans-theoretical experience" and Ken Wilber's (2000a) effort to create a "comprehensive intellectual map of all experience," Bill sometimes calls Ken's four-quadrant All Quadrants All Levels model the Flat Four (because they all are cognitive categories that tend to keep our attention fixated within the single thinking territory) and the four territories of experience, the Deep Four. The words for the Deep Four are obviously also cognitive categories, but, as the "deep" four, these terms invite us, not just to "think" the categories, but also to experience the pre- and postconceptual realities to which they refer (e.g., the color and texture of the "outside world," the "inner sensing" of our own breathing and moving, and the kind of "attending" that can glimpse thinking, sensing, and the external "other" all at once).

The Practical and Empirical Basis for the Developmental Theory

Early on during his PhD program in administrative sciences at Yale, Bill chose as his dissertation project to spend 2 years (1966–1968) studying himself creating, with his colleagues and their students, the Yale Upward Bound War on Poverty Program. In his quasi-autobiographical book about the Upward Bound program (Torbert, 1976), Bill constructed what he then called "action science," and what he now calls "developmental action inquiry," to describe the process of studying oneself and others, empirically and phenomenologically, while simultaneously taking an active role as a participant. It seemed to him that a truly useful, enlightening, and transforming social science would consist as much of studying oneself in interaction with others (first-person research/practice), and of a team or organization studying itself in the midst of its ongoing projects (second-person research/practice, as of studying others at a distance (third-person research/practice). So he reviewed many of the tape recordings of staff meetings and school meetings in real time, attempting to increase the efficacy of his actions and of the way the staff and the whole school worked together from week to week. After the 2 years, as he reviewed the tape recordings again, along with multiple other sources of data, he constructed a theory of organizational development to explain the spirals of development that seemed to occur not only during each 7-week summer residential program, but also (a) within the core staff itself, (b) during planning and staff development periods each spring, and (c) during the program's overall 2-year development.

Reviewing prior developmental theorizing at the individual, group, and organizational scales, he eventually wrestled Erikson's (1959) theory of interpersonal development into a 3×3 box, where the vertical columns represent thesis, synthesis, and antithesis, and the horizontal rows represent the three inner territories of experience, our direct, moment-to-moment experience of embodiment and performance, our thinking or strategizing as it occurs, and our transcognitive attention. He next removed the Eriksonian names (Birth, Trust, Autonomy, Initiative, Industry, Identity, Intimacy, Generativity, Elder) from the nine boxes and in their place generated organizational names that seemed to fit the empirical events at the school. Table 3.1 shows the organizational names, in their 3×3 symmetry.

Given the analogy found between individual and organizational development, this version of developmental theory had a fractal, scalable, complexity-theory quality to it from the start, making it possible to analyze micro-developmental octaves within a single person or a single meeting (Torbert, 1989), or macro-developmental octaves across IBM's 100-year history (Torbert, 1987), as well as issues of leadership in organizations as these emerged in real time.

Later (Fisher & Torbert, 1995; Torbert, 1987, 1991), Bill explicitly retrofitted this organizational model to the personal scale of development. He named the developmental positions "action-logics" rather than "stages" because "stage" has a relatively static, structural, mental quality, whereas "action-logics" has a relatively dynamic, multiterritory connotation, which is more evocative of later-action-logic experience and of the multiterritory ontology underlying the theory. Table 3.2 shows the names for the personal action-logics in their Fischer & Torbert (1995) symmetry.

Table 3.1. Sequential Organizational Development Action-Logics

Conception	→ Investments	→ Incorporation
Experiments	→ Systematic Productivity	→ Collaborative Inquiry,
Community of Inquiry	→ Liberating Disciplines	→ ?

Note: Adapted from "Creating a Community of Inquiry" from W. Torbert, 1976. London: Wiley Interscience. Reprinted with permission.

Table 3.2. Sequential Personal Development Action-Logics

Impulsive	→	Opportunist (3)*	→	Diplomat (4)
Expert (5)	→	Achiever (6)	→	Strategist (8)
Alchemist (9)	→	Ironist (10)	→	Elder

Note: *numbers represent "Stage."
Adapted from "Managing the Corporate Dream," by W. Torbert, 1987. Homewood, IL: Dow Jones-Irwin.

Analogously, the developmental action-logic names for social scientific paradigms are listed in Table 3.3.

On the personal scale, let's follow, very briefly, how the developing child (corresponding to the first row) first gains relative mastery of the "outside world" territory through the Opportunist action-logic (Stage 3; e.g., learning to ride a bike), and then relative mastery of the "own performance" territory through the Diplomat action-logic, Stage 4, e.g., learning how to act in conformity with peer-group norms). Next, the adolescent may begin the process of relative mastery of the "cognitive, strategizing" territory with a focus on predefined arenas at the Expert action-logic, Stage 5, e.g., subjects at school, games, or crafts). As one takes on responsibilities in the work world in one's 20s or 30s, one may develop from Expert, Stage 5, into the Achiever action-logic, Stage 6,

Table 3.3. Developmental Action-Logics Applied to Social Scientific Methodologies/Paradigms

Anarchism	→	Behaviorism	→	Gestalt Psych/Soc
Empirical Positivism	→	Multi-Method Eclecticism	→	Postmodern Interpretivism
Ecological Cooperative Inquiry	→	Developmental Action Inquiry	→	?

Note: Adapted from "A Developmental Approach to Social Science: A Model for Analyzing Charles Alexander's Scientific Contributions" by W. Torbert, 2000a, *Journal of Adult Development*, 7, and "Transforming Social Science: Integrating Quantitative, Qualitative, and Action Research," by W. Torbert, 2000b, in F. Sherman & W. Torbert (Eds.), Transforming Social Inquiry, Transforming Social Action. Boston: Kluwer. Reprinted with permission.

with more complex cognitive and emotional capacities for coordinating the three territories of thought, action, and outcomes through single-loop feedback and error-correction in action with others. Some adults later come to recognize that different people and situations operate on the basis of different action-logics or frames, and they develop the capacity to "deconstruct" assumed frames, Individualist—Stage 7, and may come to co-construct shared frames, Strategist—Stage 8. Strategists gain the capacity to coordinate thought, action, and outcome through both single- and double-loop (transforming) learning. Finally, a very few adults develop into the bottom row action-logics, Alchemist, Stage 9, Ironist, Stage 10, or Elder, with a taste for an ongoing, increasingly moment-to-moment engagement with the "attending/intending" territory that grants them awareness of the particular action-logics they are expressing at any given time. According to this version of developmental theory, Alchemists and their Ironist and Elder mentors seek simultaneous awareness of all four territories and their relative congruity or incongruity with one another at any given time, and of the nondual background—the undifferentiated aesthetic continuum—from which the differentiatable territories emerge. They seek triple-loop change in the present (e.g., "Am I [are we] saying what I [we] mean, doing what I [we] say, and accomplishing what I [we] intend?").

The Evolution From Loevinger's SCT to the Harthill LDP and the Continuing Validity Testing of the LDP

Because Bill was trained in action research and because at Boston College he and his colleagues were trying to create an MBA program that could have a developmentally transforming effect on all its participants—first and foremost those of its students inspired by the opportunity to learn to act in fundamentally more effective ways—he wanted, from the outset of his use of Loevinger's SCT, to transform it in a variety of ways that would increase its face validity and its pragmatic utility as a diagnostic tool and as a developmental support for adults taking leadership responsibility, and that would robustly test its external validity in terms of predicting real-world actions and outcomes.

New Stems, New Scoring Criteria, and New Names for Increasing Face Validity and Construct Validity

First, as the Loevinger SCT had no work-related stems, Bill decided to increase the measure's face validity for adults in general and manager/

leaders in particular, without diminishing its internal validity. He was fortunate to discover a recent doctoral thesis that had developed and initially validated several work-related items, such as "A good boss . . ." (Molloy, 1978, as later improved by Cook-Greuter, 1999). In recent years, the Harthill LDP has included additional new stems about teams and time and power to replace older gendered stems (e.g., "Men are lucky . . ." "Women are lucky . . .") that generate responses with the lowest correlations to overall protocol ratings. The validity testing and reliability testing among scorers is ongoing (until recently, Cook-Greuter and Herdman Barker typically scored alone, with regular reliability checks; now Harthill has several trained scorers, with every protocol that is initially scored postconventional being reviewed by Herdman Barker). At this point, the most recently added six stems have proven to correlate with overall protocol ratings better than the dropped stems, and slightly better than the average of the remaining old stems. In toto, the Harthill LDP now includes 27 Loevinger stems and 9 different stems that increase the emphasis on work and time management and reduce the emphasis on gender.

The second major difference between the Harthill LDP and the Loevinger SCT is that the LDP has now twice refocused the definitions and scoring manuals for the later action-logics, aligning them more closely with the Alchemist and Ironist constructs, Stages 9 and 10, found in Cook-Greuter's (1999) and Torbert's (1987, 2004) work. The first refocusing came through Cook-Greuter's dissertation (1999), wherein she based new definitions of and scoring manuals for the latest, "third-row" action-logics on *analyses of the actual responses to the SCT by persons scored at those action-logics.* Contrary to Pfaffenberg's critique in Chapter 2, this seems a highly plausible, empirically and phenomenologically based improvement. Loevinger (Hy & Loevinger, 1996) conceived of her highest stage, 9, in a bare bones way as an integrated self-actualizing identity, but suggested, most peculiarly, that "because this stage is rare in most samples and there are major differences among qualified raters both as to the description of this level and application of the description in specific cases, under most circumstances it is best combined with the Autonomous stage, Stage 8" (p. 7). She did not imagine, or theorize, or research the possibility that integrity may be the fruit of developing a postcognitive, observing, listening attention that registers ongoing transformation across all four territories of experience and all action-logics. Thus, for example, she offers neither theory nor method for scoring the "I am . . ." sentence stem when it is completed as follows: "I am—*finally, in the long run, mostly unfathomable, but I enjoy the process of trying to fathom*"

(Cook-Greuter, 1999, p. 31). Cook-Greuter comments that this statement can reasonably be interpreted as meaning that the person "is abdicating the search for identity in favor of being a witness to the ongoing process of self-becoming." The fact that fewer sentence stems get scored Alchemist using the Cook-Greuter procedure (see Pfaffenberger, Chap. 2, this volume) seems to us one confirmation of its greater validity.

At the same time, our theoretical and experiential sense of the Alchemist, Stage 9, action-logic has led to a further revision of the Harthill LDP Alchemist scoring manual, including additional new criteria. One of these criteria is whether the sentence completion "treats attention/conscience/consciousness as a process distinct from thinking and acting" (e.g., "I am . . . '*I am, therefore I think'—Descartes got it the wrong way round. Our thoughts and emotions are an inevitable aspect of our being—delightful, painful, exciting, infuriating—but can hide our inner depths from us*"). Another criterion is whether the sentence completion is a "passionate, artistic self-expression, *not* hyper-rational" (e.g., "I am . . . *a riot of differing roles and impulses held together in a loose alliance by something I call me, I am mostly happy and amazed, by any rational analysis my existence is such a staggering improbability that delighted laughter is the only possible response*").

In other words, our scoring criteria for Alchemist are emerging from a theoretical perspective that treats it as critical to distinguish simultaneous experiential contact with the four territories of experience from sheer cognitive complexity and clever, fashionable, postmodern wordsmithing. We are looking for a weave between cognitive and relational strands and for a unique and glimmering oddness that shines through Alchemists we meet. Additionally, based on our coaching, consulting, and workshop contacts with people scored at postconventional action-logics (described in a later section), we have raised the number of Alchemist stems and the number of categories those stems must fall into for a total protocol to be scored early Alchemist or full Alchemist. All this, we believe, increases the construct validity of the Alchemist designation when it is used to summarize the center of gravity action-logic represented by a person's LDP.

Harthill recently sponsored a measurement validity study of the LDP, conducted by Reut Livne-Tarandach and yet to be published in detail. The study includes two factor analyses, one of all 36 items in Achiever, Stage 6, and earlier protocols and one of all postconventional protocols (Individualist, Stage 7 and later). This study permits us to see whether there are any differences in the factors produced by conventional and postconventional protocols and whether such differences support the construct validity of the developmental distinctions. The results show, not only significantly different factors in the two sets of protocols, but also a significant difference in the structure of the factors. For the earlier action-logics, stems loaded on 8 factors and most stems loaded on a single factor (only two stems load on 2 factors). For the postconventional action-logics, stems loaded on 11 factors, and 52% of the stems loaded on 2 factors or more, with seven loading on 3 factors and three loading on 4 factors. These results are consistent with theoretical predictions, the earlier action-logics generating a relatively simple mental map with distinct, independent categories, and the later action-logics generating a more complex mental map with systems-oriented, interdependent categories.

A third project in the evolution from the Loevinger SCT to the Harthill LDP was to reinvent the key names and descriptions of the Harthill LDP to become more descriptive and actionable and less evaluative and abstract than those associated with the Loevinger SCT. Not only did these changes seem to us an improvement in accuracy and objectivity, but they also made it feasible to give individual participants and institutions involved in the action research we conducted in real-life situations useful feedback that might generate or support double-loop, developmentally transformational learning (as well as contribute to testing the external validity testing of the LDP, as discussed later). Thus, we reconstructed such terms as "from lower to higher stages" to "from earlier to later action-logics." We changed particular "stage" names from Conformist, Stage 4, to Diplomat, from Self-aware, Stage 5, to Expert, and so on; likewise, we fully rewrote and continue to amend the 20-plus pages of action-logic related feedback that anyone taking the Harthill LDP today receives as part of the feedback package (along with introducing a 200- to 300-word commentary written for that particular protocol). All these changes make it feasible and effectual to use the instrument and to offer feedback on people's performance on it in action research situations, thus providing external validity tests of the LDP, to which we now turn.

Measuring the External Validity of the LDP

As readers familiar with validity research on the Loevinger SCT know, there is an extensive body of internal validity research about it (Westenberg, Blasi, & Cohn, 1998), but there was very little external validity data available when Bill began his work. Because it was pragmatic, real-world validity with which he was primarily concerned, both in his own first-person efforts to use the theory to make his own leadership more timely, effective, and transformational and in his second-person teaching, coaching, and consulting efforts to help others become more effective, most of his methodological work has been dedicated to generating and measuring the external validity of the LDP measure.

Offering feedback and coaching to people who take the measure has permitted one set of external validity tests. For example, developmental theory suggests that people at earlier action-logics are more likely to avoid feedback, especially of a double-loop nature that questions their current action-logic, whereas people at later action-logics will increasingly seek out such feedback and associated transformational opportunities. When we offered a purely voluntary opportunity for feedback on their measured action-logic to 281 adults who had taken the measure, we found that an increasing proportion of each later action-logic in fact chose to receive it. None of those measured Diplomat, Stage 4, sought feedback, and only a small minority of those measured Expert, Stage 5, did so. A bare majority of those measured Achiever, Stage 6, sought feedback, whereas a large majority of those measured as Individualist, Stage 7, or later did so. This rank order correlated perfectly with the theoretical prediction and thus confirmed the validity of the LDP in a powerful new, unobtrusive way (Torbert, 1994).

Qualitative External Validity Testing

A second, more qualitative and ongoing way of testing the external validity of the LDP is to triangulate its finding with a first-person estimate of one's own action-logic and a second-person action-logic estimate. In our teaching, coaching, and consulting work, we ask our participants to make a first-person estimate their own action-logic, based on reading *Action Inquiry* (Torbert & Associates, 2004). Additionally, we are frequently in the position to do an analysis with participants of difficult, unsatisfactory conversations they have had with one another in work situations (Rudolph, Foldy, & Taylor, 2007). From the small group's analysis of the actual frames and actual actions that a person has been using in crafting how he or she speaks in the difficult conversation, it is possible to infer the person's action-logic. Very frequently, the first-, second-, and third-person methods correlate precisely, or differ by no more than one action-logic (with the second-person conversation analysis usually yielding the most conservative estimate). On the rare occasions when there are significant discrepancies among first-, second-, and third-person estimates of a person's action-logic, we have found that the first-person estimate is usually most at variance and that careful exploration of the discrepancies can become a powerful catalyst, not just for the personal development of the participant in question, but also for the team and organization within which the exploration is taking place (McGuire, Palus, & Torbert, 2007).

Moreover, although, as stated previously, we have found that persons are more likely to initiate a search for feedback and transformation at later action-logics, we have also found that, when coached by LDP-authorized, postconventional consultants, managers scored as early as the Expert (Stage 5) action-logic can move beyond initial resistance to this feedback and to the notion of transforming beyond their current approach. The quality of reflecting, with positive regard, upon the structure and implicit limitations of one's action-logic frequently ignites a realization of the very presence of a structure, thus validating the LDP's finding. In observing one's tendency to be subject to an event, double-loop insight erupts; the nature of Expert action-logic (Stage 5) becomes visible and felt to the Expert. Moreover, in workshops and coaching sessions, it often is the individuals profiling at this action logic who express heartfelt moments of realization and, it is about these individuals that we hear tales of change, redirection, and hope feeding back from the organization.

For example, Elaine worked with Michel (not his real name) two years ago, when he profiled at the Expert action-logic, Stage 5, and was a senior vice president of operations in the aviation industry. Initially, Michel expressed his resistance, in a workshop, to the LDP. Questioning its validity and reliability, he focused his attention on the technical accuracy of this third-person feedback, effectively distancing *himself* from the inquiry. "Explain the statistics to me. . . . How do I have more scores in Diplomat but still profile at Expert. . . . I did this in a rush. How does that affect the rating? . . ." Although such questions are helpful, there was an air of dismissal around Michel. Whereas the rest of the group sat forward, intrigued by the framework, drawing on personal experiences, delving into the guts of the theory and engaging in robust inquiry, Michel, consistent with the Expert action-logic, first opposed and then withdrew.

Later, in a one-on-one conversation, it quickly emerged that he believed that it would not further him to go beyond a set way of working; an approach to management that he had held for many years. Eight years before, following an MBA and under the tutelage of a coach and mentor, Michel split away from old limiting habits by adopting a code, of sorts, that focused on personal mastery. It became, he believed, the mainstay of his success. By the time of the workshop, however, Michel was struggling to excel in an environment that required more than individual excellence. Although he was still improving incrementally (through single-loop feedback), he was standing still developmentally (i.e., in terms of double-loop change that could expand his capacity), and that, until this one-on-one conversation, had escaped his notice. The content of his code was irrelevant; its importance lay in its being a structure; an unquestioned and unquestioning way of relating to the world. In describing his approach and its limitation Michel began to make visible his assumptions—he quickly seized the moment: "I've not changed my thinking in 8 years . . . I've not questioned my approach despite new experiences. I've kept to a prototype . . . it didn't dawn on me to notice 'it.' "

Michel's way of organizing himself and his interrelationships moved on during the workshop; his manner of speaking began to invite feedback and he expressed personal vulnerability and doubt. One participant observed, "most of us expected you to stand miles away from this type of discussion. I felt uncomfortable, at first, when you were so defensive . . . I thought, here we go, Michel's going to block this. . . . I could not have predicted your reaction and your support." Eighteen months later, Michel was acknowledged as one of the more collaborative and supportive leaders in the organization and a strong performer. To an observer it would be difficult to imagine him otherwise.

Quantitative Laboratory and Field Experiments That Test the External Validity of the LDP

In addition to these up-close, qualitative external validity tests of the measure, we have conducted laboratory and field tests of the external validity of the LDP. For example, we have found statistically significant differences in managerial performance between conventional and postconventional action-logics on in-basket tests (Merron, Fisher, & Torbert, 1987) and in an interview study (Fisher & Torbert, 1991). Postconventionals are more likely to (a) reframe presenting problems and constraints; (b) recognize diverse frames or action-logics and to deliberately seek to create shared vision; (c) use a collaborative inquiry process in implementing solutions; and, (d) spot incongruities among their own territories of experience, such as between what they advocate and what they actually do.

What kind of leadership and organizational processes support personal and organizational transformations? The simple theoretical answer is postconventional leadership, starting with Strategist (Stage 8) and postconventional organizing, starting with Collaborative Inquiry (Stage 8). Several studies we have done offer empirical support for this answer. For example, one study (Torbert & Fisher, 1992) showed that voluntary participation in groups (formed and guided by an Alchemist action-logic, Stage 9, practitioner) that encouraged first-, and second-person action inquiry over a 2- to 4-year period (a Collaborative Inquiry, Stage 8, organizing process generated transformation to postconventional action-logics among 22 of the 24 participants). By contrast, only 3 of 165 persons in a control group, who started the same MBA program at the same time as the participants, showed positive developmental transformation over the same period when retested. Thus, according to Goodman and Kruskall's tau statistic, participation in the self-inquiry group increased participants' likelihood of developing to a later action-logic by 81%.

We also found statistically significant differences that account for an unusually high proportion of the variance between conventional and postconventional CEOs in their success in leading organizational transformation over 4-year periods, with the support of consultants (Rooke & Torbert, 1998). Of the 10 organizations studied, 5 were led by CEOs at the Strategist, Stage 8, action-logic and 5 by conventional action-logic CEOs (two Achievers, Stage 6, two Experts, Stage 5, and one Diplomat, Stage 4). All five of the postconventional Strategist CEOs generated successful organizational transformation, but only two of the conventional CEOs succeeded. After the initial study was published, we reanalyzed the data, adding the consultants' action-logic scores (three measured as Strategists, Stage 8, one measured at Alchemist, Stage 9). The consultant measured as Alchemist, Stage 9, had been the lead consultant in the two cases of conventional CEOs who gener-ated successful organizational transformation, suggesting that, as the theory would predict, Alchemists are more effective at working with action-logic discrepancies than Strategists. The re-analysis showed that the combined action-logic scores of CEO and lead consultant in each case accounted for 59% of the variance (according to the Spearman Rank Order test, beyond the .01 level of significance) in whether the organization successfully transformed (Torbert & Associates, 2004).

Why and how would leaders' action-logics be so critical to suc-cessful organizational transformation, especially given the paradox that their intent is to generate more empowerment, more initiative, and more distributed leadership throughout the organization? A qualitative re-analysis of the 10 organization study suggests that later action-logic CEOs and consultants tend to engage increasingly often in an increasing proportion of 27 types of action research (first-, second, and third-person research × first-, second, and third-person practice × past, present, and future; D. Chandler & Torbert, 2003). This increase in, and intensifica-tion of, interpersonal and organizational Collaborative Inquiry, Stage 8, increases the likelihood of generating organizational transformation. In short, each later postconventional action-logic person or team engaged in a more nearly constant inquiry process to determine what action is timely now, thus generating more instances of single-, double-, and triple-loop change in conversations, meetings, procedures, and strategies than conventional action-logic leadership does.

The most recent and most comprehensive review of literature on whether and how different versions of developmental theory and their concomitant measures advance our understanding of leadership (McCauley, Drath, Palus, O'Connor, & Baker, 2006) calls for more research, such as reported above, that is longitudinal rather than cross-sectional; that explores how to generate developmental change rather than simply looking at differences in style of leaders with different action-logics; that includes organizational action-logics as well as individual action-logics; and that is cumulative.

In general, what one sees in the transformation of the Loevinger SCT into the Harthill LDP, as we use it in our research and practice, is typical of developmental transformations from conventional action-logics to postconventional action-logics. First, the third-person, Expert, Empirical Positivist, Stage 5, scientific base of the original instrument is preserved and enhanced. Second, new, postconventional action-logics are conceived, defined, and operationalized through Cook-Greuter's, Herdman Barker's, Rooke's, and Torbert's work. Third, the third-person measure is reoriented so that it can play a role in a wider field where the effort is to integrate it with practitioners' first- and second-person research and practices in the midst of daily work and life. Thus, Loevinger's SCT transforms from a relatively early action-logic Empirical Positivist, Stage 5, psychometric measure toward a relatively late-action-logic Developmental Action Inquiry, Stage 10, psychometric-measure-as-part-of-an-integral-system-of-mutually responsible-action-and-inquiry.

New Understandings of Postconventional Leadership

As we engage more deeply with colleagues, clients, and organizations who are volunteering for development beyond the conventional, a more and more differentiated portrait of Individualists, Stage 7, Strategists, Stage 8, Alchemists, Stage 9, and Ironists, Stage 10, is emerging. We focus primarily on the distinctive features of Strategists, Stage 8, and Alchemists, Stage 9, in the following comments. For example, as we have just documented, Strategists, Stage 8, in roles of power (e.g., CEO) wield that power in a more creative, inquiry-supportive, and transforming way than leaders operating at conventional action-logics. Similarly, we find that Strategists, Stage 8, operating in "middle" roles and within the shadow of "top" conventional power may also *begin* by asking "What is it that we do not currently envisage or experience?" They also may be less likely than conventional action-logic managers to shy away from the risks of uncertainty and befuddlement; and they may be more likely to sit in-wait for the unexpected. Strategists, Stage 8, in noticing the system of which they are a part, are akin to comedians, more able to touch the nerve of the organizational body, and this is a mixed blessing for their subordinates—usually conventional action-logic line managers—who may develop an allergic reaction to nerve touching. This can, in turn, lead mid-level Strategists, Stage 8, to turn their backs on transformative intervention and quietly yield to the organizational momentum. They do so based on their conventional desires for acknowledgement, safety, community, and so on.

Even Alchemists, Stage 9, report withdrawing from the fray as they choose their version of survival. Indeed, using the LDP, observation, journals, and interviews with participants in a group relations conference, McCallum (2008) recently found that participants at all action-logics experienced "fallback" periods during the stressful and ambiguous event, when they acted from earlier action-logics. The difference among the action-logics was that the later the action-logic the quicker the recovery of one's center of gravity action-logic, with the Alchemist, Stage 9, in the study often being aware of the regression as it was occurring and being able to recover and learn from it within seconds.

This withdrawal and caution of some Strategists, Stage 8, in the shadow of conventional power raises questions of organizations in how they support and work with individuals in this action logic—that is, if the organization wishes to retain and nurture Strategist-like double-loop inquiry and transforming power. From research interviews conducted by Herdman Barker and Rooke and experience of coaching and consulting to Strategists, Stage 8, the following emerge as simple but helpful organizational interventions. First, as part of a talent management and development process, spot and acknowledge the Strategists', Stage 8s', contributions as different and distinctly valuable, if perhaps at odds with leadership stereotypes in the organization. Second, find someone (be it senior manager, coach, or even PA) to help Strategists, Stage 8, at the mid-levels of large organizations navigate through the system. Third, create high trust meetings that liberate individuals or teams from the need to be unfailingly competent and knowing (presenting the "glossy front page"), so that inefficacies and lack of alignment within and among individuals and groups can be tackled. Fourth, at least acknowledge and face, and at best temper, the double bind that accompanies attempts at transformational change, namely organizational impatience for delivery and outcome at the very same time as a longer-term change is being sought. Fifth, create small, senior- or consultant-supported communities of mutual inquiry for mid-level Individualists, Stage 7, and Strategists, Stage 8, within which they can seek coaching in conceptualizing and enacting challenging dilemmas. Sixth, offer Strategists, Stage 8, roles in which they can satisfy their (sometimes almost intoxicated) desire for development; the development of self, colleagues, organization, and the organization's overall impact on the environment. And seventh, use a Strategist, Stage 8, propensity to be drawn to broad, systemic interventions; brush strokes that have, at their center, an intergenerational concern.

A final new study (Nicolaides, 2008) helps us understand the relative context-dependence of Strategists, Stage 8, by comparison to Alchemists, Stage 9, in a way consistent with the developmental action inquiry theory and methods presented throughout this chapter. Nicolaides conducted in-depth interviews, on their relationship with ambiguity, with nine persons scored at postconventional action-logics: one Individualist, Stage 7, two Strategists, Stage 8, two Late Strategists/Early Alchemists, Stage 8/9, three Alchemists, Stage 9, and one Ironist, Stage 10. She found that, unlike people at conventional action-logics who tend to try to avoid ambiguity, all of her postconventional sample saw positive, creative potential in ambiguity. But within this broad similarity, she found four distinctive responses to ambiguity: the Individualist, Stage 7, *endured* it; the Strategists, Stage 8, *tolerated* it; the Alchemists, Stage 9, *surrendered* to it; and the Ironist, Stage 10, *generated* it. More generally, Nicolaides found that the Individualists, Stage 7, and the Strategists, Stage 8, worked with ambiguity on particular occasions for particular ends; whereas, in a figure–ground shift, the Alchemists, Stage 9, and the Ironist, Stage 10, experienced ambiguity as the creative, ongoing element of all experience. This finding is consistent with the change from a primarily cognitive–structural approach to experience to a primarily attentional–spiritual approach in the shift from Strategist, Stage 8, to Alchemist, Stage 9, described in the 3×3 model earlier in this chapter.

We conclude this chapter with the hope that we have not only provided new glimpses into the postconventional personality, but have also provided a useful introduction to fellow developmental researchers to the evolution of the Harthill LDP and to the many new ways of ongoingly testing the validity of this measure when one adopts a postconventional set of methodologies, such as those in the developmental action inquiry paradigm (Stage 10).

Finally, to study oneself and others in action, as well as generating after-the-action reports like this one, requires long-term commitment and typically involves relatively small numbers of participants. We see our research as just one among the beginning efforts of this kind (Reason & Bradbury, 2007; Shani, Mohrman, Pasmore, Stymne, & Adler, 2007), and we believe much more of this kind of research is called for. Thus, we invite our readers to join in this kind of effort to bridge the worlds of scientific inquiry and social action.

4

A Report from the
Scoring Trenches

Susanne R. Cook-Greuter

In the following chapter, I offer some observations on the shifting winds in the field of ego-development theory and testing from the perspectives of both a veteran scorer with a scientist-researcher mindset *and* a seasoned practitioner in applying the results to support people in their developmental journeys. In this brief expose I take the pulse of the field from my unique vantage point. It is no exaggeration to say that in recent years there have been fundamental social and cultural changes affecting the *business* of scoring.

It is hard to believe that I have dedicated most of my adult career as a psychologist to the Washington University Sentence Completion Test (SCT; Hy & Loevinger, 1996; Loevinger & Wessler, 1970; Loevinger, Wessler, & Redmore, 1970) and its exploration. With more than 8,000 SCTs of various forms rated and studied for patterns and salient markers, I have become an authority in this field. My initial hunches about being able to distinguish subtler qualitative differences at the high end of Loevinger's scale than she predicted have been borne out and have kept me intellectually and personally fascinated with meaning-making and how to assess it ever since my first encounter with her theory and instrument back in 1979. Unlike Loevinger, however, I have not felt a loss of freedom in this choice. Loevinger's (1998a) last contribution to the field in a postscript called *Completing a Life Sentence* is a poignant tribute to the level of dedication and responsibility she felt toward the theory and the instrument she had been pivotal in creating. This volume investigates the ongoing legacy of her efforts and ingenious contribution to developmental theory and personality testing.

The high-end ego stages, the Construct-aware, Stage 9, and the Unitive, Stage 10, and the corresponding scoring categories and scoring rules that I proposed, have been generally accepted by those who posit that human beings have the capacity for self-realization and development beyond the personal realm toward ego transcendence (Cook-Greuter, 1999, 2000). Loevinger's conviction (personal communication, 1982) that such distinctions cannot be made because of lack of data and researcher limitations has been proven premature. It took 15 years of scoring to get enough data to test and validate my earlier hypotheses of what these higher levels might look like and how to measure them. The result of this effort at testing the hypothesis is a 1999 Harvard dissertation, *Postautonomous Ego Development: A Study of Its Nature and Measurement* (Cook-Greuter, 1999). It is both a critique of Loevinger's theory and measurement and an endorsement of her seminal contribution to adult development theory, her psychometric creativity, and scientific objectivity.

This chapter addresses various topics and emergent tendencies in an impressionistic fashion. I begin in the voice of researcher-scorer, then I mention observations gained as a practitioner with a developmental grounding. I first report some recent data about the later stages that raise some fascinating questions of what it means to have one's center of gravity[1] at the boundary between personal and transpersonal ways of meaning making. Following, I remark on general trends and collaborative efforts in refining, disseminating, and applying ego-development theory and its measurement in the professional world.

From Rare High-End Material to a Sizable Collection

From inception, I have kept systematic logs of all the high-end data crossing my path. Table 4.1 shows the simple distribution stats based on the data set of 3,397 protocols scored from 2000 to 2007. The test form used is predominantly the SCTi-MAP, a form we developed to respond to the demand for more business-oriented stems. In 95% of cases, I alone scored the protocols using the high-end distinctions. In all cases including research projects designed by others, the higher cut-off numbers were used, as indicated in my dissertation.

Stage 10 protocols continue to be rare (.06%). Among the 948 protocols rated at the postconventional tier ($N=34,128$ sentence completions), the following are the numbers of completions that were scored at each of the stages:

Table 4.1. Summary of C-G Scoring Data

| Stages | Percentage Number | Average (%) | TWS | Age Range | Gender | | |
					Female	Male	n/a
2–6	2,449	72.09					
7–10	948	27.90					
7	525	15.45	259	22–70	266	240	19
8	305	8.98	284	20–78	138	151	16
9	99	2.91	315	18–85	39	58	2
10	19	0.55	335	33–60	8	11	0
Total	3,397	100.00			451	460	37

n/a, not available

- Stage 7 (*n*=9,599)
- Stage 8 (*n*=5,568)
- Stage 9 (*n*=1,878)
- Stage 10 (*n*=426)

Unlike the dissertation, which covered a broad, representative sample of the general population (*N*=4,510), this newer data set is from individuals who often self-selected to be tested, and thus it is not representative. Still, it is interesting to notice that in certain subcultures up to 27.9% of the participants do test at the postconventional levels compared with the 18.2% in the pre-1999 sample. I discuss more about the shift in who takes the test and for what reasons later. People as young as 18 years of age seem to be able to make high-end distinctions and produce postautonomous protocols. These young people seem to be able to take on complex perspectives that did not occur to most of our generation until midlife. It remains to be seen whether these younger individuals can sustain their early advantage and whether they are given the societal supports and opportunities to make good use of their precocious insights and impressive mental capacities.

The percentages of postconventional protocols cited earlier are based on cut-off numbers different from those used by Loevinger. In 1990, I upped the cut-off numbers for Stages 9 and 10 to minimally four responses each in order to do justice to the average number of postautonomous responses actually appearing on protocols at that time. How does one decide how many responses are necessary to assign a preliminary protocol score to a given SCT? Introducing Bayes' theorem to determine the cut-off numbers was one of Loevinger's psychometric masterstrokes. Her reasoning appreciated the rarity of high-end responses at the "extremes" (Loevinger & Wessler, 1978, p. 234) of her samples and the relative weight each of these responses therefore had in terms of symptomology. The rarer the symptom, the greater its predictability, as we know from medical diagnostics.

Given current response distributions, these numbers seem not stringent enough as the average of responses for people who do get rated at the Construct-aware and the Unitive stages are considerably higher. Currently, the average number of responses from Stage 9 for Stage 9 protocols is 9.5, and 1.9 from the Stage 10. The numbers for the Unitive stage are on average 11.8 responses from Stage 9 and 7.8 responses from Stage 10, respectively. This shows clearly a very different picture from the one Loevinger encountered. I suggest that if someone's center of gravity for meaning-making truly is at these later stages, the number of responses the person produces is commensurate with the concept of center of gravity, namely the perspective from which one tends to *routinely* process experience. Clearly, there is a need to create even more stringent cut-off numbers based on the available evidence. The question is whether and to what degree to tailor the psychometrics to best reflect the findings or whether to *honor* a method now seemingly suboptimal in light of the data. How to do this in a valid psychometric fashion without employing Bayes' theorem is the challenge. As a developmental measure, based on empirical evidence, the SCT requires new theory and new measurement approaches when the data changes. Another pertinent and practical question is at what point in time does one introduce radical changes to an established measure including new metrics and recalculate, readjust older samples in light of the new evidence?

Meanwhile, the lines of research started by Loevinger continue. Various studies are being conducted in applying the measure in new contexts, with new populations, longitudinally, in different cultures, all in order to answer some of the questions raised about human potential and adult development. As we gather more evidence, the proposition that some adults develop beyond formal operations as defined by Piaget (1977, 1978) is less controversial than it was in Loevinger's times. Beginning in the 1960s, Kohlberg (1969), Loevinger (1976) and later Commons and Richards (1984) posed a challenge to Piaget's theory by investigating how much adult development is possible beyond formal operations.[2] Along with this line of inquiry, various measurement tools have been developed. The SCT is one of the few projective personality measuring tools that have stood the test of time. This is so because of its psychometric robustness, proven effectiveness, world-wide database, and its cost-effective, predictive power useful beyond research. The SCT's conventional research applications were last examined in Westenberg, Blasi, and Cohn (1998) and its technical foundations in Loevinger (1998a, 1998b, 1998c), whereas our more dynamic, evolutionary perspective on ego development was identified as essentially postconventional by Torbert and associates in 2004.

Dissertations and Studies Exploring Upper-End Development

In recent years, several doctoral candidates have undertaken to test the new high-end stages, Stages 9 and 10, and categories in order to validate and/or refine the distinctions and categories at the high end or to explore possible correlations with specific capacities or other measures (see, e.g., Boyer, 2005; Hewlett, 2004; McCallum, 2008; Nicolaides,

2008). Some researchers apply the theory to specific subpopulations. Page (2005, see also this volume) focused on renunciates from different religions. A title such as "The Magic in Adult Transformation to a Construct-aware Worldview" (Meents, 2003) gives one a taste of the abiding interest in late-stage development. Others, including Pfaffenberger (this volume), assess ego-development theory and the tool from a more traditional overview perspective. Of special interest in today's climate of mind–body–spirit research is the question of whether and how meditation might accelerate development to the later stages (H. Chandler et al., 2005) and to what degree sophisticated brain measures correlate with ego development (Harung et al., 2009).

In order to spread the information about constructivist adult development theory, practitioners also are beginning to write articles meant for the general reader rather than for academics. A summary written by Cook-Greuter (2004), as well as one by Metcalf (2008), explain the basic tenets of ego-development theory and how thinking in terms of developmental levels may enhance individual and organizational viability.

Intimations of Subtler Distinctions

Research in ego development inevitably also reflects on one's own meaning-making capacities. Loevinger faced her limitation with her Integrated stage, Stage 9. It became a catch-all stage for everything she deemed higher than her Autonomous stage, Stage 8. According to her definition of stage, any new stage has to be qualitatively different and exemplify ways of meaning-making not available at any earlier stages. However, unlike the others stages on Loevinger's scale, her Integrated stage is just an amalgam of earlier material. In defining Stages 9 and 10, I made sure they were not just more complex combinations of material and ideas from earlier stages, but could be identified by their unique emergent qualities and perspectives.

I discovered in hindsight that my own boundary at the time I did my original research was the Unitive Stage (Stage 10). Exploring and expanding ego-development theory then has this additional benefit: It ironically and inevitably illuminates the researchers' own powers and limitation of understanding. Postconventional meaning-makers are aware of being participant-observers who influence the theory. It is perhaps this self-referential or introspective aspect of theory-making that creates the most resistance to high-end ego-development theory. As experience shows, formal operations are sufficient to evaluate the formal aspects of any theory including ego-development theory or to create a purely cognitive theory of development.

Based on some very unusual and salient Stage 9 protocols, I have recently postulated that there may be a substage to the Construct-aware stage that constitutes a missing link between Stages 9 and 10. I have called it *Ego-aware*. It shows the ego in its death throws just before it either solidifies at the Construct-aware level or relinquishes its hold on being the center of interpretation. Expressed more accurately, it represents the condition before an ego-transcendent view can place the ego in its proper context, neither denying nor overestimating its function and power.

Despite a collection of more than 400 recent Stage 10 responses, I have so far not been able to distinguish further levels at the Unitive stage. That such distinctions are plausible is based both on theory and on hundreds of treatises about the path from early ego transcendence to Unity consciousness. Brown (1986) charted 18 levels of increasingly subtle transpersonal attachments on the path to enlightenment in Buddhism. Thus, I am delighted that O'Fallon has begun a study to discern distinctions at the Unitive stage. She plans to look at the SCTs of spiritual masters, advanced students of spiritual disciplines, and other highly evolved subjects in order to determine whether finer distinctions can be made using the SCT, grounded theory, and interview data.

An additional hurdle one faces at these very late ego stages is trying to tease apart ego development from spiritual development as these can look similar on the surface. Wilber (2006) recently introduced a critically important distinction between structure stages and state stages of consciousness (see also the chapter by Combs, this volume). What most developmentalists do agree on is that people interpret their altered states and peak experiences through the lens of their current developmental level. The ancient East has given us extraordinary first-person accounts of the spiritual journey; the modern West has provided a unique objective, scientific view of how human beings develop through a spectrum of increasingly broader and higher perspectives. People who have meditated for years and achieved sustained levels of enlightenment states, may or may not also operate from higher ego development stages as the structure stages and state stages paradoxically seem to be both independent and influence each other in a variety of ways.[3] How these interactions work has yet to be researched. Based on existing data and experience, we have as yet untested hypotheses of how we can tell apart those who have access to transpersonal perspectives in peak moments only and talk about their insights on the SCT through the filter of an earlier position from those who more steadily live out of a

Unitive perspective. Can high be *faked*? Even when high-end responses are in someway contrived (espoused theory) is there a benefit in terms of accelerating overall growth in consciously accessing higher states on occasion and thus having access to later perspectives?

Adapting the SCT to Contemporary Sensibilities and Uses

Some users of the SCT add their own domain-specific stems that do not have manuals to the test in order to reflect more contemporary professional concerns. The Hy and Loevinger (1996) manual edition still contains many stems that a busy professional may look on as irrelevant such as "When a child will not join in group activities . . ." or see some items as intrusive or illegal in today's antiharassment climate, such as references to sex in item stems. Given the SCT's Freudian heritage, these kinds of stems hardly are surprising, but they no longer match the research and application environments of today and do not necessarily pass current institutional review boards.

Overall, various new stems and manuals with various levels of validity have been introduced. "A good father" for instance has been replaced with "A good boss" (Molloy, 1978). Our current master list contains 60 different stems. Unfortunately, most self-made manuals are not nearly as psychometrically rigorous as those of Loevinger. They often draw from a limited range of the scale, conventional to early postconventional, and represent a best guess of their creators. Rather than tapping into different aspects of a person's experience, they may repeatedly focus on a specific thematic interest of the researcher. From a psychometric perspective, the fewer facets of experience are explored, the less valid is the result as a measure of a person's ego development. On the other hand, this approach may provide new insights into a particular topic. Moreover, from a purely practical stance, less fully developed manuals may be sufficient and functional when coaching and personal development are the goals rather than rigorous research. Ideally, creating a preliminary manual is only the first step in a complex procedure carefully described in Loevinger and Wessler (1970) in Chapter 2, "The Construction of a Manual." We also are introducing and testing a number of new stems and building manuals for them in order to be more contemporary and responsive to the current demands for items relevant to today's professional contexts.

Current Research and Manual Construction Efforts

Cook-Greuter and Associates is in the process of making a concerted effort to create cross-stem categories for Stage 8. Both in my dissertation and in the interrater reliability work with certified scorers, we have found that Loevinger's Stage 8 creates the greatest disagreement among all scorers because it is ill defined and poorly illustrated. There were likely not enough Stage 8 responses for grounded research in the original data and few of the researchers working with Loevinger on the different manuals may have made distinctions at Stage 8, Autonomous, or later themselves. With the additional data we have, we hope to be in a position to remedy this uncertainty and create consistent Stage 8 categories that will more clearly distinguish this stage from both earlier and later stages.

It is with great satisfaction that we also are creating a new updated 36-item manual in collaboration with our associates. It will incorporate 25 years of notes, observations, amendments, and additional categories for some levels. It also places certain responses at a given position in the scale for theoretical reasons such that the particular progression of a concept from rudimentary to fully explored can be more easily and logically traced. Structure and content are considered separately as much as possible with structural markers deemed more telling than content ones. Most uniquely and importantly, the new manual will include examples of postautonomous responses for all item stems that are in use.

Other Practical Concerns

Some researchers change the test forms to allow for considerably more space for sentence completions than recommended. This has both advantages and disadvantages. Too little space, and respondents may choose not to write at the level of complexity they are capable of as they understand the space limit as a tacit invitation to brevity. Limited, but adequate space allows later stage participants to express themselves more fully and in more richly modulated ways. No doubt, more space also invites some test takers to write whole paragraphs and stories that are no longer related to the stimulus stem. It is for this situations that the scoring rules are paramount in adjudicating whether or not multiple sentences should be treated as a whole which presents a more complex picture than its constituent parts or whether we just dealing with run on story telling or lists of ideas not integrated into a larger whole.

As demand for the SCT for large-scale testing and interventions has grown, so have requests and efforts to computerize the SCT. Considering that responses at the highest stages become very unique and inventive, so that no matches with any manuals can be found, it is unlikely that scoring the postconventional tier can be successfully automatized. Only deep theoretical knowledge of mature ego development and the high-end scoring categories as well as the sophisticated use of the scoring rules for compound sentences (Loevinger & Wessler, 1970) can guide the rater in determining the most appropriate stage at the postconventional tier. Although some automatization of scoring may be accomplished for Stages 2 through 7, it is unlikely ever to replace a highly experienced and insightful human scorer at the upper end.-

The role of translations of the SCT in spreading the use of the measure also has changed. The SCTi-MAP has been translated into several languages and is currently used in German, French, and Spanish (see more about translations in Loevinger, 1998a, 1998b, 1998c).

Certification of Scorers and Training in Developmental Coaching

As the demand for the test grows, so does the supply of people who feel themselves capable of scoring the later stages and interpreting them to their clients. In order to retain the integrity of Loevinger's approach and to share what I have learned in the wake of all those years of immersion into sentence completions, I teach a 16-month scoring certification course with stringent requirements for admission, training, and final exams for getting certified. The criteria for passing include a thorough knowledge of developmental theory in general, ego-development theory in particular, high interrater reliability along the whole scale, and excellent content interpretation skills.

Scoring at this level of expertise includes assessing each protocol according to the established procedures using all available manuals, doing a qualitative analysis and providing unique commentary about the structure, style, and pertinent content of each individual protocol. The comments serve as a basis for feedback and coaching dialogues with clients directly or they support coaches who work with their clients using a developmental lens. Although scoring is mostly a science, commenting and making recommendations is closer to an art. It requires that the scorer not only be accurate in gauging the level of development according to the established procedures, but also be able to empathetically tailor his or her observations and recommendations for *development practices* to the stage from which the subject has responded. I believe that boilerplate commentary and automated output shortchanges the power of the instrument to reveal a person's utterly unique meaning making propensities and patterns.

Those who are skilled in interpreting the SCT are continuously fascinated with how much one can deduce—and intuit—about a person's experience of life from just those 36 sentences. What does not appear on someone's radar and thus remains unexpressed is just as informative about their level of ego development as what is expressed in so many words. Additionally, late-stage responses can be inspiring and in themselves transformational for those who are privileged to assess them. The following is an e-mail testimonial to this from a certified scorer:

> I'm looking at one [protocol] that is clearly a late Stage 9—I rated some items at Stage 10—a first for me! Very exciting . . . there was a beauty to some of the responses that tipped the scale for me. (March 18, 2008)

We also offer regular training for coaches, consultants, and change agents who want to use a developmental perspective in their institutions and with their clients. This is naturally exciting and, at the same time, raises many ethical questions. At what point does developmentalism become another tool for pigeonholing people and cultures? When is the developmental perspective not the most salient and effective perspective to take on a person's experience? The easier it is to understand a developmental theory initially, the more likely it can be abused and ill applied as has been seen with Spiral Dynamics (Beck & Cowan, 1995). Thus, instilling a mindful approach to using a developmental lens in one's work is very much part of our training along with a caution about the current *transformational* bias.[4]

A Shift From Adult Constructivist Developmentalism as a Foster Child of Psychology to a Major Focus in Ken Wilber's Integral Theory

In 2000, Wilber founded the Integral Institute, a multidisciplinary think tank, to disseminate Integral Theory as a comprehensive approach to exploring the human condition. With such books as *The Marriage of Sense and Soul* (1998b) and *Integral Psychology* (2000a), Wilber sparked a much wider interest into developmental levels as a major source of difference among human beings. Before that adult development was a subspecialty of psychology with few people engaged in its investigation. Thus, Wilber's writings and the Institute have been instrumental in bringing developmental thinking and appreciation of levels of consciousness into the main stream. By citing Loevinger's seminal work and my revisions of it, Wilber has brought attention to the later stages in ego-development theory and the SCT.

Given current opportunities for my knowledge to be shared in a more direct, interactional, and public way, I also have changed my focus from mostly research and scoring to applying developmental psychology in support of professional development. Teaching, lecturing, leading workshops, and coaching provide deep personal fulfillment at this stage of my life as well as increasing appreciation of just how difficult it is to be an adult in today's complex world.

Major Shift From Using the SCT for Research Only to Applying It in Coaching and Change Interventions

Along with adapting the SCT to current cultural givens and data, there also has been a major shift from academic research only to applying developmental thinking and testing in the professions for the purpose of change work with individual, teams, and whole organizations. One of the first to expand the application of the theory into the managerial world was Torbert (1987; see also this volume). He coined new labels for the levels he identified and introduced the term *action-logics* for ego-development stages to make the theory more suitable for business. Some of the purposes other than traditional studies for which the SCT is currently used are as follow:

1. Testing whole cohorts in academic programs in order to tailor the program to those involved, or to measure potential gain in pre-/postintervention studies (see Boyer, 2005).

2. Testing to transform people as part of the current, and in my view, ill-conceived but likely unexamined desire of the transforming agents to *help* others move to later stages regardless of need, preference, or fit with work demands.

3. Testing as an additional mirror for those interested in their own development. Here the goal is to better understand, celebrate, and accept where one is on the developmental trajectory. Although most coaching aims to be transformational, our own position is that being an adult is difficult enough under any circumstances. Therefore, assisting people in becoming at home in life where they are without pressure to transform will indeed allow growth to emerge both horizontally (expanding capacity within the level one is already) and vertically (acquiring greater

perspectives and new, more comprehensive worldviews) in a natural, organic way.

4. Testing to get a general sense of the stage constellation in a team or organizational division, most often at the executive level. Team profiles or organizational chart profiles can be used to find optimal matches between a person's capacity, his or her responsibilities, the people the person reports to and supervises, and the task environment.

5. Testing is sometimes employed for high-potential selection and retention as well as part of a battery of tests toward employment selection. Because of existing laws, the latter is not as common in the United States as in other countries.

As a consequence of the new interest in development, testing with the SCTi-MAP is being carried out in organizations of all sizes, including the U.S. military and the government, especially at the executive level. Evaluating individuals' level of ego integration or leadership maturity is thus no longer simply an academic concern. This has created new challenges regarding quality control and psychometric rigor. It requires an ongoing balancing act between scientific considerations and practicality.

Shift in Testing From Research Projects to Individual Test-Takers and Corporate Projects

Another shift has occurred in terms of how the results of an SCT are used. In research, subjects generally do not get their SCT results or at most as a group aggregate. Today, feedback about the results is often part of the agreement in both individual testing and in corporate contexts. Results are variously used for individual growth support, as part of team exploration and cohesion, and as part of overall organizational change strategies.

The former often includes feedback to the client that is uniquely tailored to his or her current growing edge and personal concerns as revealed on the SCT. Indeed, it takes as much or more time to write the 150- to 200-word summary interpretation that accompanies the test profile as it does to score a protocol. The more insightful these comments, the more both the client and/or the coach, who commissioned the profile, can use the material to further explore the client's meaning-making preferences and underlying assumptions about life. Each feedback session is used as a test of the test and its face validity. In general, there is very high agreement between the suggested stage or center of gravity on a profile and the recipient being able to find him or herself in the description, thus resonating with the comments. Recommendations outline stage-specific practices. These help clients in consolidating and expanding their capacity within the current stage. Stage-specific practices also may suggest areas of greatest leverage at their growing edge if the clients seek, welcome, or are mandated to expand their perspectives beyond where they are.

Increasing Demand for High-End Scoring and Coaching

As people become more aware of the SCT through others' experience and advocacy or through Web-based searches, we also receive more protocols that are high-end outliers in various ways. As mentioned previously, people enthused with Integral Theory and those dedicated to a spiritual journey often volunteer to take the test for purposes of deeper self-knowledge. Confusion between access to transcendent states and ordinary stages is common. It takes a very highly trained scorer to be able to differentiate between mature, integrated high-end test-takers and participants who seek to be at later stages.

Trying to prove to oneself that one is at a later stage is another hazard that comes with more information now available about what these later stages look like and what the criteria are by which we evaluate their attainment. In general, test-takers are more sophisticated and educated in developmental theory than prior generations. Upper-end protocols often come from people versed in the integral writings of Wilber (2000b) or other developmental theories. The participants are no longer naïve as to some of the criteria that count for higher ratings. Sometimes they produce protocols almost entirely situated in the postconventional tier, Stages 7 to 10, in an attempt at expressing their deep longing to attain ego-transcendent perspectives or to confirm their own sense of making meaning at the later stages. To distinguish between genuinely mature, integrated protocols (theory in practice) and those that consciously or unconsciously try to *game* the test (espoused theory) has become a salient aspect of training certified scorers. It remains a difficult issue. In the spirit of development, such efforts at expressing one's highest potential and seeking personal transformation are laudable, regardless of capacity. They are a testament to the human spirit and to the evolutionary mandate. Yet any such *effort* also is contrary to authentic later stage integration. According to the current theory, the mature ego is flexible, has access to the whole spiral, and is less attached to any given outcome—be that on a test or in life. As mentioned in Cook-Greuter (1999, p. 82), becoming aware of existential paradox is one aspect of late-stage insight. Thus, in order to assign a Stage 9 rating, we look for how conscious participants are of the paradox that their very seeking of detachment and ego transcendence is in itself an expression of attachment.

In conclusion, I look forward to many more years of interesting theoretical research as well as refining and developing the SCTi-MAP and its manuals—only this time in collaboration with others equally fascinated by the theory and the tool. I remain intrigued and animated by the power, beauty, and the growing influence of developmental thinking in the public consciousness and of the SCTi-MAP as a tool to measure differences in ego maturity. Being a coach and teacher to people on their journey through adulthood toward greater resilience, self-acceptance, wisdom, and compassion is a privilege and a continuing joy.

Notes

1. *Center of gravity* is the felicitous term coined for the concept of stage by W. James in 1902 (1902/1961).

2. Piaget characterized *formal operations* as the acquisition of the ability to think abstractly, reason logically, and draw conclusions from the information available and offered this form of reasoning as the apex of adult meaning-making in Western society. Loevinger's Conscientious stage (Stage 6) exemplifies this view of adult functioning. Adults are expected to be able to understand such things as motivations, logical proofs, hypothetical situations, and shades of gray and act with self-agency.

3. The *dual center of gravity* model of development, which Wilber writes about in his yet-to-be-published books, *Overview* and *Superview*, provides a remarkable view of the human journey, from birth to enlightenment. It outlines how individuals move through a clearly defined vertical spectrum of structure stages of development, allowing them to take increasingly deeper and wider perspectives, and how they move through a horizontal spectrum of state stages, progressively deepening their ability to witness the arising of all gross, subtle, and causal phenomena.

4. A quick search on Google brought 4,440,000 hits for books on transformation.

Part II

Emerging Research About
Postconventional Development

The second part of this book is devoted to studying postconventional individuals and asking questions about their unique development pathways. Various authors report their empirical research concerning postconventional development.

5

The Issue of Highest Stages in Structural-Developmental Theories

Tobias Krettenauer

Highest stages always have been a troublesome issue for structural-developmental theories, both on theoretical and empirical grounds. According to structural-developmental theories, highest stages are better than lower ones because they can be considered better equilibrated, higher on integrative complexity, and more adaptive. Thus, proposing a sequence of developmental stages implies a value judgment. Structural-developmental theories combine descriptive and evaluative elements in conceptualizing development and, as a consequence, run counter to the common, but highly debatable idea that modern science is value free. This problem, however, is not limited to structural-developmental theories but applies to all research that draws a distinction between development and mere age-graded change. Proposing a highest stage requires structural-developmental theorists to explicate their evaluative criteria, which, in turn, renders this type of theory more vulnerable to objections against value implications of theoretical approaches.

The problem of value implications is external to structural-developmental theories. That is, it may diminish the attractiveness of structural-developmental theories in some scientific communities. However, it does not affect the architecture of the theories themselves. On the contrary, the second major problem associated with highest stages has important theoretical ramifications: As was borne out by hundreds of studies, highest stages, generally, tend to be very rare. This is true for all domains in which structural-developmental theories have been proposed. With regard to cognitive development only about one-third of adolescents or young adults reach the highest stage of full formal operations (Piaget, 1972; Neimark, 1985; Shayer, Demetriou, & Pervez,

1988). In Kohlberg's system (Colby & Kohlberg, 1987), only a very small number (approximately 2.5%) of respondents, achieve the post-conventional Moral stage (Stage 5). Kohlberg's Stage 6 turned out to be virtually nonexistent (Colby, Kohlberg, Gibbs, & Lieberman, 1983; Snarey & Keljo, 1991). Last but not least, in Loevinger's (1976) model of ego development, the highest Autonomous or Integrated levels are very infrequent (Manners & Durkin, 2000; Pfaffenberger, this volume). Similar findings were obtained in areas where cognitive, moral, and personality development overlap. For instance, in Perry's (1970) seminal study on intellectual and ethical development in the college years, only very few participants reached the highest level of commitment in relativity. Following Perry's work, Krettenauer (2004) found that only 13% of 19- to 20-year-olds had achieved the highest level of meta-ethical reasoning, a dimension of intellectual development that is closely associated with identity formation and the self-integration of moral values (Krettenauer & Eichler, 2006; Krettenauer, Malti, & Sokol, 2008).

As a first reaction, the scarcity of highest stages in cognitive, moral, and personality development may be blamed on the lack of developmental opportunities in society. After all, it is not the fault of the theories that so many individuals fail to reach their full potential as defined by highest stages of development. However, externalizing the problem in this way appears to be premature. Structural-developmental theories are half empty from an empirical point of view. Highest stages do not define a real end point of development, but function as a regulatory idea that helps to order lower stages and bring them into a developmental sequence. If researchers wish to understand cognitive or moral excellence, as it in fact exists, they need to rely on accounts different from structural-developmental theories. Indeed, in the field of moral development, for instance, researchers ceased to focus on post-conventional reasoning as an important outcome of moral development and started to devote their attention to moral excellence in terms of extraordinary moral commitment. Research on so-called *moral exemplars* showed that higher stages in Kohlberg's sense are neither necessary nor sufficient for developing sustained moral commitment (Colby & Damon, 1992; Damon, 1996). Thus, studies on moral exemplars set up a research agenda that is completely devoid of Kohlberg's cognitive-structural model (Hart, 2005; Walker & Hennig, 2004). If structural-developmental theories fail to account for outstanding developmental achievements, they are bound to lose relevance.

At the same time, the scarcity of highest stages contradicts the basic tenet of structural-developmental theories claiming universality of internal processes and mechanisms that enable individuals to reach the best equilibrated, most integrative and best-adapted stages of psychological functioning (Edelstein & Krettenauer, 2004). Structural-developmental theories assume powerful internal devices that move individuals toward higher stages of greater psychological maturity. If this organismic view of development is valid, a much higher incidence of higher stages could reasonably be expected. Thus, there is a conflict between the assumption of internal processes of equilibration and disequilibration that naturally move individuals toward highest stages on the one hand, and the general scarcity of these stages, on the other. Any attempt to solve this conflict requires, at least partial reconstructions of the theory.

Strategies of Dealing With the Issue of Highest Stages

In the following, I discuss various strategies that have been developed in dealing with the conflict that arises from the fact that so few individuals actually reach stages that are assumed to be an outgrowth of general developmental dynamics inherent in cognitive, moral, and personality growth. In the first part of this chapter, I outline four complementary, but mutually nonexclusive ways to deal with the issue of highest stages in structural-developmental theories. In this section, I repeatedly refer to research in the area of moral development as illustrative examples. Although Kohlberg's model of moral judgment development and Loevinger's (1976) conception of ego development are not identical, it can be safely assumed that both models are fair representations of the family of structural-developmental theories: First, there are striking parallels in the description of stages and levels between Kohlberg's (Colby & Kohlberg, 1987) and Loevinger's models. Second, there is the same dearth of individuals reaching the highest levels in both approaches. Third, there are substantial correlations between the moral stage and ego level (Lee & Snarey, 1988). Last but not least, ego development and moral development evidence similar growth curves, with a growth spurt in adolescence and leveling off in early adulthood (Cohn, 1998). All of these findings support the family resemblance of Kohlberg's and Loevinger's models. In the second part of this chapter, I address the issue of highest stages in Loevinger's model of ego development from an empirical point of view, and provide empirical support for the adequacy of one of the four strategies in dealing with the issue of highest stage.

The Highest Stages: A Problem of Measurement

A possible way to deal with the lack of empirical evidence in support of the existence of the highest stages is to take it as a problem of measurement. The empirical procedures commonly used to assess highest-stage competencies may be too demanding to actually reveal these competencies. This argument is supported by many studies that demonstrate how slight changes in measurement procedures can reveal competencies in young children that typically have been ascribed to older individuals only. Hundreds of studies in the field of cognitive development showed that standard Piagetian tasks often lead to false-negative errors (Lourenço & Machado, 1996). That means these tasks fail to evidence competencies that children actually have as evidenced by task performance under more supportive conditions. In the moral domain, using a method different from Kohlberg's dilemma-based Moral Judgment Interview (Colby & Kohlberg, 1987), Turiel and colleagues demonstrated that young children already at the age of 3 or 4 have developed an intrinsic understanding of moral rules according to which moral norms are universally binding, unchangeable, and non-contingent on authoritative commands (Smetana, 2006; Turiel, 1998). Thus, in essence, a postconventional understanding of morality cannot be measured reliably with Kohlberg's Moral Judgment Interview. In a similar vein, research on Rest's Defining Issues Test using a recognition rather than a production procedure for the assessment of moral stages typically reveals a much greater percentage of postconventional reasoning in adult samples (Rest, Narvaez, Bebeau, & Thoma, 1999). Thus, changing the assessment procedure may have a substantive impact on finding the incidence of highest stages.

At first glance, this finding leaves structural-developmental theories intact because revisions are only required on the level of measurement procedures rather than the theoretical level. However, a closer look at the changes of the measurement procedures reveals that the competencies that are assessed by easier tasks typically are not equivalent to highest stage competencies (Lourenço & Machado, 1996). Thus, what is asked for by these tasks are competencies that bear some resemblance to highest stages, but lack important features of these stages. Obviously, cognitive and sociocognitive competencies can be articulated at different levels of explicitness that cut across various developmental levels. Colby and Kohlberg (1987) dealt with this idea by introducing a level of *intuitive* postconventional moral reasoning that can be reached at lower stages of conventional moral reasoning, called Type B reasoning (see Krettenauer & Edelstein, 1999). According to Colby and Kohlberg (1987), judgments of Type B reflect an intuition of moral judgments typically articulated by moral Stage 5 and 6 reasoners, yet they lack the organization of moral judgment around a clearly formulated moral principle. Thus, individuals assigned to Type B argue as if they were postconventional. However, they are not able to express and justify their viewpoint in a truly postconventional manner.

The idea that developmental levels or stages can be expressed at different levels of explicitness is an important extension of structural-developmental theories. It suggests that a higher developmental level may be implicitly present even though on an explicit level an individual is operating on a lower stage. The exact relation between implicit and explicit levels of competence needs to be spelled out for each theory. Implicit concepts may be important precursors of highest stages of explicit competence, but must not necessarily be so; this means they may be neither necessary nor sufficient for achieving the highest stage in a developmental sequence. On the implicit level individuals probably need more contextual support to articulate their competencies and therefore performance factors play a greater role when assessing competencies on an implicit rather than an explicit level.

The Highest Stages: A Problem of Conceptual Definition

A second strategy that was used to address the issue of highest stages is to revise and extend their conceptual definitions. In general, researchers rely on a very limited number of sample cases for the definition of highest stage. Consequently, highest stages may be defined too narrowly. An extension of the conceptual definition may yield more comprehensive and cultural-fair conceptions of highest stages and better reflect individuals' actual competencies. Following the critique raised by Carol Gilligan (1982), Kohlberg, Levine, and Hewer (1984) explicitly acknowledged that care-based reasoning might not be sufficiently represented in Kohlberg's stage sequence. Consequently, Kohlberg, Boyd, and Levine (1986) extended the definition of moral Stage 6 to include welfare considerations that complement the justice orientation of higher stages. In a similar vein, Snarey and Keljo (1991) identified a "Gemeinschaft voice," such as considerations around communal interconnectedness, upholding tradition, social harmony, and unity that is largely missing in Kohlberg's description of higher stages. They argued that a Gemeinschaft-like, communitarian morality might not only occur at the conventional but at the postconventional level as well. Such extensions in the conceptual definition of highest stages are important as they help to overcome restrictions in stage conceptions. However, these extensions have been largely conceptual so far and it is unclear whether they in fact lead to an increase in the number of individuals assigned to highest stage. Moreover, extensions of stage definitions carry the risk for becoming overly extensive. If stage descriptions are overly extended they may become theoretically inconsistent.

Highest Stages: A Problem of Model Specification

The most common reaction to the scarcity of individuals reaching highest stages has been to consider it a problem of model specification. According to this view, highest stages are not stages in the same sense as lower stages are. They do not naturally occur in the course of development but require highly specialized training. Higher stages, therefore, are not part of general developmental structures, but reflect special skills that are domain-specific. Students who major in physics, for instance, tend to be better formal operational thinkers with regard to the pendulum problem than political science students, who, in turn, outperform physics students in a political science problem that requires formal operational thinking (De Lisi & Staudt, 1980). With regard to moral development, Gibbs (1979, 2003) formulated a "Piagetian revision" of Kohlberg's stage sequence arguing that postconventional moral stages are not natural moral stages but mere philosophical reconstructions of moral reasoning structures that emerge earlier in development. These philosophical reconstructions start from basic stage assumptions but do not form stages by themselves. According to Gibbs (2003), moral development consists of two overlapping phases: standard and existential. For the standard phase of moral development that typically lasts from childhood to adolescence, an invariant developmental sequence of immature to mature forms of moral reasoning can be assumed. The existential phase, however, cannot be characterized in the same way. In this phase, individuals may develop an explicit moral philosophy as a particular kind of expertise that depends on an individual's reflective competence as it is typically trained during college education.

The idea that achieving a highest stage requires training of particular skills in highly specialized domains of expertise demands some plausibility when applied to areas that allow for professional specialization. However, it becomes less plausible with regard to developmental dimensions that are integrative in nature, such as personality or ego development. Because everyone faces similar challenges and needs to cope with the same fundamental issues, everyone can claim expert status in this area. Psychological maturity in personality characteristics is difficult to conceive of as an expertise that depends on specialized skills training. However, this restriction did not prevent researchers from conceptualizing personality growth in terms of acquiring expertise in a particular field of knowledge. Baltes and Staudinger (2000), for instance, developed a conception of wisdom as an ultimate goal of personality growth that defines wisdom as an expert knowledge system concerning the pragmatics of life. In an attempt to clarify what role professional experience plays in developing this expertise, they found that clinical psychologists, who were supposed to have intensive engagement with questions of life planning, life management, and life review, received the highest scores in wisdom related performance. Notably, on average this group of experts scored well below the theoretical maximum of the scale. Similar to the highest stages in ego development, wisdom in this theoretical framework seems hard (if not impossible) to attain. Whereas wisdom-related performance increased over the adolescent years (Pasupathi, Staudinger, & Baltes, 2001), no significant relation between age and wisdom was found in adult samples (Baltes, Staudinger, & Lindenberger, 1999). Consequently, it is life experience and not merely age that accounts for personality growth beyond an average level of psychological maturity. Such findings are well known from structural-developmental theories (Manners & Durkin, 2000). Recasting the issue of the highest stages in a theoretical framework of expertise development provides a different theoretical perspective. However, when it comes to empirical results it does not change the picture fundamentally.

Highest Stages: A Case for Developmental Discontinuity

Two-phase models like those proposed by Gibbs (2003) imply developmental discontinuity, both on the level of description and on the level of explanation. On the level of description, stage-like development does not continue from lowest to highest stages. On the level of explanation, it is assumed that those factors that promote development beyond modal levels are fundamentally different from factors involved in development that lead to modal levels of adulthood.

A less radical view concerning developmental discontinuity is to leave stage models intact on the descriptive level while assuming discontinuity only on the level of explanation. From this perspective, stage models provide a valid description of development from lowest to highest stages. However, development is not considered an outgrowth of one unified developmental process that accounts for all stage transitions. Instead, those factors that promote development on lower levels could be systematically different from factors that account for the achievement of highest stages. This view regarding developmental discontinuity provides a solution to the paradox pointed out above that structural-developmental theories assume an intrinsic developmental dynamic that moves individuals toward highest stages of psychological maturity, yet evidence a general scarcity of these stages. At the same time, it opens up new opportunities for empirically investigating factors that contribute to the attainment of highest stages without having to deny the validity of stage models as valid descriptions of development.

In the following, I present findings from an empirical study that is meant to further substantiate the discontinuity view in particular with regard to Loevinger's (1976) model of ego development. This study investigated long-term correlations among various cognitive, sociocognitive, and behavioral measures in childhood and adolescence and ego-level attainment in early adulthood. Assuming that the discontinuity hypothesis is valid, it is expected that developmental conditions promoting the attainment of highest levels of ego development are different from those leading to average performance or middle-level development.

Discontinuity in Ego Development: Empirical Example

The study reported here is based on a longitudinal project, Individual Development and Social Structure, carried out in Iceland from 1976 to 1992 (for an overview see Edelstein, Keller, & Schröder, 1990). The study was designed to investigate individual differences in cognitive, sociomoral, behavioral, and emotional development as a function of macro- as well as micro-social context. Children who participated in the study came from different social classes and grew up in either urban or rural environments. At the onset of the study, subjects were 7 years old and had just entered the first grade. At that time, children were tested with a battery of Piagetian tasks assessing cognitive development. Children's social cognitive development was assessed using a semi-structured interview about a friendship dilemma. The procedure was repeated at the ages of 9, 12, 15 and, partly, 17 years. Additionally, from the age of 9 to the age of 15, the main classroom teacher rated children's classroom behaviors. Overall, a wealth of data was assembled to represent various dimensions of individual development. Many of these dimensions have been demonstrated by previous research to be linked to ego development.

Sample

Of the 165 children at onset of the study, 103 participated in the entire longitudinal project from childhood (7 years) to early adulthood (22 years). These 103 participants constitute the sample of the present study. Of these participants, 45 were male and 58 female; 64 were from the original urban sample and 39 from the rural sample; 62 from the lower social class, and 41 from the higher social class. At the age of 22, participants had attained diverse educational levels: Some had attended preacademic high schools until the age of 18 or 19 years and were enrolled in university studies ($n=45$). In the following these participants are referred to as the "higher educated." By contrast, others had either no postsecondary education beyond the mandatory level (Grade 10 around age 16) or had received vocational training only ($n=58$). These participants are referred to as the "lower educated."

Measures

EGO LEVEL IN EARLY ADULTHOOD

In general, ego development as described by Loevinger (1976) and assessed by the Washington University Sentence Completion Test (SCT; Hy & Loevinger, 1996), moves through a sequence of eight levels with the lowest levels labeled as *Impulsive* and *Self-protective* (Stages 2 and 3), the intermediate levels as *Conformist* and *Self aware* (Stages 4 and 5), and the highest ones as *Conscientious, Individualistic, Autonomous,* and *Integrated* (Stages 6–9). John, Pals, and Westenberg (1998) demonstrated empirically that these eight ego stages can be combined into three groups that represent different achievements with regard to ego development. The Impulsive and Self-protective levels (Stages 2 and 3) represent the preconformist group; the Conformist and Self-aware levels (Stages 4 and 5) represent the conformist group, and the Conscientious, Individualistic, Autonomous, and Integrated levels (Stages 6–9) define the postconformist group of ego levels.

In the present study, ego stage was assessed at the age of 22. Three independent raters scored protocols of the SCT (Form 11-68) according to the procedure detailed by Loevinger and Wessler (1970). For detailed information regarding interrater agreement see Krettenauer, Hofmann, Ullrich, and Edelstein (2003). In the sample, the following distribution of ego levels was found: Stage 2 (Impulsive) $n=1$; Stage 3 (Self-protective): $n=15$; Stage 4 (Conformist): $n=9$; Stage 5 (Self-aware): $n=56$; Stage 6 (Conscientious): $n=17$; Stage 7 (Individualistic): $n=3$, Stage 8 (Autonomous): $n=2$. Thus, the majority of the participants (53.8%) were assigned to Stage 5, the modal level in adulthood. Nonetheless, a broad range from Stages 2 to 8 was present in the sample. Sixteen participants had not developed beyond preconformist Stages 2 and 3,

64 belonged to the conformist group, and 22 participants had attained one of the postconformist levels.

SOCIOCOGNITIVE DEVELOPMENT

At each measurement point sociocognitive development was assessed by an interview about a friendship dilemma. Responses were coded for the child's level of perspective taking (for details see Keller & Edelstein, 1991).

INTERNALIZING AND EXTERNALIZING PROBLEMS

At the ages of 9, 12, and 15 years, participants' main classroom teachers rated behavioral problems using a questionnaire assessing classroom behavior. Factor and scale analyses of the questionnaire yielded the two band factors of externalizing and internalizing behavior problems. The scale for the assessment of externalizing problems comprises 17 items that indicate lack of impulse control and aggressive and disruptive behavior in the school setting. The scale for assessing internalizing problems consists of 18 items that indicate social withdrawal, anxiousness, and depressive mood.

Results

To explore whether the different socialization conditions as represented by the sample characteristics as well as the various dimensions of individual development are related to ego-level attainment in early adulthood, first a multiple analysis of variance (MANOVA) was conducted with the three ego-level groups (preconformists, conformists, postconformists) defined as between-subjects factor, whereas gender, context of socialization, social class, educational attainment, cognitive development, sociocognitive development, and externalizing as well as internalizing problems were the dependent within-subjects factors. Subsequently, two planned comparisons between (a) preconformists versus conformists, and (b) conformists versus postconformists were conducted in order to identify variables that could potentially be related to the attainment of postconformist levels. For all analyses, the repeated measures of cognitive and sociocognitive development, and behavioral problems were averaged over the assessments at ages 9, 12, and 15 years.

The MANOVA yielded a significant multivariate F value, $F(18, 184) = 2.49$, $p<.01$. Thus, the sampling factors and the various dimensions of individual development were shown to relate to the three ego-level groups. The subsequent unique F tests provide a more detailed view of the nature of this multivariate effect. Overall, participants' level of education, their cognitive and sociocognitive development, as well as their externalizing and internalizing behavioral problems were related to differences between the three ego-level groups (see Table 5.1). By contrast, gender, urban versus rural origin socialization context, as well as social class were unrelated to ego-level attainment. In summary, person variables were related to ego-level differences, whereas social structure variables were not.

The planned comparisons (*a priori* contrasts, $p<.05$) between preconformists versus conformists, on the one hand, and conformists versus postconformists, on the other, call for a differentiation of this general picture. They indicate that the sample characteristics and the developmental measures are differentially related to the transition from the preconformist to the conformist level, and to the transition from the conformist to the postconformist level. None of the variables under scrutiny were significantly related to *both* developmental transitions (see

Table 5.1. Ego-Level Attainment in Early Adulthood and Differences Between Ego-Level Groups

	Overall	*A priori* Contrasts Between Groups	
		Preconformists vs. Conformists	Conformists vs. Postconformists
	$F (2, 100)$	$t (100)$	$t (100)$
Rural (0) vs. urban (1) ecology	1.02	0.85	0.93
Lower (0) vs. higher (1) social class	2.25	0.31	1.95
Lower (0) vs. higher (1) level of education	8.43[b]	1.52	3.38 [b]
Male (0) vs. female (1)	2.80	1.99 [a]	0.81
Cognitive development	4.89 [b]	1.94	1.95
Social-cognitive development	5.59 [b]	2.46 [a]	1.66
Externalizing problems	5.02 [b]	−2.18 [a]	−1.75
Internalizing problems	9.19 [b]	−1.38	−3.65 [b]

[a] $p < .05$, [b] $p < .01$

Table 5.1). In view of the transition to the conformist levels, socio-cognitive development, as well as externalizing behavioral problems were particularly relevant: Conformists were more advanced in social cognition during childhood and adolescence than preconformists, and they had fewer externalizing behavioral problems. Additionally, a gender difference was found, with females more often assigned to conformist than to preconformist levels.

A different pattern of findings emerged with regard to the transition from the conformist to the postconformist level. Conformists and postconformists did not differ significantly with regard to sociocognitive development, externalizing behavior, and gender. Instead, they differed with regard to level of education and internalizing behavioral problems, with higher-educated participants who had fewer internalizing problems achieving postconformist levels more often.

Conclusion

The findings as described in this chapter merely illustrate an important strategy in dealing with the issue of highest stages. They do not provide an exhaustive list of all factors that account for discontinuities in ego development. By providing this example it is not implied that assuming discontinuity in developmental factors is the only useful strategy when dealing with the issue of highest stages and that it should be granted priority over others. Other strategies have their own merit. The various strategies as outlined in this chapter even may be combined in meaningful ways. For instance, it is theoretically possible to propose developmental models that differentiate between implicit versus explicit levels of postconformism, that broaden the definition of higher stages and, at the same time, look for developmental discontinuities in the attainment of highest ego stages. Investigations into such enriched models of ego development would turn the (deadly) issue of highest stages that has long beset structural-developmental theories into a viable and vibrant research enterprise.

6

Exploring Facilitative Agents that Allow Ego Development to Occur

Paul W. Marko

A facilitative agent is a hypothetical construct that provides the impetus for ego development to occur or signals the occurrence of ego development. Change models dealing with this subject present both a gradually unfolding process and one marked with sudden breakthroughs in development. This chapter documents a search for the triggering agents involved in the breakthroughs that facilitate vertical growth. Finding these agents is important to increasing the understanding of how the growth process unfolds, and may provide keys to engendering development.

Loevinger's (1976) stage model of ego development coupled with Cook-Greuter's (1999) augmentation at the most expanded ranges of that model provides a conceptual framework for understanding the development of personality. Many studies demonstrate substantial support for both the validity and conceptual soundness of Loevinger's theory (Cohn & Westenberg, 2004; Manners & Durken, 2001). The veracity of Cook-Greuter's additional delineation is shown through her own rigorous research using both qualitative and quantitative methods (Cook-Greuter, 1999). Her work also illustrates how the reconceptualization of worldview changes as consciousness matures throughout life.

In developmental models characterizing consciousness evolution, a worldview is held in place by the adoption of assumptions and moved forward when those assumptions are exchanged for broader, more encompassing ones (Kegan, 1982; Loevinger, 1976; Wade, 1996; Wilber, 1986). Put another way, development happens when persistent inconsistencies appear and cannot be incorporated into the individual's current paradigm. In these instances, reorganization to a higher order of integration occurs (Hy & Loevinger, 1996; Wade, 1996). Inputs for these inconsistencies at the lower stages are thought to arise from interactions with the child's physical environment or as a consequence of brain development (Kegan, 1982; Piaget, 1965). Behaviors or ideas typical of a certain level simply do not work effectively and must be modified or automatically evolve into another type of reasoning to meet upcoming demands. In the higher levels of development, however, the origin of these inconsistencies is thought to be not only from feedback from the environment but may be from nonphysical, transcendent sources (Cook-Greuter, 2000; Wilber, 2000c). Only sketchy evidence currently exists to indicate that movement through the lower stages of development may also involve, to some extent, a similar type of transcendent consciousness (Wade, 1996). Regardless of the source or the cause of the perceived inconsistency, growth proceeds by shedding one worldview or set of assumptions about reality and adopting another.

Models depicting conceptualizations of how changes in worldview and human growth might take place are prolific (Beck & Cowan, 1995; Kegan, 1982; Piaget, 1952; Wilber, 2000a), but may not describe all of the mechanisms involved in these shifts in worldview. These change models depict the building up of conflicting ideas causing stress and dissatisfaction with the current state of affairs. They also describe a resolution process that takes place when ego development occurs in which the individual reconfigures his or her worldview around another set of assumptions and moves to a more sophisticated level of development (Cook-Greuter, 1999; Kegan, 1982; Maslow, 1971; Wade, 1996). An alternate perspective, however, might be that it is possible for changes of this magnitude to take place simply because of a new awareness, a new feeling about life or suddenly seeing something previously hidden. All of these possibilities may employ an enabling factor to allow or cause the change to happen. These *facilitative agents* could occur anywhere along the change continuum moving it incrementally forward or through a bolt of sudden awareness completely replacing the gradual process for this type of change.

The presence of facilitative agents has been alluded to in literature throughout history. Around the turn of the 20th century, scholars described sudden life-changing events related to the conversion experience chronicled in Christian literature (Bucke, 1901; James, 1961/1902). Peak experiences, which are sometimes sudden and unexpected, appear to propel both curative and growth-inducing changes (Maslow, 1971). In the field of modern transformational learning, the fact that rapid advancements can be made due to epochal events is recognized, but a requisite for this discipline is that the event only can take place as a natural unfolding of lived experience (Parks Daloz, 2000; Mezirow, 2000). While studying episodes of near-death experience (NDE), which are characteristically both sudden and unexpected, authors note that a worldview metamorphosis appears to take place after many such events. Looking closely at the results of these happenings reveals viewpoint changes consistent with ego-development levels (Groth-Marnat & Summers, 1998; Ring, 1984; von Lommel, van Wees, Meyers, & Elfferich, 2001).

It appears through the literature that facilitative agents exist whether engendering complete, instantaneous shifts in worldview, or motivating incremental events slowly sculpting a new viewpoint. Logically, these agents would take place in relation to life situations because most theories of the evolution of individual consciousness argue that the contextualization of life's experience is essential for progress. Attainment of the subsequent level of expansion is contingent on lessons learned in their current worldview (Beck & Cowan, 1995; Kegan, 1982; Torbert, 2004). Even sudden events unrelated to everyday lived experience, such as an NDE, may require years of contextualization before transformation occurs. In the therapeutic context, Wilber (2000a) referred to such a phenomenon as "curative catalysts" (p. 99). Curative catalysts provide the key concept required to release the individual from his or her existing paradigm and facilitate movement through the current circumstance to a new consciousness level. These concepts may appear at any age, perhaps experienced as new attitudes, feelings, morality lessons, insights, visions, or contrary ideas.

Studying the Lived Experience of Change

An empirical study (Marko, 2006) sought to investigate whether these facilitative agents or ideas that act as triggers or tipping points exist and if found, to explore their role in the reauthoring of core life assumptions and ego growth. The study sought to answer the following questions.

1. Do facilitative agents exist and if so, what are the agents (conceptual or affective triggers) that cause the rejection of assumptions that hold individual development at one stage and allow a reorganization of worldview to accommodate the successive level?

2. How do facilitative agents appear as lived experience?

3. Are there particular times, states of mind, or other environmental circumstances that might allow the facilitative agent to influence vertical growth?

4. Are there common facilitative agents for individual levels and if so what are they?

To find the answers, individuals who, based on their developmental level, had experienced many growth transitions, were asked to complete questionnaires and participate in interviews. Background information was gathered on related subjects from each of the participants. The results revealed a predominately homogeneous group of White, middle-class women. Only 5 of the 36 participants were male. All of the males were White professionals ranging in age from 41 to 58. The women participants were racially mixed, thus showing more diversity than the men. Three Asian and two Black women joined the study. The ages of the female participants ranged from 28 to 70. Their professions spread across many occupations from body worker and Jin Shin Jyutsu practitioner to contract negotiator. Participant ego-level scores as revealed by the Washington University Sentence Completion Test (SCT), ranged from Level E-7, the Individualistic stage, the minimum requirement for the study, to Level E-10, the Unitive stage, the highest stage able to be measured by the instrument. Nine participants scored at the E-7, Individualistic level; four scored at the E-8, Autonomous level; four individuals scored at the E-9, Construct-Aware level; and four participants scored as functioning at the E-10, Unitive stage of the Loevinger/Cook-Greuter model.

The participants were asked to recall a critical incident that they felt changed their perspective or way of being. Additionally, participants were queried regarding attitudes, feelings, and situations before and after the incident to determine if there had been an ego-level shift. Incidents that appeared to trigger a shift were regarded and reported as facilitative agents. Finding facilitative agents necessitated the exploration of examples of ego development and incidents that played a role in that change. The shift was analyzed using characteristics descriptive of ego level to ascertain if growth had taken place. If a determination of a change was made, then the incident was labeled a facilitative agent regardless of the nature or source of the incident. The design of this study involved a three-step assessment using a standardized measure, a questionnaire, and a follow-up structured interview.

To bring clarity to the presentation of findings, a certain amount of interpretation was necessary to delineate the role played by the facilitative agent regarding the ego-level change. Although this constitutes a somewhat subjective judgment on my part, without these decisions the findings would lack structure and understandability. To illustrate these findings in an easily understandable manner, they are presented in the context of three categories with examples. The first category consists of agents reported to have signaled the beginning of a change cycle. Participants described this type of agent as presenting an opening or awakening, beginning a long path of discovery or as a coming home, allowing a relaxing into whatever manifests. Many incidents found in this study comprised a second category, those occurring throughout the process allowing a series of incremental changes in viewpoint that eventually culminated in a new stage of development. The third category appeared to take place on the end of the change cycle signaling the final letting go of the old ego-level concepts and the embracing of new realizations provided by the expanded level.

Facilitative Agents Occurring at the Beginning of the Change Cycle

From the critical incidents and surrounding circumstances reported by the participants, several contained evidence that a facilitative agent occurred in the beginning of the change cycle and either provided impetus for the change or presented an opening for self-discovery. Participant Q appeared to surface from Level E-6, the Conscientious stage, and progress to Level E-7, the Individualistic stage, due to a sudden awareness of the depth of trauma she had experienced. The participant, 32 years of age at the time of the study, described an incident that took place only 2 years earlier in a couple's counseling session she attended with her partner. Q describes the incident as follows:

> I was in couple's counseling and the therapist had Jay and I draw our family charts. She spent a lot of time on mine, asking questions and drawing arrows for violence, alcohol/ drug abuse, divorce, sexual assault, etc. She then looked up at Jay and said, "do you understand how much trauma Q has sustained in her life . . . how every man in her childhood has violated or abandoned either her or her mother?" This statement was profound for me.

Subsequent to this event, Q felt relief and hope, having discovered that there was NOT "something permanently wrong with me." This feeling of relief, however, did not constitute her initial reaction to the revelation. Q said that at the time of the incident she became short of breath, hot, sweaty and experienced an unusual phenomenon with her eyes that she labeled as disassociation. This incident began 2 years of intense psychological work and self-discovery where Q became acutely aware of her bodily reactions to lived experience, her habitual patterns of life, and how her trauma affected her entire outlook. Psychological counseling during the intervening 2 years after the incident was done in an effort to relieve symptoms of post-traumatic stress disorder (PTSD). Positive outcomes related to the PTSD symptoms appear to have been accompanied by a rise in ego-development level.

This facilitative agent acted to awaken Q to the reality of her dilemma, and motivate her to move toward resolution. According to her SCT score, Q currently is functioning at the E-7 level. Her descriptions of herself before the incident and differences described between her approaches to life at the time of the study as compared with before the incident suggest that she experienced the event while functioning at the E-6 level. Q described herself before the incident as someone totally focused on success and self-improvement. According to Loevinger (1976), the achievement motive reaches its apex at the E-6, Conscientious stage. At this stage, the individual is concerned with objective accomplishment, and this motivation combines with a strong desire for self-improvement. Because of this concern for achievement, the individual at the Conscientious stage sees procrastination, wasting time, and disorganization as major problems (Loevinger & Wessler, 1970).

One of the differences between the E-6 level and the E-7 stage is the degree and way these two differing perspectives view the relationship between the inner life of the mind and the body. Whereas the E-6 individual sees a dichotomy between mind and body, the E-7 person sees interaction and integration. There is an increase in differentiation between thoughts and feelings, processes and outcomes. As the E-7 person develops, conflicts seem to be internal in addition to being between one's needs and society's requirements (Hy & Loevinger, 1996; Loevinger & Wessler, 1970).

Facilitative Agents Occurring Throughout the Change Cycle

Participant M offered a complex set of incidents that may describe a facilitative agent's involvement in an ego-level change. These occurrences may have been instrumental in allowing her to undertake and finalize a shift in conscious awareness between the E-6, Conscientious stage and the E-7, Individualistic stage. Whereas Q recounted a transformational path between these same two levels and identified the facilitative agent that initiated that process, M chronicles several incidents along a continuum between Levels E-6 and E-7. Like Q, M experienced ego development as a by-product of another type of pursuit involving a life struggle.

It has been postulated that adjustment to a difficult time, especially divorce might play a role in ego development (Bursik, 1991). Participant M described a detailed anatomy of that shift of consciousness through adversity, complete with the possible facilitative agents involved. Her intense introspection and self-examination as she left a 24-year marriage provided useful insight into the change process that facilitated growth. A similar phenomenon is demonstrated by Torbert's action inquiry process where life events are studied in an effort to spur ego growth and increase management effectiveness (Torbert, 1994, 2004).

According to M, her divorce, and her assumed rise in ego level, was promoted by three revelations that came to her in the form of metaphors. The first signaled a release or unfreezing from her existing situation. The second metaphor contained a pivotal conceptual shift that commonly undergoes a metamorphosis between Levels E-6 and E-7. This shift between ego levels likely occurred when the reconceptualization revealed in the second metaphor became totally embraced and incorporated into M's worldview. The adoption of this new paradigm was likely facilitated by the third metaphor.

The first metaphor brought into her awareness the thought that she and her husband may not be headed in the same direction. "Unconnected to any one event, I experienced—like a bolt out of the blue—that a larger change was looming . . . it is as if we are were crossing the same river but on different bridges, leading us in different directions." In this passage, she describes the first metaphor and perhaps revealed a clue to her ego level at the time. Through the image of the bridges leading in different directions, M allowed herself to accept the grave realization that her marriage may be ending. M, looking through the eyes of someone functioning at the E-6 level, felt guilt for not being able to do something to avoid it and was overcome with a deep sense of injustice. "The E-6 [E-6 Conscientious] subjects have a strong sense of responsibility and duties. When they feel guilt, it is more likely to be over consequences of actions than over breaking rules. . . . Along with responsibility goes a sense of rights, justice and fairness" (Hy & Loevinger, 1996, p. 16).

The second metaphor followed with a new concept that was to shatter her existing paradigm from that point forward. This second revelation, like the third, came in through a drawing that she made in a class.

> I remember doing this drawing and . . . what it meant to me. I had put my goals up at the top, which was this forest of trees and then I had done this . . . rock wall but it looked like marble, not jagged and rough but really smooth, so it was really hard to get a foothold. Then . . . I realized that I'm on this slippery slope . . . I go up to my goal that way by trying . . . and slipping backward, I could do that forever.

Frustration and feeling foolish that somehow her friends had seen the futility in her attempts to save her marriage gave rise to a new insight. M thought, that *if other people saw my situation differently, if my husband conceived it differently, how could this change the situation?* The metaphor gave rise to new concepts more commonly found on the E-7, Individualistic level. "Suddenly it was so obvious to me that I thought, 'Why haven't I seen this before?' It was a complete shift in perspective that in turn really affected my whole attitude."

Although Loevinger and Wessler (1970) state that the E-6 individual does relate to the perception of multiple possibilities and choice, at the E-7 stage, the person puts an increasing effort forth to discover and cope with reality and make a greater effort to be more objective about what is outside and what is felt inside (Hy & Loevinger, 1996). Intrapsychic conflict begins to appear at the E-7 level and comes into full bloom at Level E-8. At the E-7, Individualistic stage, how one conceptualizes life becomes much less egocentric and the person embraces a broader view of life as a whole (Loevinger & Wessler, 1970). Individuals begin to realize that things are not necessarily what they appeared to be at earlier stages and that reality depends on perspective. This conceptualization forms the groundwork for the progress made due to the third metaphor.

This metaphor, again appearing in a drawing, formed the basis for severing M's relationship and perhaps surfacing to the new ego paradigm. As with the drawing of the slippery slope, the significance was not apparent to M immediately. She began to see the waterfall as a metaphor for her making a decision to let go of her relationship, "You can't prevent the water from going over the edge." Unlike her reaction to the first metaphor, however, M saw this image as positive. Although at the time of this study, she was still building her new life, according to her SCT, she was approaching life from the E-7, Individualistic perspective. Obviously, there are many more events and elements that were involved in M's divorce and perhaps her transitional journey from Level E-6 to E-7, however, she regarded the above as critical incidents along the path that could be referred to as facilitative agents.

Facilitative Agents Occurring Near the End of the Change Cycle

In this study, several incidents either appeared at the end of the change cycle or provided breakthrough knowing that could have hastened the completion of the change. These incidents are organized in ascending order of E-level, beginning with transitions from the *Self-protective* to the E-4, Conformist stage through incidents that describe the shift from the E-9, Construct-aware to the E-10, Unitive level of development.

The journey from the Self-protective stage of development to the E-4, Conformist stage usually takes place during the child's early school years. Loevinger uses the title Self-protective stage, because of the child's emerging, albeit somewhat innocent, notion of self-control. "Controls are at first fragile, and there is a corresponding vulnerability and guardedness, hence we term the stage Self-Protective . . . his main rule is 'Don't get caught' " (Loevinger, 1976, p. 17). Blame lies exclusively externally and getting caught becomes the measure of right or wrong. Loevinger describes the mode of operation at this stage as "opportunistic hedonism" (Loevinger & Wessler 1970, p. 4) where life is a zero-sum game—"your loss is my gain."

Around school age, most children progress to the Conformist level, Stage 4 (Hy & Loevinger, 1996; Loevinger, 1970; Loevinger, & Wessler, 1970). This level is characterized by the development of identification with a group and the authority of the group. The child, or adult, displays an obedience for rules, not out of fear of reprisals as in the Self-protective stage, but because these rules are accepted by the larger group. This accompanies an association with, and an entrusting of, his or her welfare to the larger group. At the Conformist stage, individuals put a great deal of effort into conforming to social conventions and standards (Loevinger, 1976). Individuals, at this stage, are preoccupied with appearance, material possessions, and social acceptance. They often disapprove of hostility and aggression, unlike individuals at the Self-protective stage who often flaunt their aggression (Loevinger & Wessler, 1970). The shift is dramatic and moves the individual from a self-serving, self-centered entity working for his or her own ends to a person able to understand the rules and roles in a society. Participants N and U describe incidents that appear to mark the beginning of the Conformist stage.

Participant U was 41 years old during the study, but even as an adult recalled vividly an incident that happened to him 34 years earlier when he was a child.

> When I was 7ish, I was in a fight with my friend Kenny, only it really wasn't a fight. He just stood in front of me with his arms crossed, saying nothing, and I pushed him down. He got up, arms crossed, saying nothing, just looking at me. I pushed him down again . . . he stood up . . . I pushed him down. . . . He never fought back, never said a word. Finally, I stopped and ran away . . . and I hid and I cried and I prayed for the first time in my life. I was ashamed of what I had done.

U was suddenly and unexpectedly questioning his motives, who he was, and why he would hurt his friend Kenny. U reports a permanent change in his attitude after the incident. The impact of this realization that he was now responsible for his actions to the world certainly is not characteristic of the Self-protective stage of development. This might be an example of a facilitative agent bringing to the surface the newly emerging ego level and marks the first conscious awareness of that new perspective. The two stages bridged by U's incident stand as dramatically different in their orientation toward how others are treated, especially toward common roles like friends and family members. Another example of this shift is characterized by an incident recalled by participant N.

> I dreamt that I was at the bottom of a hill and when I looked around, there was a big fire and people . . . were helping to put out the fire. I started looking around for my mother . . . no one could find her. There was a deep sense of fear that she was caught in the fire and I started crying in my sleep.

During the interview, N recalled many details of this lucid dream a full 34 years after it occurred. Immediately following the dream, N reports having two major shifts in her perspective on life. She had a change in the way she viewed her relationship with her mother and how she conceptualized right and wrong. Additionally, her view of death, its meaning and importance, was altered. Both of these changes could be evidence that she had completed the shift from the Self-protective stage to the Conformist stage.

N emerged with a new sense of responsibility and a transformed idea of death. N realized after this dream how important her mother was to her, and that she wanted to strive constantly to please her mother. This sense of responsibility to her mother, perhaps as a symbol of a relationship to a protective society, seemed to be elevated to her conscious awareness by this dream. A strong sense of right and wrong emerged. Additionally, she found that she also was left with a new conceptualization of death. From the time of the dream, N became very aware of the inevitability of dying and the purpose of life and obsessed with using time effectively. Both of these shifts may be indicative of ego development.

The Conformist stage of ego development, the fourth level, is almost universally described in developmental models (Beck & Cowan, 1995; Kegan, 1994; Wade, 1996; Wilber, 2000a). Although Loevinger does not specifically refer to the reconceptualization of death at this stage, Wade, whose model parallels Loevinger's in many respects, considers shifts in perspective on the issue of death to be specifically indicative of level change. Wade describes the idea of death that is held at the stage that precedes her Conformist stage as an adversary to be out maneuvered. It looms as an enemy force that can be avoided by not getting caught. This conception changes drastically at the Conformist stage, where death is seen as an inescapable biological process. This shift in supposition changes everything regarding life orientation for the child. "The certainty of death means that Conformist people live to control their fate when that eventuality overtakes them. . . . The notion of reciprocity extending over linear time (a "fair" cosmos) creates morality, the need to do good and control today in order to be rewarded eventually" (Wade, 1996, p. 127). Whether or not N or U consciously thought of eventual punishment or reward after their experiences remains unknown; what is certain is that their orientation toward good and bad, and relationships was transformed. After the experience of these concluding facilitative agents, they both took actions to form bonds with society and not, as in the Self-protective stage, totally focus on self-interest. These incidents demonstrate a dramatic, sudden, and highly contrasting switch of viewpoint.

Just as dramatic as the shift from Level E-6 to E-7 experienced by Q and M, and the change from E-3 to E-4 by the two 7-year-olds is the transformation from E-8, the Autonomous stage to the E-9, the Construct-aware stage. Participant K scored in the E-9 range on the

SCT. She had been involved in human growth and introspective activities for many years prior to the incident. K felt that human unfolding is a gradual process, but portrays these incidents as turning points or milestones in her development.

K's incident appeared in a dream that occurred a few days after she enrolled in a "Shaktipat Intensive" given by Siddha Guru. She felt that she was a "seeker" but understood spiritual awakening only on an intellectual level, and had not made the leap to direct experience. In 1989, she had a dream in which she received spiritual awakening or initiation. According to K, a radiant man with a beard and robes appeared in a dream. He seemed very affectionate toward her. She reports after the dream, "I woke up, feeling aware for the first time that I was unconditionally loved, and that the essence of everything, including myself, was this love." Unaware who this Guru was, his connection to her remained an enigma.

A major difference between the E-8, Autonomous stage and the E-9, Construct-aware stage appears as an increased access to intuition, bodily states, feelings, dreams, and other transpersonal knowing. In the Construct-aware stage, Level 9 in the Cook-Greuter (2000) system, these sources of knowledge rival rational deliberation as a way of making sense of life experiences. Although K was not adverse to direct experience, her incident reinforced the importance of turning inward rather than looking outward for answers. K reports that now there are times of regression, where she senses less of a connection, but she no longer feels isolated. She feels that she can always turn inward and reconnect with that ultimate love. Cook-Greuter (2000) refers to E-9, Construct-aware individuals as being intuition-directed. They have had the experience of direct knowing and seek it as a permanent type of awareness, but it is not fully available to them. The intermittent direct knowing of the E-9, Construct-aware individual as described by Cook-Greuter (2000) includes a yearning for more constant access to transpersonal experience. "It seems that for some people, once awakened, the desire to go beyond the judging mind becomes all-powerful. They want to be free of endlessly categorizing and labeling experience" (p. 236). This seems to be apparent in the E-9 participants in the study; however, there also appears a counterpoint, a mysterious, holding back that also may be common at this level. How can a person exist in a rational world having seen this vastly different reality? This conflict and unsolvable paradox vanishes at the E-10, Unitive stage of ego development. At the Construct-aware level, an attachment remains to old habits of the mind, to parse, judge, and rationalize. Additionally, there appears to be a conscious or subconscious reluctance to totally let go and live in direct knowing.

Discussion

The findings indicate that facilitative agents exist, although their location and role are not exclusively that of a conceptual or affective trigger to signal a change of ego level. The findings describe developmental processes that are not always "seamless." Rather the processes could better be characterized as a gradual unfolding punctuated by facilitative agents that occur in places along the course and serve to move the growth along. These agents appear in many ways at times subtle and other times quite dramatic. Although facilitative agents can occur in normal waking consciousness, they seem to happen more often in alternative or altered states. Additionally, when they take place in normal waking consciousness they happen in extreme states such as a time of great focus, as when participating in a highly absorbing endeavor or in an extremely excited or anxious state. In this small sample, common facilitative agents were not found specific to any developmental level. There are, however, indications that facilitative agents play different roles at different levels, depending on the change process that is occurring.

Of the facilitative agents in this study only a small percentage occurred in waking consciousness the rest took place in altered or alternative realms. Of the incidents reported in altered consciousness, three took place in states altered by ritual, such as meditation or trance, and three in consciousness altered by hallucinogenic substances. It is interesting to note that none of these transpired in participants scoring at the E-7 level, all arose in the Levels E-8 and above. Three of the incidents happened during lucid dreaming. Of the five that took place in normal waking consciousness, one took place while experiencing the extreme stress of PTSD in remembering a past trauma, another occurred in an inspired state where the participant was blind to the significance of a drawing until after the creative state had passed. One incident took place during a healing by nonphysical means, not generally undertaken in an ordinary state of consciousness. It appears, therefore, that only two incidents occurred in the everyday normal waking state. Although this is a small sample from which to draw conclusions, and the participants were not selected randomly, it is interesting to speculate why this was the case. Perhaps the all-encompassing control demanded by the ego is less able to discredit or disregard data inconsistent with its viewpoint in an altered or alternative state. In addition, the alternative or altered state may provide an avenue for direct contact with the subtle or casual realms of the mind (Wilber, 2000c), which contain ultimate wisdom. More work is needed to explore either of these hypotheses.

There appeared to be three developmental processes at work in these examples. Additionally, certain processes seem associated with particular ranges of ego levels. Dividing the levels into three groupings; the lower range of development, before Level E-5; the middle range of development, E-5 through E-7 or E-8; and the upper range, E-9 and E-10. These three ranges featured different change processes. On the most elementary level, the two children who likely moved to the E-3, Conformist level immediately following a memorable event changed through still another process. They both had sudden realizations. Again, with the small number of samples, nothing can be said definitively, but it is a consistent observation. In the middle range of the model, the dilemma-based growth pattern is evident. This model is commonly described by scholars who have studied growth through adversity (Bursik, 1991; Helson & Roberts, 1994; Helson & Srivastava, 2001; Kegan, 1982; L. King, 2001). Those models characterize a process that begins with the stable ego. Then the individual is presented with a dilemma containing factors that create dissonance with the ego's current paradigm. If the ego cannot integrate these new factors it may release its current worldview and begin to embrace the higher-level viewpoint.

The E-9 and E-10 group describes a somewhat different process. In these changes, the participant becomes a seeker, someone who desires to see beyond their current paradigm. They pursue growth-inducing practices or experiment in a serious manner with alterations of consciousness. Growth for these individuals comes through a series of incidents or revelations and breakthroughs that frequently are self-induced. In many examples, the final release into the new ego level was triggered by a spiritually oriented event or happening. Evidence of the dilemma-based growth pattern, however, did appear with one high-level participant. All of the other higher-level incidents involve this searching and then finding change process. In closing, it should be noted that many of the shifts in awareness described in critical incidents that are not mentioned in this chapter, did not involve an elevation of ego level.

7

The Postconventional Self

Ego Maturity, Growth Stories . . . and Happiness?

Jack J. Bauer

This chapter explores the postconventional self in the context of growth, happiness, and optimal human development. I use the term *postconventional self* as a label for how people at the postconventional stages of ego development (Loevinger, 1976), Stages 7 to 9, think and feel about their lives. That is, the postconventional self is the self-identity of these individuals.[1] A growing body of research suggests that the postconventional self represents an important but partial portrait of optimal human development. In this chapter, I attempt to establish the following claims:

1. A central feature of the postconventional self is the concept of growth. In other words, people with a postconventional self tend to identify with the concept of growth.

2. There are different kinds of growth. The postconventional self does not, on average, focus on the kinds of growth associated with happiness and well-being.

3. As it turns out, research also demonstrates that the postconventional self is not necessarily a happy self: Ego development itself tends not to correlate with well-being.

4. The concept of optimal human development should include qualities not only of ego maturity but also of well-being.

As such, the postconventional self represents only half the picture of optimal human development.

5. Self-actualization may pose an exception to this rule. New data presented here tentatively suggest that the highest postconventional stage involves both ego maturity and well-being.

6. Research on intentional self-development suggests that growth-mindedness, and different forms of it, might not only lead to optimal human development but might also be a skill that can be learned.

The Postconventional Preoccupation With the Idea of Growth

The postconventional personality has numerous characteristics that suggest high levels of development (for a review, see Pfaffenberger, 2005). The postconventional self, however, is not merely a self-identity that has grown to a high level. The postconventional self is also a self-identity in which the concept of growth is central to the meaning of the self-identity itself. In this section, I outline the notion of growth as a subjectively construed concept and how the person at postconventional stages of ego development conceptualizes growth in an increasingly more complex or integrative manner.

A Preoccupation With the Concept of Growth

As typically studied, growth in a person's self-identity means that the self-identity *has attained* growth, as when a person's self-identity becomes more structurally integrated, more conceptually complex, more interdependent, or otherwise more mature (e.g., Damon & Hart, 1988; Kegan, 1982; Labouvie-Vief, 2005). Such theories, notably Loevinger's (1976) theory of ego development, perhaps better reflect the structural complexity of self-identity than its content (McAdams, 1985). Yet Loevinger's theory does claim that each stage tends toward particular value orientations. For example, individuals at the postconventional level have a *preoccupying concern* for growth. With this observation, the view of growth switches from growth as an objective pattern of progress over time to growth as a person's subjective concept of progress (i.e., on growth as a mental construct that is used to make sense of events over time).

Structuring the Concept of Growth at the Postconventional Stages

Regardless of a person's ego-development level, periodic assessments of growth may be necessary for keeping levels of well-being afloat (Ryff & Keyes, 1995). Most people will, from time to time, interpret their lives in a way that suggests growth, even if it means they have to retrospectively underestimate their past abilities in order to make it appear as though they have grown since then (Ross, 1989). However, in the earlier stages of ego development, one does not need to identify primarily with the concept of growth in order for that person's self-identity to grow. It just will grow—on average in modern, industrialized societies—to the conventional level.

Individuals at the postconventional level of personality development—people who have a postconventional self—routinely use concepts of growth to make sense of their own lives. They are not merely aware of their own growth; they routinely value growth and look to it as a primary source of meaning in their lives. These individuals identify themselves with the ongoing process of growing. They evaluate themselves according to whether they are growing—and, especially at Stage 8, *Autonomous*, whether they are helping others grow also. They judge actions in terms of whether those actions promote growth. In short, they are preoccupied with growth.

Loevinger (1976) described the person at Stage 7, Individualistic, as preoccupied with development, as one who can routinely distinguish between process and outcome. Whereas the subjective concern for development arises more haphazardly for individuals at the Conscientious stage (Stage 6), or prior, individuals at Stage 7 more routinely interpret events not only in terms of outcomes but also in terms of process. Thus, these individuals interpret events and people within broader contexts, notably in terms of incremental or unfolding processes. The concept of growth becomes no longer a matter of periodic assessments of whether growth was attained. It becomes a subtler matter, a matter not of merely attaining some end point but rather of progressing. The end point itself is also perceived in a more subtle fashion, less in terms of appearances and more in terms of abstract principles, as moving toward the principles of postconventional moral reasoning or self-actualization (Kohlberg, 1969; Maslow, 1968). Additionally, end points or goals are viewed in a more flexible fashion, such that previous conceptions of end points may change or have alternative appearances as a process unfolds (Brandtstadter, Wentura, & Rothermund, 1999; Vaillant, 1977). The person at the Individualistic stage is beginning to do this but still struggles with thinking about psychosocial conflicts as internal. For example, from the perspective of a woman at the Individualistic stage who is conflicted over family and work issues, "If only society or (my) husband were more helpful and accommodating, there need be no conflict" (Loevinger, 1976, p. 22). That conflict is part of the human condition is not routinely recognized until the Autonomous stage (Stage 8). Still, the self-identity at the Individualistic stage—the early postconventional self—is concerned with the process of growth, even if the perception of one's own growth is more outcome-bound and individualistic than it will become at the next stage (Bauer, 2008).

By the time the person reaches Loevinger's Autonomous stage of ego development, the person's focus on growth includes a more dynamic, process-oriented, interdependent view of the self and others. Self-fulfillment or self-actualization takes center stage as a personal concern, and the person becomes more tolerant and accepting of others' perspectives—as well as of conflicting perspectives and motivations of one's own. At the Integrated stage (Stage 9), the emphasis on self-actualization continues, although probably in a less-rigid fashion than in the Autonomous stage, where the goal of self-actualization was first adopted as a primary concern.[2] Self-actualization itself becomes at the Integrated stage less something to attain and more something that is approached—less an outcome called "self-actualization" than a progressive process of self-actualizing (Maslow, 1968). The person at the Integrated stage is less concerned with the problem of identifying oneself as "self-actualized" than at the Autonomous stage.

Furthermore, around the Integrated stage, people routinely understand that their concepts of growth—and other concepts of self, others, and so on—are just that: concepts, ideas, mental constructs (Cook-Greuter, 2000). Cook-Greuter calls this the Construct-Aware stage because people at this stage are keenly aware of the fact that their understanding of the world (and here, self-identity) is in fact constructed. But it is not that people at this stage merely understand this idea; this idea can be grasped at earlier stages, albeit in a more abstract, impersonal manner. It is that these people understand this fact personally, *in situ*, as something that shapes their experience in the present moment. They draw on this knowledge in the moment when evaluating the self and others and when deciding what to do in a given situation. For people at the Construct-aware stage, knowledge of the linguistic limitations of concepts, including growth and self-identity, is so well understood that it routinely influences the individual's reactions to people and events. For example, a person at the Construct-aware stage is less likely to judge others—and even the self—based on particular views of growth that he or she knows might not be appropriate to the situation at hand. Similarly, the person's experience with trying to live out idealized versions of self-actualization has taught him or her the limitations of particular concepts of self-actualization. Whereas people at Individualistic, Stage 7, and especially Autonomous, Stage 8, use the concept of growth as a primary source of meaning in their self-identity, people at the Integrated level, Stage 9, might understand more fully, and accept the inevitability that the concept of growth itself is a concept, with all the linguistic baggage that implies. This acceptance helps guard against identifying with overly idealistic notions of growth.

Growth Stories and the Postconventional Self

The preceding section attempts to establish that persons at postconventional stages of ego development are preoccupied with the idea of growth. This section focuses on the medium of thinking through which these people use as the idea of growth to construct a meaningful self-identity. That medium is the personal narrative or life story. In short, the postconventional self is a growth story. However, there are different kinds of growth, and therefore different kinds of growth stories. Research on narrative identity has demonstrated what these kinds of growth look and sound like.

The Empirical Study of Narrative Identity

People make sense of their lives by creating a self-identity, and they do this by creating life stories (McAdams, 2008). People interpret the events in their lives in narrative form, and people link those events together in narrative form. This process takes place in everyday life, as people participate in activities, talk about them with others, think about other's perspectives on them, and reflect on how all these things fit together. In doing so, people engage in an ongoing process of constructing and reconstructing their life stories and self-identity, as well as co-constructing those stories with others (McLean, 2008; Pasupathi, 2001; Pasupathi, Alderman, & Shaw, 2007; Thorne, 2000).

Life stories, like stories generally, make use of characters, plots, themes, tones, and other narrative elements to convey meaning (McAdams, 2008). Themes, which have been widely examined in narrative research, are especially important for this chapter. Themes give meaning to a life story by linking personal events to personally held values repeatedly throughout the episodes of a life story. Two of the great themes in life stories and life-story research are agency, such as power and mastery, and communion, that is intimacy and sharing (McAdams et al., 2006; Woike, Lavezzary, & Barsky, 1995). In addition to these two, a third theme—growth—is receiving increasing attention and is the topic of the next section.[3]

The Growth Story: Thematic Content of the Postconventional Self

A growth story is a personal narrative that emphasizes a theme of development or developmental processes (Bauer, McAdams, & Pals, 2008). In other words, a growth story uses the concept of growth as a theme to give the story meaning. To the degree that a person's life story is a growth story, that person values and identifies with the concept of growth. That person uses the concept of growth to interpret meaning in the past (growth memories; Bauer, McAdams, & Sakaeda, 2005) and to plan for a meaningful future (growth goals; Bauer, 2009; Bauer & McAdams, 2004a). For example, in a growth memory, a person describes an event as important explicitly because he or she grew—or a relationship deepened, and so on—as a result of that event. Growth goals are goals that aim explicitly toward personal growth. People at the postconventional level of ego development, compared with those at earlier levels, express more growth memories and growth goals when talking about their lives. In other words, the postconventional self is filled with growth memories and growth goals.

In the broadest sense, growth themes in narratives emphasize growth in the sense of Maslow's (1968) notion of growth versus safety, where growth involves a concern for things like progress, deepening, learning, and exploration, rather than protection, preservation, conservation, and defending. In a nutshell, the prototypical growth story conveys an *underlying concern* for *personally meaningful, progressive processes* over time (for elaboration, see Bauer & McAdams, 2010). Yet growth themes come in different forms or kinds.

What Growth Sounds Like: How Growth Themes Relate to Ego Maturity

When one detects a growth theme in someone's life story, what does growth sound like? Over the past several years, based on research by others and myself, I have distinguished two, higher-level growth themes: intellectual and experiential. Intellectual and experiential growth themes deal with the thinking and feeling facets of personality development. Intellectual growth themes emphasize one's increasing capacity to *think complexly* or *integratively* about the self and others, whereas experiential growth themes emphasize one's increasing capacity to *feel good* about the self and others. These two growth themes come in agentic or communal types, representing the intrapersonal and interpersonal facets of either intellectual or experiential growth.

Intellectual Growth Themes

Intellectual growth themes emphasize the seeking and integration of new conceptual perspectives. These are perhaps more accurately called sociointellectual growth themes, as they involve the integration of particularly sociointellectual perspectives (Bauer & McAdams, 2004a). These are the growth themes that have the strongest ties to postconventional stages of ego development. Intellectual growth memories are called by different names, such as accommodation in meaningful life events (L. King, Scollon, Ramsey, & Williams, 2000; L. King & Noelle, 2005); causal connections between life events and one's broader concept of self (Pals, 2006a); and gaining insights, learning lessons, and exploring new perspectives (Bauer & McAdams, 2004b; Bauer et al., 2005; McLean, 2005; Pals, 2006a). Intellectual growth goals have been referred to as learning goals (Dweck, 1999), goal complexity (McAdams, Ruetzel, & Foley, 1986), elaboration of possible selves (L. King & Smith, 2004), and exploratory goals (Bauer & McAdams, 2004a). In these studies, intellectual growth memories and goals show consistent ties to higher stages of ego development and other measures of psychosocial maturity.

Experiential Growth Themes

Experiential growth themes emphasize a deepening in the felt experience of one's life, but *not* necessarily with an emphasis on gaining a deeper *conceptual* understanding of the self or others. In this way, experiential growth themes are relatively more socioemotional than the intellectual themes, which are more sociointellectual; the distinction being a matter of relative emphasis (Bauer & McAdams, 2004a). In general, experiential growth themes are focused on whether one's actions match with humanistic rather than materialistic values (e.g., on cultivating personally meaningful skills and on fostering meaningful relationships rather than on seeking status, appearances, material gain, and others' approval; Kasser & Ryan, 1993). Experiential growth themes may be agentic, such as a strengthened sense of self (Calhoun & Tedeschi, 2001) or communal, such as intimacy or generativity (de St. Aubin, McAdams, & Kim, 2004; McAdams et al., 2006). But again, intellectual growth may or may not be part of this focus on experiential growth. Studies consistently show that experiential growth memories and goals correlate with well-being (e.g., Bauer et al., 2005; L. King et al., 2000; Pals, 2006b). However, experiential growth themes typically do not correlate with ego development or other measures of psychosocial maturity. In other words, experiential growth themes are not characteristic of the postconventional self.

Is the Postconventional Self a Happy Self?

If ego development is so great, then the postconventional self should be a happy self, right? Yet study after study shows that higher stages of ego maturity do not correlate significantly with measures of happiness, well-being, or psychological health (Bauer & McAdams, 2004b, 2008; Bauer et al., 2005; Block, 1971; Bursik, 1991; Helson & Roberts, 1994; Helson & Wink, 1992; L. King & Noelle, 2005; L. King & Raspin, 2004; L. King et al., 2000; L. King & Smith, 2004; Pals, 2006b; Vaillant, 1977; Westenberg & Block, 1993). In other words, people at the postconventional level of ego development are just as likely to be happy as unhappy. But how can this be? After all, ego development has been hailed as "one of the most comprehensive constructs in the field of personality development" (Westenberg & Block, 1993, p. 792). Plus, Western thought has a history of lumping together psychosocial maturity, such as wisdom, virtue, moral reasoning, meaning-making, and happiness (Flanagan, 1990). How can it be possible that Loevinger's (1976) ego development, which taps into so many facets of psychosocial maturity, actually has nothing to do with happiness and well-being?

To start, Loevinger herself claims that ego development is not a theory of psychological health. Generally speaking, structural theories of development (e.g., Piaget, 1970a)—those that chart how the mind organizes information—tend to have a more intellectual than emotional emphasis, corresponding more to measures of intelligence than of health and well-being.[4] Thus the lack of correlation between ego development and well-being amounts to empirical support of the theory itself.

Additionally, the claim I made earlier that "the postconventional self is a growth story" was too general. The research demonstrates that the postconventional self is more specifically an *intellectual* growth story. People at higher stages of ego development tend to have intellectual growth narratives but not necessarily experiential growth narratives (Bauer & McAdams, 2004a, 2004b, 2008; L. King & Noelle, 2005; L. King & Raspin, 2004; L. King et al., 2000; L. King & Smith, 2004).

And only experiential growth narratives, not intellectual growth narratives, correlate with well-being. In other words, people at the postconventional level of ego development do not appear to be especially concerned with the kinds of personal growth that lead toward happiness and well-being, and they are not especially likely to be happy or have higher levels of well-being.

Optimal Human Development

Based on the previous observations, for people at the postconventional level of ego development, just as for people at preconventional and conventional levels, ego maturity and well-being seem to function as two distinct paths of personality development (Bauer & McAdams, 2004a). A more optimal and well-rounded portrait of human development would seem to integrate both paths, as portrayed in Maslow's (1968) concept of self-actualization and Rogers' (1989) concept of the fully functioning person.

Toward the Good Life: Eudaimonic Growth

People who have high levels of both ego development and well-being are said to be living the "good life"—not in terms of the materialistic American Dream, but rather in terms of a philosophical notion of the good life that dates at least to Aristotle (Bauer et al., 2005; L. King, 2001). Aristotle's term for the good life, *eudaimonia*, applied to the person who had cultivated a high degree of virtue as well as pleasure. In modern psychology, eudaimonic well-being refers to a combination of meaning, growth, and hedonic happiness (see Deci & Ryan, 2008; Ryan & Deci, 2001). Here meaning and growth often translate into psychosocial maturity, which includes virtue and moral reasoning but extends to psychosocial perspective-taking more generally, as is aptly captured by Loevinger's ego development (Bauer et al., 2008). As for empirical measures of change over time, a combined growth in both levels of ego development and levels of happiness has been called eudaimonic personality development, or eudaimonic growth (Bauer, 2008; Bauer & McAdams, 2010).

Eudaimonic Growth and Self-Actualization: Data Analysis

The postconventional self seems to represent half the picture of eudaimonia. However, perhaps a fuller picture can be found in a subset of the group of people at the postconventional level—those at the highest, Integrated stage, Stage 9. Loevinger (1976) equates her Integrated stage with Maslow's (1968) concept of self-actualization. In addition to having very high degrees of ego maturity, self-actualization is characterized as the pinnacle of psychological health (Maslow, 1968). Maslow described self-actualization not only in terms of a deep understanding of the human condition, that is, ego maturity, but also in terms of self-acceptance and the capacity to enjoy oneself. Given the tie to self-actualization, it seems intuitively reasonable that people at the Integrated stage would report higher levels of well-being than those at other stages. To attempt some empirical test of this, I reanalyzed data from four samples published previously (Bauer & McAdams, 2004a, 2004b, 2008; Bauer et al., 2005).

Methodology

The four studies in total included 331 participants (see Table 7.1). Studies employed the Washington University Sentence Completion Test (SCT; Hy & Loevinger, 1996). In each study, an advanced graduate student spent several months in training to code the SCT and attained high levels of agreement ($\geq 80\%$) with test items. In the new analyses, for each sample, I compared levels of well-being among people at the highest stage of ego development versus those at lower stages. In two of the studies, no participants scored at the Integrated stage, so for those studies I ran analyses of those at the Autonomous stage (Stage 8) versus all other stages (figuring that they represented the highest stage, relative to the others in that sample). Well-being was measured via two, widely used, self-report scales of well-being. The Satisfaction with Life Scale (Diener, Emmons, Larson, & Griffen, 1985) asks participants to rate five items with a seven-point Likert-type scale that address how satisfied they are with their lives (e.g., "I am satisfied with my life" and "If I could live my life over, I would change almost nothing"). The Psychological Well-Being scale (Ryff & Keyes, 1995) uses 54 items and a six-point Likert-type scale to measure six dimensions of eudaimonic well-being: autonomy, environmental mastery, personal growth, positive relationships, purpose in life, and self-acceptance.

Results

Across the four studies (see Table 7.1), there was a distinct, although not always statistically significant, trend: Participants at the highest stage of ego development appeared to be happier and more focused

Table 7.1. Happiness and Self-Actualization? Comparing People at the Highest Stage of ED versus Other Stages in Terms of Well-Being and Experiential Growth Narratives

Study	ED group (n)	Well-being M (SD)	Test	Exper. Growth Themes f		Test
				Low	High	
1	ED = 9 (2)	PWB = 44.67 (0.94)	t = 1.91++	0	2	X² = 2.00++
	ED ≤ 8 (49)	PWB = 42.80 (4.97)		25	24	
2	ED = 9 (2)	PWB = 68.33 (0.71)	t = 5.34**	0	2	X² = 1.38
	ED ≤ 8 (123)	PWB = 64.04 (6.95)		49	70	
3	ED = 8 (3)	LS = 28.67 (3.06)	t = 3.35*	0	3	X² = 3.05+
	ED = 7 (64)	LS = 21.95 (7.60)		33	31	
4	ED = 8 (3)	LS = 29.33 (3.51)	t = 1.19++	0	3	X² = 1.30
	ED ≤ 7 (85)	LS = 25.65 (5.29)		26	59	

++p < .20. +p < .10. *p < .05. **p < .001.

Note: Studies 1 and 2 = Adults and students, respectively (Bauer & McAdams, 2004a; Bauer et al., 2005). Study 3 = Adults (Bauer & McAdams, 2004b). Study 4 = Student longitudinal (Bauer & McAdams, 2010). ED = ego development. "ED = x" or "ED ≤ x" = grouping of participants by ED stage or stages. PWB = psychological well-being. LS = life satisfaction. Exper. Growth = experiential growth themes. f = frequencies of participants in each category. Low, High = Below or above the median.

on experiential growth than participants at lower stages. As for well-being, participants at the highest stage always had a mean level of well-being that was higher numerically (although not always statistically significantly) than those at lower stages. As for experiential growth narratives, participants at the highest stage always had more than the median number of growth narratives, whereas participants at lower stages were more evenly split above and below the median (differences in actual numbers, not statistical significance). Additionally, participants at the other postconventional stages did not come even close to having higher levels of well-being or experiential growth memories than people at lower stages, including those at the Autonomous level, Stage 8, in Studies 1 and 2 of Table 7.1.[5] Despite the fact that most differences were not statistically significant, these data suggest that people at the highest stage of ego development not only might possess heightened ego maturity but also might be happier and more focused on experiential growth.

Optimal Development: The Fully Functioning Person and Transcending Self-Interest

Self-actualization and eudaimonic growth have a parallel in Rogers' (1989) fully functioning person, who essentially has high levels of ego maturity as well as well-being. But high levels of functioning alone are not sufficient, for full functioning "is not any fixed state" (p. 410). The fully functioning person, according to Rogers, has an overarching, subjective concern for the ongoing processes of growth. Earlier I emphasized that high levels of ego development by definition involve a concern for intellectual growth. In contrast, high levels of well-being do not; one need not think deeply about one's life to be happy. However, the data reported in this chapter suggest that people at the higher end of the postconventional levels also might think deeply about their lives in ways that foster happiness. This means they are concerned with themes of experiential growth. In other words, these people not only have high levels of ego maturity and happiness, but they also tend to think about their lives in ways that foster growth both in their conceptual self-understanding and in their nonconceptual experience of life.

The present findings, coupled with past research, suggest two paths to happiness: The simpler one involves being satisfied with what one has in life, not that this is always *simple* to do, regardless of ego maturity. As such, happiness functions as a personality disposition that seems to have a sizable genetic component (Diener et al., 2006). Haidt (2006) has likened the genetic endowment of happiness to "winning the cortical lottery." The other path involves thinking deeply about life—a path that yields happiness only if one scales the heights of ego development (if the preliminary data are correct). L. King (2001) calls this path "the hard road to the good life." This path comes with some seeming paradoxes, such as developing happiness only when one ceases to idealize growth and happiness, and that detachment from one's own self-interest leads to a more fully engaged and enjoyable life (Bauer, 2008).

Intentional Self-Development: Fostering Ego Maturity and Happiness

This section addresses two questions: First, can people intentionally cultivate higher levels of ego maturity and happiness by interpreting and planning their lives in terms of growth? Second, can such growth-mindedness be taught?

The Intentional Cultivation of Ego Maturity and Happiness

The following research suggests that people's intellectual-growth narratives foster subsequent increases in ego maturity, whereas people's experiential-growth narratives foster subsequent increases in well-being.

Intentional Ego Maturity

To test people's intentional efforts to foster intellectual growth, my colleagues and I conducted a 3-year longitudinal study enrolling persons during and after college. Participants on average showed an increase in ego maturity by approximately one ego stage over the 3 years. But a significant portion of this increase was explained by whether participants had intellectual growth goals. Participants who had more intellectual growth goals were more likely to show increases in ego development three years later, controlling for initial levels of ego development and beyond normative increases in ego development (Bauer & McAdams, 2010). In other words, they planned for intellectual growth, and their capacities for psychosocial thinking increased. Similarly, in a 2-year longitudinal study, gay and lesbian participants provided narratives of their gay and straight "best possible selves" (L. King & Smith, 2004). Greater conceptual elaboration of straight best possible selves predicted increases in ego development two years later, suggesting that the thoughtful exploration of alternate life paths may promote ego development. Turning to mostly cross-sectional research, older adults are more likely than younger adults to tell life stories that emphasize psychosocial meanings rather than merely life facts (Pasupathi, 2001; Pasupathi & Mansour, 2006). In one data set, older adults had marginally higher levels of ego development, as well as more growth narratives, than younger adults (Bauer & McAdams, 2004a; Bauer et al., 2005). Furthermore, the greater tendency to have intellectual growth goals, and not age itself, turned out to account for higher levels of ego development. These studies with adults are especially important because ego development tends to plateau around the period of emerging adulthood, roughly 18 to 25 years of age (Westenberg & Gjerde, 1999). Because ego development is not the norm in adulthood in most studies, intellectual growth memories and goals constitute some of the few predictors of significant increases in adult ego development.

Intentional Happiness

One study demonstrated that people who intentionally changed their actions in a personally meaningful way had increased levels of well-being three months later, whereas people who reported externally initiated, positive changes in their lives did not show increases in well-being (Sheldon & Lyubomirksy, 2006), indicating the importance of intentionality in fostering happiness. In the 3-year longitudinal study mentioned earlier, participants with more experiential growth goals showed increases in well-being 3 years later (Bauer & McAdams, 2010). In other words, people who set goals to develop themselves in a personally meaningful manner and to deepen their relationships, although not necessarily in terms of intellectual growth, were happier 3 years later. Furthermore, experiential growth memories and goals have explained age differences in well-being across adulthood: Older people's higher levels of life satisfaction were explained by the degree to which they had experiential growth memories and goals (Bauer & McAdams, 2004a; Bauer et al., 2005; see also Sheldon & Kasser, 2001). These findings are all the more impressive when considering that levels of well-being tend to fluctuate around and return to a baseline level across adulthood (Diener, Lucas, & Scollon, 2006). Of the approximately 25% of people whose well-being does increase or decrease, the research discussed here suggests that it is important to consider whether people are thinking about their lives in terms of experiential growth.

Intentional Eudaimonic Growth

In the 3-year longitudinal study, individuals who had both intellectual and experiential growth narratives showed increases in both ego development and well-being (i.e., eudaimonic growth; Bauer & McAdams, 2010). In another longitudinal study of college students over the course of one academic year, self-concordant, that is, internally motivated, goals predicted goal attainment later that semester, which predicted greater self-concordance in goals for the next semester, which predicted greater goal attainment the second semester, which in turn predicted increases in both psychosocial maturity and adjustment to college over the course of the year (Sheldon & Houser-Marko, 2001). In that study, growth goals did not relate to eudaimonic growth directly but rather depended on whether progress was made toward those goals.

Can Growth-Mindedness Be Taught?

Very few studies have addressed whether growth-mindedness is a skill that can be taught. In a longitudinal intervention study, adults who received training in "building better relationships"—a course in interpersonal perspective-taking and self-understanding—showed increased levels of ego development, on the average of one stage, over the 10-week intervention course (Manners, Durkin, & Nesdale, 2004). Increases were sustained 4 months later. Research on teaching growth-mindedness may be scarce, but research on growth goals, growth memories, and other forms of growth-mindedness may well offer roadmaps to the intentional self-development of ego maturity and happiness. In another study over the course of a semester, college students went through a growth-oriented goals training program (Sheldon, Kasser, Smith, & Share, 2002). Results showed that participants' growth goals going into the program led to increases in well-being. However, participation in the training program itself did not. Still, as those authors suggest, the null results may well be due to flaws in the training program itself rather than to a human inability to learn skills for growth-mindedness. The notion that individuals can indeed learn skills to foster maturity and happiness is deeply embedded in American ideals. Much research needs to be done in the future to demonstrate systematically the ways this notion actually works—and does not work.

Conclusion

This chapter makes several claims concerning the postconventional self, about how people at postconventional stages of ego development (Loevinger, 1976) think and feel about their lives. To start, the concept of growth is a central feature of the postconventional self. But on a closer look, the postconventional self uses a particular concept of growth—intellectual growth—that has little to do with happiness and well-being. By standard, empirical definitions of happiness and well-being, the postconventional self is just as likely to be happy as unhappy—except perhaps at, and only at, the highest end of the postconventional level, where well-being and a focus on both intellectual and experiential growth *might* also be common (the data are quite preliminary). Still, the differing natures of ego development and well-being suggest that optimal human development involves a combination of two separate paths toward contemporary psychological notions of the good life (Bauer et al., 2005; King et al., 2001). Ego maturity, that is, high capacities and concerns for meaningful growth and integrative human systems, is a necessary but not sufficient condition for optimal or well-rounded development, just as happiness is necessary but not sufficient. How to foster such optimal human development? The research suggests that the intentional self development of both ego maturity and happiness may well start by constructing personal narratives that emphasize themes of both intellectual and experiential growth.

Notes

1. Some definitions are in order. I view the *postconventional level* as the Individualistic stage (Stage 7) and higher. To distinguish the *postconventional personality* from the *postconventional self*: Personality is the broader term that includes both objective and subjective assessments of the individual's characteristics. *Self* is the subjective facet of personality, the side of personality that can only be known by listening to what the individual has to say about his or her life (McAdams, 2008).

2. As at any new level of development, the goals of the previous level are viewed through the lens of experience, which allows the person to see those goals more objectively, less idealistically, and more pragmatically and flexibly (Kegan, 1982; Labouvie-Vief, 2005).

3. Researchers can reliably identify themes in people's life stories, so themes have been studied not only qualitatively but also quantitatively. Such research allows for a measure of interrater agreement of narrative content (approximately 80% agreement generally is accepted) as well as comparisons between narrative themes and quantitative measures of personality and development, such as ego development and personality traits (see McAdams, 2008).

4. However, ego development appears to be distinct from intelligence when compared with various measures of personality (Cohn & Westenberg, 2004). The difference seems to be that intelligence deals with the complexity of *thinking generally*, whereas ego development deals with the complexity of *psychosocial thinking*, more specifically.

5. If *postconventional* is defined as only the Autonomous (Stage 8) and Integrated stages (Stage 9), but not Individualistic (Stage 7), then the postconventional level involved well-being only when no participants were identified at the Integrated stage.

8

Postconventional Ego Development and Self-Transcendence in Religious Renunciates

Heidi Page

Human beings are meaning-making machines (Kegan, 1982). Without a framework to make sense of reality we flounder and lose direction. Ego-development theory asserts that the meaning we attribute to life is determined by the lens through which we view our world and ourselves, and that for most of us this lens naturally increases in transparency as we move from childhood into adulthood. The thicker the lens, the more literal and concrete our perceptions, the thinner the lens, the more capacity to hold ourselves apart from the objects of our perceptions, including thoughts and emotions, and to recognize these as impermanent experiences rather than the very nature of our being. At the highest measurable stages of ego development even the lens through which we view the world is recognized as another cog in the meaning-making wheel, and content of experience takes a backseat to process: *How* one thinks is more at issue than *what* one thinks (Cook-Greuter, 1999; Loevinger, 1997; Wade, 1996; Wilber, 2000b). Worldview is thus seen as a self-constructed phenomenon, which leads naturally to the question of how a person's reality is created, sustained and transformed over time. If I am not the content of my thoughts, if I am not what I feel and think, if I am not what comes and goes, then who or what am I?

The purpose of this study was to examine how an individual's ego-development level contributed to his or her sense of spirituality and how this conceptualization either supported or diverged from contemporary theories and definitions of spirituality. The relationship between postconventional ego development and ego transcendence was explored through the lens of the data as a means to postulate the role that ego development plays on the road to enlightenment. Finally, the ongoing debate between the personal growth emphasis of Western psychology and the personal transcendence orientation of Eastern spirituality is reviewed and discussed from the perspective of participant responses.

Twenty-two monks, nuns, and priests from three religious traditions participated in interviews and completed the standard format of Loevinger's Washington University Sentence Completion Test (SCT). SCTs were scored by Cook-Greuter and ego-development level was compared with emergent themes from a content analysis of interviews. This sample consisted of 7 (32%) males and 15 (68%) females; all were White and all were native English speakers. Eight individuals self-identified as Buddhist, seven as Christian, and seven as Hindu. Ego stage varied and included one participant at Loevinger's Conformist stage, Stage 4, four at the Self-aware stage, Stage 5, seven at the Conscientious stage, Stage 6, six at the Individualistic stage, Stage 7, three at the Autonomous stage, Stage 8, and one at Cook-Greuter's Construct-aware stage, Stage 9, which replaces Loevinger's Integrated stage, Stage 9. I collected the data in India and the United States in 2004. The small sample size allowed for preliminary answers, and the study highlighted some surprising outcomes, offering a map for further exploration. I begin with a review of postconventional themes that emerged from the data and explore how these themes support definitions of spirituality as either the highest level of a line of development, or as a separate developmental line itself (Wilber, 2000b). In this process, I differentiate phenomenological states of being, or *states stages* from the developmental *structure stages* (Wilber, 2006) of ego development. Next, I examine SCT results against expected norms and inquire into the role that postconventional ego development plays on the path to spiritual awakening. I conclude with a fresh look into an age-old debate: Does one need an ego in order to transcend ego?

Postconventional Themes

As expected, themes elicited from postconventional individuals were complex, abstract, and often paradoxical in nature. Ten primary concepts emerged among individuals measuring at postconventional Stages 7 to 9, the highest stage captured by this study. In order of the highest percentages of postconventional responses, these themes were as follows:

- feeling acceptance for self and experience as is   100%
- questioning assumptions   100%
- analyzing doubt   100%
- seeing suffering as a means to increasing
  compassion for self and others   80%
- perceiving experiences of synchronicity   80%
- valuing patience   80%
- valuing living in harmony with others   75%
- viewing reality as nonconceptual   71%
- recognizing interdependence   71%
- valuing nonattachment to objects and experiences   71%

Seven of these themes can be found in the ego-development literature while three are unique to this religious sample, including (a) nonattachment, (b) awareness of experiences of synchronicity, and (c) the quality of patience.

The theme of nonattachment was found primarily at postconventional levels of development in this population and can be viewed as integral and important to spiritual practice, and in particular to the practice of renunciation. Paradoxically, at higher levels of ego development, the bonds of ego and ideas of self are loosened (Cook-Greuter, 1999; Kegan, 1994; Wilber, 1996). True renunciation, and its corollary nonattachment, may only become possible when there exists a capacity to differentiate from, rather than be merged with the needs of the individual self.

Recognition of synchronistic occurrences is a unique theme not found in the ego-development literature. It appeared almost exclusively among postconventional respondents in this study. Carl Jung described synchronicity as an archetypal expression of the Self, an outer event connected to but not caused by an inner state, and therefore bordering on the mystical. Jung (1952/1972) believed that synchronicity held meaning and was intended to guide the ego, albeit in an unconscious manner. Perhaps the awareness of synchronicity occurs more frequently when the unconscious has been closely examined, as is assumed to be the case in postconventional individuals.

Finally, the quality of patience stands out as a unique theme that appeared most frequently among postconventional respondents. One might assume that as individuals plod along the spiritual path, expectations are tempered by the reality that the goal of the path is, in the end, not an external object—enlightenment out there—but rather the everyday chop-wood-and-carry-water existence of the path itself. This quality is important for religious renunciates, for without patience, the aspirant may soon despair. In contrast, attention to the quality of courage, an attribute that may be viewed as shoring up the individual self-sense, was found only among conventional-level participants.

Spirituality as the Highest Level of a Line of Development

Integral theorist Ken Wilber (1999) concluded that at least a dozen developmental lines move through basic structures of consciousness. These different lines, which develop at different rates and at different times, include morals, affects, self-identity, psychosexuality, cognition, creativity, altruism, and various lines that he called "spiritual," to name a few. The postconventional themes described here can be viewed as the highest levels of a spiritual line of development.

The concept of developmental lines, referring to areas of development that evolve independently of ego-development stage, is important to this study because it may explain anomalous results that do not otherwise fit neatly into the linearity asserted by the progression of development from one stage to the next. Why, for example, are certain themes articulated by these renunciates with a depth of awareness and concern that appear to surpass their core ego-development levels? In particular, the themes of self-awareness, the helpful role of suffering, and especially the desire to be of service appear to be highly developed in participants regardless of ego-development level.

Among conventionally scored respondents, Stage 4 to 6, of all three religious traditions, the focus and commitment to service seems to exceed their level of ego development. One Buddhist states the wish, "that my life be directed towards others and not toward my own comfort and happiness and safety." A Christian respondent expresses genuine concern for the welfare of more than 180 individuals for whom he provides daily intercessory prayers. A Hindu respondent similarly states "[my] responsibility is to get myself straight so that I contribute something positive back to the earth." Another suggests that she would as soon forget about her own emancipation from the cycle of death and rebirth in order to come back and give her life in service. Hy and Loevinger (1996) described individuals at the conventional level as people who may "wish to supply guidance and a supportive environment for the miscreant and others" (p. 15). Statements such as those made by participants in the current study go far beyond simple support; rather they are embodied as a central value, suggesting integration at a level exceeding what was defined by the SCT. They exemplify "The transpersonal, transrational, post-postconventional levels of any of the lines, such as our highest cognitive capacities (e.g., transrational intuition), our most developed affects (e.g., transpersonal love), our highest moral aspirations (transcendental compassion for all sentient beings)" (Wilber, 1999, p. 6).

States of Being and State Stages

In addition to viewing postconventional responses from conventionally situated participants as the highest level of a line of development, these responses also express a depth of inner experience that support the notion of *states of being* as accessible to all people at all levels. This is true at least in part because phenomenological states are embodied in the natural human activities of waking (gross state), dreaming (subtle state), and deep sleep (causal state). Per the wisdom traditions, meditative training may unfold these *state stages* in a linear fashion to include the increasingly subtle experiences of witness and nondual consciousness, but peak experiences of even these highest states can occur in individuals at postconventional, conventional, and even preconventional levels of development. To provide a more concrete visual, Wilber and consciousness researcher Combs map this grid with developmental or structure stages, along the vertical y-axis and state stages along the x-axis (Wilber, 2006). This grid, also known as the Wilber–Combs lattice explains how, as individuals climb the vertical ladder of ego development, they can at any moment veer right into the world of states of being, opening the door to a variety of mystical experiences.

It is no surprise that participants in this study appear naturally more attuned to those qualities many would consider defining of spirituality, qualities such as altruism and service. Most participants reported that they came to this lifestyle not by premeditated choice, but rather because a life of renunciation, often through a relentless intuitive calling, chose them. Perhaps these inner experiences of God, Guru, and No Mind that underlie the calling to spiritual life are located along this horizontal axis of states of being, which are then interpreted through the perspective-taking capacity of each individual's position along the vertical axis. As Wilber (2006) explains, this clarifies how advanced spiritual teachers who have developed an ability to access exceptionally subtle states of being, can simultaneously hold very concrete views, or in worst-case scenarios even act out in pathological ways.

Spirituality as a Separate Line or Structure of Development

Unlike state stages, structure stages, as seen in the progression of ego development, cannot be skipped over even as a temporary peak experience. A conventional-level individual can experience a temporary nondual state of awareness, which will then be interpreted from a conventional perspective, but that same individual cannot experience a postconventional stage of development. This linearity occurs because stages of development always include and then transcend what came before (Cook-Greuer, 1999; Kegan, 1982; Loevinger, 1997, Wilber, 2000b; Wade, 1996).

> From Clare Graves to Abraham Maslow; from Deirdre Kramer to Jan Sinnot; from Jurgen Habermas to Cheryl Armon; from Kurt Fischer to Jenny Wade; from Robert Kegan to Susanne Cook-Greuter, there emerges a remarkably consistent story of the evolution of consciousness. . . . They all tell a generally similar tale of the growth and development of the mind as a series of unfolding states or waves. (Wilber, 2000b, p. 5).

Scholars such as Huston Smith (1991), Arthur Lovejoy (1964), and Ananda Coomaraswamy (1943) have founded their work on the ideas inherent within the *perennial philosophy*: a theory that posits a common core of many of the world's great spiritual traditions and proposes that reality is composed of increasingly subtle levels of recognition, culminating in nondual awareness.

Following is an example of how construction of spiritual meaning evolved in this sample as ego development progressed, and how it crossed into the transpersonal at the highest levels. In response to the question, "What is enlightenment?" a conventional Stage 4 respondent replied in a simple, straightforward, and honest manner, "I've heard [enlightenment] expressed many different ways, and I don't feel like I can say anything that would not confuse anybody who heard it more." There was no exploration of the subject, even if that exploration was only a repetition of what had been understood rather than experienced.

Two developmental levels further a conventional respondent at Stage 6 described enlightenment as a wish for an ideal state, rather than an experience grounded in her reality. "[Enlightenment means] a state beyond all struggles. [An enlightened person would] be more steady and peaceful, and not affected to the same degree . . . about hard things in life."

Moving into the postconventional realm, at Stage 8 a respondent described an enlightened person as someone who has a translucency about him or her. Unlike conventional levels, the descriptive language used had a personal feel, a touching into inner experience. "Two words I would use to make it a little more concrete would be a sense of playful joy . . . a joy that's not heavy, it's not overwhelming, it's not Bang! It's not Wow! But it's a playful light joy, and a nothingness of the person. There's not a whole lot there."

At the highest recorded level in the current study, a Stage 9 respondent moved beyond theory entirely; her response was both personal and simultaneously impersonal. This participant provided multiple examples of experiences too lengthy to report here, but in summary she had this to say, "I mean it's not really enlightenment because enlightenment means that you know you are one [with everything]. But it was certainly much more than a normal experience. I wasn't even there, I was witnessing the whole day."

These four examples from conventional to postconventional show a movement from concrete to abstract, from beliefs and concepts to personal experience. The postconventional examples provide a taste of enlightenment as lived experience, and support the definition of spirituality as its own line of development.

In summary, data from the current research reveal postconventional themes both expected and unexpected from a sample of religious renunciates. Participant responses lend credibility to the placement of spirituality as the highest level of a developmental line, which in this sample exceeds core ego development levels (e.g., altruism and service), and explain spirituality also as phenomenological states of being, highlighting the process of unfolding states stages in spiritual growth. Spiritual development is then defined as a separate line of development, identified through the increasingly complex responses of participants as ego development progresses. Although these examples demonstrate how developmental perspectives act as interpretive lenses into spiritual experience, one question posed by numerous transpersonal researchers (Alexander, Heaton, & Chandler, 1994; Welwood, 2000; Wilber, 2000a) remains unanswered: How important *is* postconventional ego development on the path to enlightenment?

Postconventional Ego Development and Ego Transcendence

In this study, none of the participants scored at Unitive Stage 10, Cook-Greuter's highest and the only identified transcendent level of development. There were, however, a far higher percentage of participants at postconventional stages (45%) than is typically found in the general population (10%). Although it is impossible to ascertain to what degree a life of renunciation contributed to psychological growth among participants in this study, renunciation does appear to support above-average ego development. It also is possible that a life of renunciation self-selects for individuals with higher than average levels of ego development.

Transpersonal theorists both past and present (Alexander et al., 1994; Ferrer, 2003; Goleman, 1988; Huxley, 1962; Leonard & Murphy, 1995; Underhill, 1929; Walsh, 2001; Wilber, Engler, & Brown, 1986), described progressively refined states of consciousness as a direct result of either spiritual or integral psychological practices. Given that many participants in this study had spent at least 10 years committed to a religious path, it was postulated that the practices associated with this life would propel at least a few of them past the stages of postconventional development and into transcendent modes of organization. This was not the case.

The absence of transcendent-level findings among respondents in this study may relate to the limitations inherent in a language-based assessment tool. A modality that does not rely on cognitive reasoning seems necessary to determine nonconceptual, or transcendent-level functioning. If we assume that the SCT, despite being language-based, points at minimum to the beginnings of ego transcendence, then the absence of individuals at Stage 10, the Unitive Stage of development, fails to support spiritual and transpersonal literature (e.g., Walsh & Vaughn, 1993). It is important to note that Cook-Greuter (1999) herself makes no claims that her highest stage denotes the achievement of ego transcendence, only that it advances Loevinger's final stage in a way that allows for continuing demarcation of human growth and development at stages beyond the personal realm.

Another explanation may be that the movement from postconventional to transcendent consciousness is a leap not of steps or stages, but rather of a different order of magnitude altogether (Alexander & Langer, 1990; Cook-Greuter, 2000; Fink, 1995). Cook-Greuter (1999) remarks that the shift from postconventional Stage 9 to transcendent Stage 10 represents "a quantum leap in experience and outlook, which is discontinuous from the previous pattern of gradually reframing and expanding one's perspective" (p. 52). Fink (1995) likewise suggests that transcendent functioning is not so much a natural progression from its predecessor, the postconventional stage, as it is an entirely different way of knowing, a knowing described in the world's major

religious traditions as Buddhist *nirvana*, Hindu *nirvikalpa samadhi*, and the Christian *gnostic abyss*. All of these ways of knowing spring from the same deep internal structure: a condition of formless, objectless awareness (Wilber, 1980).

The question of how a spiritual seeker attains objectless awareness as a permanent structure is addressed by different religious and philosophical schools. A branch of Hinduism known as Advaita Vedanta, hereafter referred to as *nondualism* due to its emphasis on the underlying unity of all experience, proposes that enlightenment is an accident; not something that can be achieved through effort. It either happens, or it doesn't happen (Balsekar, 1999). Likewise, Ferrer (2003) stated that neither spiritual practices nor psychological ego development leads inexorably to this state of formless, objectless awareness. Perhaps, at best, these practices simply make the spiritual seeker more accident-prone. This is summed up by a Zen Buddhist teacher who suggested, "We cannot achieve it by willing it, nor can we intentionally bring it about; all we can do is to prepare ourselves for it. This preparation is the chief aim of all man's existential self-exploration and practice." (Durckheim, 1990, p. 79). Spiritual practice almost certainly facilitates both psychological and spiritual growth, but the ultimate leap into the permanent state of formless awareness, hinted at in the highest stages of ego development and described in experiences of spiritual enlightenment, may have little relationship to self-effort; it may be a factor of something else entirely.

Wilber (2006) proposed that full enlightenment only can occur when both the vertical line of structure stages and the horizontal line of state stages are systematically ascended and unfolded to include the entire grid of development and experience. Without this structural capacity in place, the mystical states of being, which appear throughout all levels of development, are destined to remain as temporary peak experiences, interpreted as wholeness from vantage points only part way up the mountain. Without the unfolding of spiritual stages undertaken through disciplined spiritual practice, movement up the vertical line of development may provide a solid ego structure to be transcended but will remain insufficient preparation for a leap to ego transcendence.

And so it seems that, although spiritual practices may guide the individual toward deeper levels of self-awareness, which in turn support the movement from one stage to the next, they do not guarantee movement. The advent of full spiritual awakening may have as much to do climbing the structural stages of ego development as with the unfolding of spiritual states all the way along the horizontal path from gross, to subtle, to causal, and to nondual consciousness. The very small number of individuals surmised by Kegan (1994) to be operating at transcendent levels of ego functioning (<1%) is evidence of the fact that this process is seldom simple or immediate but rather a gradual progression. One participant at postconventional Stage 8 intuitively points to this evolution:

> Don't reject any experience you've had as inessential to the process. Everything is somehow part of the education. Don't try to shortcut the process by artificial means. As you are going through that process of seeking God you are building up an internal structure that can hold God; that can support that weight. If you take short cuts you can't support that weight—bad workmanship, bad engineering and so you're going to end up hurting. (Christian)

The East–West Debate: Ego Integration versus Ego Transcendence

Although the question of how individuals transcend ego is compelling for developmental psychologists and spiritual seekers, it is important to place this issue within the broader context of spiritual traditions that find no merit whatsoever in the notion of personality development. As stated previously, the nondual branch of Hinduism views a separate self-sense as illusory and posits formless awareness as the preeminent reality (Balsekar, 1999; Cohen & Desai, 2000; Powell, 1996). The individual personality, which most of us identify as "me," is taken no more seriously than an actor playing a role in a film. When the film is over, the role ceases. In the same way, when physical death occurs, that ever-present formless awareness continues while the socially conditioned and personally constructed "me" necessarily comes to an end. From this perspective, individual development is viewed as entirely irrelevant.

The Western psychological model (Engler & Wilber, 1986; Welwood, 2000; Wilber, 2000a), in contrast, focuses on the ultimate reality of the individual self. From this vantage point, becoming a more whole and integrated "me," is primary. As far back as the fourth century BC, Socrates admonished that the unexamined life is not worth living, suggesting that the larger purpose of life is not to embed oneself in the formless nature of reality but rather to fully and completely "know thyself."

Wilber (2000b) and Welwood (2000) attempted to resolve the ego-development versus ego-transcendence dilemma by crediting equal value to both schools of thought, highlighting the radically different assumptions from which each projects reality and noticing that emphasis on the personal versus the formless is more a matter of definition than of absolute truth. Wilber (2000c) elaborates that the conceptual difficulty with nondual reality revolves around the relation of subject and object. That relationship can only be resolved when reality is viewed *from* the nondual vantage point. In other words, we can't really get it unless we have already transcended ego, which explains why the attempt to define, explain or understand transcendence from the relative perspective results only in paradox and contradiction.

Ferrer (2002) argued alternatively that even the notion of ego transcendence as the apex of spiritual achievement, as explained by the perennial philosophy, is based on unexamined Cartesian-Kantian assumptions. These assumptions confer pregiven features upon the experience of enlightenment (e.g., nondual, monistic, impersonal); suggesting that it can be objectively known by mystics of all traditions, and that it is therefore independent of human participation. He proposes instead that these higher reaches of spiritual evolution, although not entirely subjective, must include a personal dimension that allows for "an ocean with many shores." In other words, the experience of the Buddhist *nirvana*, Hindu *nirvikalpa samadhi*, and the Christian *gnostic abyss* are not synonyms but co-created experiences that are unique to each tradition and to each individual within each tradition.

These issues are important to explore in the context of this study because they call into question the efficacy of any research that attempts to plot personal development along spiritual lines. A look at differences and similarities in the ways that respondents in this study addressed the issue of ego development and transcendence may offer new insights to this debate.

Hindu participants adhered to the *Bhakti* or devotional arm of Hinduism. Those committed to the path of Bhakti believe that the path to God-realization traverses the challenging territory of moving from the relativity of dualism to the absolute nature of nondualism by giving up personal will in a process of complete surrender to the Guru (Amritaswarupananda, 1998). Despite this emphasis on ego surrender, as opposed to ego development, there was a belief among Hindu participants that engaging the psychological self could be of substantial benefit on the spiritual path. As one Hindu respondent noted, "The mind is always the great enemy, but also the great teacher. . . . Look at it, think about it, contemplate it, and try to see what fits . . . it's a process." This type of response was not atypical and suggests that the Hindu participants in this study held a balance between recognizing ego development as useful, although ultimately not the point of spiritual practice.

Christian participants in this study practiced in the mystical tradition of Julian of Norwich. This group exhibited a profound willingness to sit in the unknown as exemplified in the following quote from interview transcripts: "Life itself is a wonder, is an unknowing . . . it's not that I don't doubt or it's not that I doubt . . . I just cannot have a verbal proposition [that says] this is completely true. I can say well . . . it opens to reality, it is a way of entering into reality . . . music, poetry, playing frisbee, these are the things." Although no Christian participant articulated the role of mind in the process of spiritual growth, the capacity to hold doubt as a verbal construct suggests an implicit use of the mind in furthering existential awareness.

The Buddhist participants proposed yet another possibility, one that offers a bridge between the apparently contradictory ideals of ego development and ego transcendence. This position suggests that ego is an invaluable tool, in fact, the only tool, that can be used to transcend the ego. Buddhists in this sample articulated a focus on the mind unlike anything found among the Hindu or the Christian participants. The majority of Buddhists emphasized the necessity of using the ego as a means to transcend the ego: using the mind to see through the illusion of the mind. Although this does not directly address the Eastern claim that residing in pure consciousness is the *real* goal (although ego development is simply part of the dream), the Buddhist orientation does suggest how to awaken spiritually in a way that both values and also necessitates working with the ego.

In summary, rather than attempting to prove that the nondual vantage point of ego transcendence represents a more "real" reality than a focus on the individual, it may be more helpful to allow the data to speak for itself. Despite the either–or dichotomy evident from a philosophical standpoint, postconventional participants in this study did not espouse dogmatic positions, but rather exhibited experiential awareness of the importance of the mind, regardless of whether the goal was personal self-knowing or spiritual awakening. It may be that the ego-development versus ego-transcendence debate is mediated more by developmental level than adherence to philosophical positions. Christian and Hindu participants, in general, seem to consider ego development as a useful if not invaluable tool, whereas Buddhist participants suggested that ego transcendence cannot be attained except through the difficult path of addressing the concerns of the personality.

Conclusion

The three themes of patience, nonattachment, and synchronicity were found to be unique to postconventionally situated renunciates in this sample. Hypotheses that long-term spiritual commitment and practice leads to ego transcendence were not substantiated. In this study, the Christian population exhibited the highest levels of ego development with more than 50% scoring at postconventional development, followed by the Hindu sample at 43% and the Buddhist sample at 38%, all far above the general population, which hovers around 10%. The Wilber–Combs lattice was presented as one possible means to highlight the necessity of integrating both vertical structural ego development and horizontal phenomenological unfolding. Consistent with findings by Wilber (2000b), Welwood (2000), Wilber and Combs (Wilber, 2006), the development of the personal self is an important tool, perhaps the only tool along with spiritual practices, that can dislodge the mind of the individual into the mind of God.

9

Leadership at Postconventional Stages of Adult Development

Bill Joiner

Do managers at postconventional stages of development make more effective leaders than managers at conventional stages? If so, in what ways, in what situations, and why? In 2002, Stephen Josephs and I began a multiyear research project designed to answer these questions in a more systematic and detailed way than had previously been done. Our findings were published in *Leadership Agility: Five Levels of Mastery for Anticipating and Initiating Change* (Joiner & Josephs, 2007). This chapter provides a synopsis of our findings, with particular attention to the distinctions between conventional and postconventional leadership.

Research Design

As lead researcher on this project, I undertook an in-depth review of an array of well-established stage-development theories, tracing human development from the first stages of life through the more advanced stages of adult growth (Cook-Greuter, 2005; Erikson, 1968, 1993; Flavell, 1963; Fowler, 1981; Kegan, 1982, 1994; P. King & Kitchener, 1994; Kohlberg, 1981; Loevinger, 1976; Richards & Commons, 1984; Selman & Schultz, 1998; Torbert, 1991, 2004; Wilber, 2000a). I then synthesized the findings of these theories into a fresh, integrated description of developmental stages. Because the focus was on organizational leadership, we named our stages to highlight how they function in this context. Table I.1 in the introduction of this book outlines these stages and shows how they correlate with those described by Loevinger and some of the other leading ego-stage theorists (Joiner & Josephs, 2007).

The research we conducted for *Leadership Agility* built on studies conducted for a number of doctoral dissertations that focused on the relationship between stage of ego development and various aspects of leadership effectiveness. Lasker's (1978) dissertation was the first to examine this relationship. Subsequent studies, most supervised by Torbert (see this volume) during the 1980s, illuminated the relationship between ego development, as defined by Loevinger (1976) and a number of variables associated with effective leadership (Merron, 1985; S. Smith, 1980).

These studies found that the mental and emotional capacities managers develop at each new stage of ego development have a strong tendency to carry over into the way they exercise leadership. They also produced statistically significant correlations showing that managers at more advanced stages of ego development are more effective than conventional managers.

Our research focused on managers at ego Stages 5 to 9, which we call *Expert, Achiever, Catalyst, Cocreator,* and *Synergist,* respectively. We examined data from 604 managers: 384 from four studies reported by Torbert (1991) and 220 managers who were our clients, interviewees, or evening MBA students. For this latter group of managers, ego-stage assessments were supplemented by either a clinical assessment, if the manager was a client, or an in-depth interview.

For this study, we consider leadership as an activity, not as an organizational role or position. Furthermore, we think of leadership in a way that is applicable for managers at all five stages: We defined *leadership* as "action taken with a proactive attitude and an intention to change something for the better" (Joiner & Josephs, 2007, p. xiii). More specifically, we looked at the leadership initiatives that managers took in three key action arenas: leading organizational change, leading teams, and engaging in pivotal, face-to-face discussions where important outcomes are at stake.

At the outset of this project, we created the grid presented in Table 9.1, which arrays our five focal stages against the three action arenas. When we mapped previous research findings onto this grid, it became clear that the existing state of knowledge on this topic was actually very spotty. In fact, a number of the cells were essentially blank.

The aim of our research project was to fill in this grid. Each manager's stage of ego development was assessed.[1] We also used in-depth interviews, client case studies, and student journals to examine the thought processes of hundreds of managers as they carried out initiatives in each of the three action arenas.[2] When the project was completed, we had identified leadership practices for each cell in the grid, as well

Table 9.1. Stage—Competency Grid

Stage	Leading Organizational Change	Leading Teams	Engaging in Pivotal Conversations
5. Expert			
6. Achiever			
7. Catalyst			
8. Co-Creator			
9. Synergist			

as the stage-related mental and emotional capacities that supported these practices. Additionally, we brought these abstract descriptions to life by selecting a real-life story to illustrate each cell in the grid.

High-Level Findings

Table 9.2 provides abbreviated descriptions of the stage-related leadership practices we identified for each of the three action arenas, along with the implicit view of leadership held by managers at each level of agility. Because this grid focuses on the *leadership practices* that emerge at each stage of development, it uses the term *level of leadership agility* rather than stage. I explain the reasoning for this terminology further in the chapter.

In the Table, our distinction between heroic and postheroic agility levels correlates with the one Torbert and Cook-Greuter (following Kohlberg, 1981) made between conventional and postconventional stages of ego development, and also with Bradford and Cohen's (1987, 1998) distinction between heroic and postheroic modes of team leadership. Percentages refer to our research-based estimates of the managers currently capable of operating at each agility level.[3] Also, keep in mind that the leadership practices that managers develop at each new level of agility both go beyond and include those they developed at previous levels.

Why Agility?

As part of our research, we also asked the following question: What is it, exactly, that develops as adults grow from one stage of development

Table 9.2. Reference Guide to Five Levels of Leadership Agility

Level of of Agility	View of Leadership	Pivotal Conversations	Leading Teams	Organizational Change
Heroic Levels				
Pre-Expert (~10%)				
5. Expert (~45%)	*Tactical, problem-solving orientation.* Believes that leaders are respected and followed by others because of their authority and expertise.	Style is either to strongly assert opinions or hold back to accommodate others. May swing from one style to the other for different situations and relationships. Tends to avoid giving or requesting feedback.	More of a supervisor than a manager. Creates a group of individuals rather than a team. Work with direct reports is primarily one-on-one. Too caught up in the details of own work to lead in a strategic manner.	Organizational initiatives focus primarily on incremental improvements inside unit boundaries with little attention to stakeholders.
6. Achiever (~35%)	*Strategic, outcome orientation.* Believes that leaders motivate others by making it challenging and satisfying to contribute to larger objectives.	Primarily assertive or accommodative with some ability to compensate with the less preferred style. Will accept or even initiate feedback, if helpful in achieving desired outcomes.	Operates like a full-fledged manager. Meetings to discuss important strategic or organizational issues are often orchestrated to gain buy-in to own views.	Organizational initiatives include analysis of external environment. Strategies to gain stakeholder buy-in range from one-way communication to soliciting input.

Post-Heroic Levels

7. Catalyst (~5%)	*Visionary, facilitative orientation.* Believes that leaders articulate an innovative, inspiring vision and bring together the right people to transform the vision into reality. Leaders empower others and actively facilitate their development.	Adept at balancing assertive and accommodative style as needed in particular situations. Likely to articulate and question underlying assumptions. Genuinely interested in learning from diverse viewpoints. Proactive in seeking and utilizing feedback.	Intent upon creating a highly participative team. Acts as a team leader and facilitator. Models and seeks open exchange of views on difficult issues. Empowers direct reports. Uses team development as a vehicle for leadership development.	Organizational initiatives often include development of a culture that promotes teamwork, participation, and empowerment. Proactive engagement with diverse stakeholders reflects a belief that input increases the quality of decisions, not just buy-in.
8. Co-Creator (~4%)	*Oriented toward shared purpose and collaboration.* Believes leadership is ultimately a service to others. Leaders collaborate with other leaders to develop a shared vision that each experiences as deeply purposeful.	Integrates his/her assertive and accommodative sides in pivotal conversations and is agile in using both styles. Able to process and seriously consider negative feedback even when highly charged emotionally.	Develops a collaborative leadership team, where members feel full responsibility not only for their own areas but also for the unit/organization they collectively manage. Practical preference for consensus decision making but doesn't hesitate to use authority as needed.	Develops key stakeholder relationships characterized by deep levels of mutual influence and genuine dedication to the common good. May create companies or organizational units where corporate responsibility and deep collaboration are integral practices.

Table 9.2. (Continued)

Level of of Agility	View of Leadership	Pivotal Conversations	Leading Teams	Organizational Change
9. Synergist (~1%)	*Holistic orientation.* Experiences leadership as participation in a palpable life purpose that benefits others while serving as a vehicle for personal transformation.	Centered within his/her assertive and accommodative energies, expressed appropriately to the situation. Cultivates a present-centered awareness that augments external feedback and supports a strong, subtle connection with others, even during challenging conversations.	Capable of moving fluidly between various team leadership styles uniquely suited to the situation at hand. Can shape or amplify the energy dynamics affecting team performance to bring about mutually beneficial results.	Develops and maintains a deep, empathetic awareness of conflicting stakeholder interests, including his/her own. Able to access synergistic intuitions that transform seemingly intractable conflicts into solutions beneficial for all parties involved.

to another, and how do these capabilities, as we came to call them, affect leadership practice? My in-depth review and synthesis of leading stage development frameworks, and our data from practicing managers, answered this question by identifying eight mental/emotional capacities that develop together in a stage-wise manner, beginning in the early stages of life. The names we have given to these capacities, emphasizing their application in leadership contexts, are *situational awareness, sense of purpose, stakeholder understanding, power style, connective awareness, reflective judgment, self-awareness*, and *developmental motivation*.

I describe these capacities and how they work together later in this chapter. For now, I highlight three key findings: First, each time a person grows into a new stage, these capacities co-develop to a new level. Second, considered both separately and together, all eight capacities are directly relevant to leadership. Third, these capacities develop in such a way that, each time a manager grows into a new level, his or her ability to respond to changing, interdependent circumstances increases.

What is leadership agility? In essence, it is the ability to lead effectively under conditions of rapid change and growing interdependence. *Agility* is increasingly being used to refer to the ability to respond effectively to just these circumstances. In fact, rapid change and growing interdependence are two of the most powerful forces shaping today's turbulent organizational environment. Because these deep trends affect all managerial levels, this competency is increasingly needed not just in the executive suite but also throughout the organization. For more than a decade, organizational change experts, acutely aware of these two deep trends, have talked about the need to develop agile organizations that can effectively anticipate and respond to rapidly changing, interdependent conditions (McCann, 2004).

To enjoy sustained success in this new century, organizations need to develop a level of agility that matches the increasing level of change and complexity in their environment. Yet, for the vast majority of companies, full-fledged strategic and operational agility remains more an aspiration than a reality. One of the major reasons for this continuing agility gap is the need to develop more agile leaders. To develop the level of agility demanded by today's turbulent global environment, organizations need leaders who embody a corresponding level of agility. It's no wonder, then, that senior executives have ranked agility among the most critical leadership competencies needed in their companies today.[4]

We found that managers at the Expert, Stage 5, and Achiever, Stage 6, levels of agility operate from a heroic mindset about leadership.

That is, they assume sole responsibility for setting their organization's objectives, coordinating the activities of their direct reports, and managing their performance. Heroic leaders can be highly effective in certain situations. However, in complex, rapidly changing organizational environments, heroic leadership tends to overcontrol and underutilize subordinates. It discourages people from feeling responsible for anything beyond their assigned area, inhibits optimal teamwork, and implicitly encourages subordinates to use the heroic approach with their own units (Bradford & Cohen, 1987, 1998).

Managers who operate at the postheroic levels of agility have a different mindset about what it means to be a leader. They retain the ultimate accountability and authority that comes with their role, yet they create work environments characterized by high involvement and shared responsibility. For a real-life example of this kind of leadership, I turn to a condensed version of a story from *Leadership Agility*.

Leading Organizational Change at the Catalyst Level

Robert faced the biggest leadership challenge of his career. A Catalyst, Stage 7, executive in a Canadian oil corporation, he had just been named president of its refining and retailing company. Competitively, his company was positioned around the middle of the pack in a mature, margin-sensitive market where long-range demand was projected to be flat. With little to distinguish it from other regional companies, its earnings were going steadily downhill. In fact, the company's future looked dismal. Within the company, morale was at an all-time low. The previous president was an Achiever, Stage 6, leader who had taken many steps to cut costs and increase profitability, including a series of layoffs; however these steps had not produced the desired results. In fact, the whole organization was in a state of fear. As Robert moved into his new position, everything was truly up for grabs.

The company badly needed a short-term increase in its stock price. But Robert wanted to do much more than that. He wanted to transform an admittedly lackluster company into the best regional in North America. In fact, his vision was to develop an organization whose business performance and innovative ways of operating would be benchmarked by companies from a wide variety of industries. Putting the stock price goal in this larger context, he decided to develop a more comprehensive set of what he called "break-out" strategies that would lead to a more innovative organization. Realizing that he and his top management team did not have all the answers, Robert hired a world-class strategy firm. He also set up ten idea factories, creative strategic-thinking sessions where employees and other stakeholders developed ideas for the top team to consider. People responded with enthusiasm, generating a huge number of ideas.

Robert then held a 2-day retreat where he and his top management group synthesized the strategy firm's ideas with those generated by the idea factories. As he put it later, "We tried to involve as many people as possible. We invested time and energy up-front to listen to people, build trust, and get everyone aligned. It paid off, because we started to think with one brain."

The new strategies that emerged went well beyond those Robert, his team, and the strategy firm would have generated on their own. They resulted in a smaller, more agile organization with a much stronger people strategy designed to catapult the company into the ranks of high-performing organizations. When the new game plan was ready, they presented it to the employees before they announced it to the market. The presentation included some bad news, but as it ended people applauded. Over the months that followed, Robert and his team repeatedly communicated their new vision and its implications for employees in many different forums. As the new strategies were implemented, they kept everyone updated on business performance. Each year, Robert met with each of the company's 20 management teams to discuss objectives and strategies and check for alignment.

Robert's participative approach to transforming his organization not only led to innovative strategies; it also developed the commitment, trust, and alignment necessary to implement them reliably and effectively. As a result, during his first three years as president, annual earnings rose from $9 million to $40 million, and cash expenses were reduced by $40 million per year. A once-faltering company had become one of the most efficient and effective refiners in North America and one of the top retailers in its marketplace.

Key Findings About
Developmental Stages and Levels of Agility

Let's now return to the question I posed at the beginning of this chapter: Do managers, like Robert, who have reached postconventional stages of development make more effective leaders than managers at conventional stages? Our research answers this question in the affirmative, with two qualifiers. First, each time a manager grows into a more advanced stage, he or she becomes more effective when carrying out leadership initiatives in rapidly changing, interdependent organizational environments. Second, managers become increasingly effective in these environments, provided they translate the mental and emotional capacities of their current stage into the way they act as leaders. Let's examine these two qualifiers in more detail.

First, what sets managers at different developmental stages apart is how effectively they lead under conditions of rapid change and interdependence. Heroic leaders can be effective over a sustained period of time, provided their work environment has not reached the level of turbulence presently found in most organizations. For example, Expert, Stage 5, leadership, with its tactical, problem-solving orientation, is most effective in relatively stable environments where interdependence is fairly low. Achiever, Stage 6, leadership, with its strategic, outcome orientation, is effective in conditions characterized by moderate interdependence and a moderate pace of episodic change.

This predominant combination of Expert and Achiever leadership worked relatively well for most companies until the waning decades of the 20th century, when the globalization of the economy ushered in an era of continuous change and pervasive interdependence. Generally speaking, consistently effective leadership in today's uncertain environment requires, at minimum, mastery of the visionary, facilitative orientation that emerges at the Catalyst, Stage 7, level of agility.

In this regard, a related finding is that, as managers advance developmentally, they retain an ability to do what we call *downshifting*, using abilities they developed at previous stages. Part of a leader's agility at the Catalyst level, is an ability to downshift into a heroic mode of leadership when the situation calls for it.

The second qualifier we discovered also is important to understand. In most cases, managers have translated the mental and emotional capacities of their current stage into the way they act as leaders. However, this is not true for all leaders. This is why we make a clear distinction between a manager's developmental stage and his or her level of leadership agility. This insight has important implications for leadership development. It is essential to work with managers simultaneously from the inside out, that is, helping them develop stage-related mental and emotional capacities, and from the outside in, that is, helping them develop corresponding leadership skills.

In conducting our research, we looked at several additional questions about the relationship between developmental stage and leadership. First, we found that managers at higher organizational levels are empirically *somewhat* more likely to have higher ego-development scores than those with lower levels of responsibility (Joiner & Josephs, 2007). At the same time, research also shows that managers at all responsibility levels, from frontline supervisor to CEO, become more effective as they reach more advanced stages (Rooke & Torbert, 1998; S. Smith, 1980). We also looked at the question of whether certain personality types, for example, as measured by the Myers-Briggs Type Indicator, correlate with particular stages or agility levels. In fact, we could find no such correlation. It appears that people of all personality types can grow through all stages of human development. The same goes for gender.

The classic understanding of developmental stages holds that they are sequential and not reversible. Our research does not contradict this view, if by stage we mean what might be called a person's center of gravity, how they understand and respond to their world most of the time. We did find that managers' agility levels, distinguished from their stage, can vary in different kinds of situations. Additionally, data from our research indicates that a manager's agility level can vary for the three categories of leading change, leading teams, or engaging in pivotal conversations. However, this variance is rarely more than half a level. The agility level of most managers, again considered as a center of gravity, is consistent across all three of these action contexts.

A manager's agility level can vary in more significant ways when considered on a minute-to-minute, hour-to-hour basis. For example, managers can experience what Daniel Goleman (1995), author of *Emotional Intelligence*, calls "emotional hijacking," which is what happens when a stressful situation triggers a strong reactive emotion such as anger, fear, depression, or professional jealousy. When the emotion takes over, the manager's usual level of agility temporarily collapses down to an earlier level.

Developmental Capacities and Agility Competencies

As noted previously, a manager's level of agility is supported by eight stage-related capacities, each of which is both mental and emotional in nature. These capacities work in pairs. Each pair supports one of four types of leadership agility. Situational awareness and sense of purpose support *context-setting agility*. Stakeholder understanding and power style support *stakeholder agility*. Connective awareness and reflective judgment support *creative agility*. Self-awareness and developmental motivation support *self-leadership agility*.

These four types of agility work together to increase a manager's effectiveness when undertaking initiatives on any scale—leading organizational change, leading teams, or engaging in pivotal conversations. As the eight stage-related capacities evolve and are translated into leadership behavior, a manager's agility moves to a new level.

Context-Setting Agility

Managers use context-setting agility to (a) scan their environment and anticipate important changes, (b) identify and score the initiatives they need to take, and (c) determine the outcomes their initiatives need to achieve. These leadership practices are supported by two developmental capacities: situational awareness and sense of purpose. A manager's level of situational awareness determines the extent to which he or she can step back and view issues and trends within a broader context. A manager's sense of purpose includes his or her strategic time frame and the extent to which his or her initiatives are motivated by a desire to serve the needs of other human beings.

For example, although Expert, Stage 5, managers know that everything exists in a larger context, they are likely to deal with the issues they face as isolated concerns, and their sense of purpose tends to be tactical rather than strategic. Achiever-level managers undertake leadership initiatives that take their larger context into account, for example, industry dynamics and customer needs. Their expanded sense of purpose gives them the ability to undertake strategic change initiatives that focus on attaining important outcomes.

When leaders grow into the postheroic levels, they expand their thinking to include relevant longer-term trends that extend beyond the boundaries of their company's industry. When the timing is right, they have the ability to undertake visionary initiatives that are both personally meaningful and beneficial for their organization and its key stakeholders. We also found that postheroic leaders are much more likely than their heroic counterparts to have a personal commitment to corporate responsibility that becomes central to the way they frame and conduct their change initiatives.[6] Virtually all the Co-creator, Stage 8, leaders we studied had a strong, principled commitment to both social and environmental responsibility. They either left the corporate world to found new companies based on these principles, or they decided to remain inside large corporations and to work to change them from within. Our small sample of Synergists, Stage 9, had similar commitments, but they were willing to take bigger, yet still manageable, risks on behalf of these core principles.

Stakeholder Agility

Managers use stakeholder agility to (a) identify the key stakeholders of an initiative and understand what they have at stake, (b) assess the extent to which their views and objectives are aligned with their own, and (c) engage with stakeholders in ways that lead to more optimal alignment. These leadership practices are supported by two developmental capacities: stakeholder understanding and power style. A manager's level of stakeholder understanding determines how deeply he or she can understand others' needs and perspectives. The versatility of this manager's power style determines how well he or she can balance and integrate assertive tendencies with his or her receptive or accommodative tendencies.

For example, Expert, Stage 5, managers have developed an initial level of tolerance for backgrounds and viewpoints that differ from their own, but they can be quick to criticize, especially when stakeholders do not agree with them. Faced with conflicting views, their *power style* tends to be either quite assertive or very accommodative, although they may flip back and forth between these stances in different situations or relationships. Achiever, Stage 6, managers have more of a capacity for empathy and therefore understand the importance of stakeholder buy-in and motivation. Faced with differing views, their power style is likely to be predominantly assertive or accommodative, with some tendency toward balance through the use of the opposite style.

Postheroic leaders have an ability to enter deeply into frames of reference that differ from their own while still honoring their own perspective. Catalyst, Stage 7, leaders seek input from key stakeholders not simply to gain buy-in, but because they feel that genuine dialogue will improve the quality of their decisions and the effectiveness of their initiatives. Their power style is one that tends to foster true dialogue. They can be both assertive and accommodative, for example, by advocating their views then immediately asking others to assert theirs, and they can be more assertive or more accommodative as the situation requires.

Co-creators often develop the capacity to deeply understand other cultures, subcultures, and ethnic groups—not just those within their institutional circle. They are committed to developing working relationships characterized by deep collaboration. Their power style, which reflects greater integration of the assertive and accommodative sides of themselves, supports them in this aim. Synergists, Stage 9, can remain fully centered in their own sense of what is needed and, at the same time, be highly responsive to the felt needs of stakeholders, even when those needs seem to conflict with their own.

Creative Agility

Managers use creative agility to transform complex, novel issues into desired results by (a) identifying the key problems their initiative needs to solve, (b) examining the causes of these problems, and (c) developing and implementing viable solutions. These leadership practices are supported by two developmental capacities: connective awareness and reflective judgment. Connective awareness is the ability to hold different ideas and experiences in mind, compare and contrast them, and make meaningful connections between them. Reflective judgment is the thought process managers use to determine what is true and what is the best course of action to take.[7]

Experts make few meaningful connections between disparate ideas and experiences, so they tend to focus on one problem at a time. Although they usually examine situational factors and consider multiple options before making important decisions, they often take for granted the conceptual framework on which their technical or functional expertise is based. Achievers, Stage 6, can hold multiple ideas and experiences in mind, so they tend to understand how various problems are related. Because they understand that their own views are subject to bias, they are more likely to test them against hard data.

Postheroic leaders begin their initiatives with a keen appreciation of the novelty inherent in the situation they are addressing, even if it seems highly familiar. Faced with complex, nonroutine problems, Catalysts can temporarily drop their own frame of reference and adopt another long enough to view a situation from a new perspective. This brings about a greater appreciation of paradox—seeing that contradictory perspectives can each be valid in their own way. Catalysts therefore understand that data alone is not enough to resolve conflicting views. Differences in stakeholders' underlying frames of reference need to be understood as well.

Co-creators are integrative thinkers who can hold multiple frames of reference in mind, note where they conflict and overlap, then develop true win–win solutions. Because they understand that organizational problems are, often unintentionally, co-created by multiple parties, they prefer to co-create mutually beneficial solutions through collaborative conversation. Synergists can hold conflicting stakeholder views and interests, even in highly charged situations, in ways that often lead to remarkable synergistic breakthroughs that benefit a wide range of stakeholders.

Self-Leadership Agility

Managers engage in self-leadership by (a) determining the kind of leader they want to be, (b) using their everyday initiatives to experiment toward this aspiration, and (c) reflecting on and learning from these experiences (see Manz & Neck, 2003).

The two developmental capacities that support self-leadership are self-awareness and developmental motivation. A manager's level of self-awareness refers to the quality of attention and reflection they bring to their own thoughts, feelings, and behaviors. It also refers to the accuracy and completeness of their self-knowledge. Developmental motivation is what motivates a manager to grow further within their current stage of development.

Experts have a strong interest in self-improvement. They want to gain the knowledge and expertise they need to be seen as accomplished professionals. Experts also can be introspective. However, because they tend to be quite self-critical, they tend not to seek feedback from others. At Stage 6, Achievers want to develop the professional competencies needed to contribute to significant organizational results and achieve long-term career objectives. Their ability to look farther back in time, as well as farther ahead, allows them to develop a stronger sense of personal and professional identity. They can be receptive to feedback, if they feel it will help them achieve desired outcomes.

Catalysts realize that their self-image is, in important ways, biased and incomplete. Consequently, they develop a strong interest in becoming aware of behaviors, feelings, and assumptions that would normally escape their conscious attention. They are motivated to increase their self-awareness and more fully align their behavior with their values and aspirations. Co-creators seek a more experiential form of self-awareness that opens them more fully to both joyful and painful emotional experiences. They place a high value on authenticity and try to live their lives in a manner that moves them toward deep self-fulfillment through expression of their innermost potentials. Synergists cultivate a present-centered awareness that grounds them in their bodies and provides direct self-knowledge of habitual mental and emotional patterns. Leaders at this level of agility find that their developmental motivation is to become more fully conscious and to bring a genuine sense of goodwill into as much of their lives as possible.

Levels of Awareness and Intent

Finally, we asked: What is it that makes growth within and between developmental stages possible? By including this question in our study, we discovered that there is a distinct level of awareness and intent that underlies each stage and makes its capacities possible. Capsule descriptions of these core capacities for each stage are summarized in Table 9.3.

Table 9.3. Levels of Awareness and Intent That Lead to Capacities

Stage	Level of Awareness	Level of Intent
5. Expert	A modest reflective capacity	To improve and accomplish things
6. Achiever	A robust reflective capacity	To achieve desired outcomes in ways that are consistent with self-chosen values
7. Catalyst	The ability to step back in the moment and attend directly but very briefly to a current assumption, feeling, or behavior that would otherwise escape attention	To create contexts and facilitate processes that are experienced as meaningful and satisfying and that enable the sustained achievement of desired outcomes
8. Co-Creator	A slightly more sustained attention to ongoing experience, giving a more robust capacity for processing difficult feelings and for fully understanding alternative frames of reference	To tap into an evolving sense of life purpose and actualize it in your everyday life through deep collaboration with others
9. Synergist	Sustained, expanded present-centered attention to one's physical presence, thought processes, intuitions, and emotional responses	To engage with life in all its fullness and to be of benefit to others as well as to oneself.

Given these levels of awareness and intent, one final finding may not be surprising: Leaders at postheroic stages are much more likely than their heroic counterparts to engage in some form of attentional practice, such as meditation, on a regular basis, which they intentionally bring into their leadership activities. In fact, successively more refined attentional practices seem to be what allows people to cultivate the levels of awareness and intent needed to grow into and stabilize increasingly advanced stages of postconventional development.[9]

Notes

1. Prior to 2002, most managers in our study were assessed using the SCT, most scored by myself. I was trained to score the SCT during the early 1980s. Between 2002 and 2005, managers in our study were assessed using

the Maturity Assessment Profile, scored by Cook-Greuter and/or Josephs and myself. We received training from Cook-Greuter in scoring what has been called the SCTi and the Leadership Development Profile (LDP) and is now called the MAP. In terms of the questions used, the MAP is a slightly different version of the SCT.

2. For more information about our research methodology, see Joiner and Josephs (2007, Appendix B).

3. To see how these percentages were calculated, refer to Joiner and Josephs (2007, Appendix B).

4. Survey of 130 senior executives and human resource professionals in Fortune 500 companies, conducted by a global career-management services firm, Lee Hecht Harrison.

5. For more on this topic, see Joiner and Josephs (2007).

6. For example, like many Catalyst leaders, Robert had a strong commitment to environmental responsibility. Becoming an environmental leader became one of the company's new strategies, and, when he retired, Robert joined the board of a nonprofit that promotes environmental protection.

7. *Reflective judgment* is a term we have taken directly from the developmental literature. See P. King and Kitchner (1994), whose work builds on earlier research by Perry (1999).

8. For more on the relevance of diverse attentional practices to stage development and leadership agility, see Joiner and Josephs (2007).

Part III

Theories of Advanced Development

The third and largest section of this book presents theoretical considerations and discussions about postconventional development.

10

Is Higher Better?

A Review and Analysis of the Correlates of Postconventional Ego Development

Tracie L. Blumentritt

In the nearly 40 years since the publication of Loevinger and Wessler's (1970) *Measuring Ego Development,* more than 1,000 articles and book chapters have been published examining nearly every conceivable aspect of the construct and measurement of ego development. In this span of time, the theory of ego development and its measurement, the Washington University Sentence Completion Test (SCT), have generally fared quite well in terms of reliability and validity. In fact, in the most recent critical review of the validity of ego development, Manners and Durkin (2001) noted that "there is substantial empirical support for the conceptual soundness of ego development and the WUSCT" (p. 541). Clearly, Loevinger's conceptualization of ego development established itself as one of the major theories of personality in the late 20th and early 21st centuries.

In the extant literature, and as can be seen from the chapters included in this volume, researchers are now pushing the limits of the traditional theory to examine and propose alternative yet still compatible conceptions and extensions of ego development (Cook-Greuter, 2000; Helson & Roberts, 1994; John et al., 1998; Manners & Durkin, 2000). One area of interest involves examining in greater depth the processes and determinants of postconventional personality functioning. Thus, in keeping with the theme of this book, this chapter focuses on the literature related to various aspects of postconventional ego development, with particular emphasis on the correlates of postconventional functioning in the adult population.

Although researchers define postconventional ego development differently, for the purposes of this chapter the stages above Conscientious, Stage 6, are considered postconventional. Thus, in the ego-development continuum, the postconventional stages are Individualistic, Stage 7, Autonomous, Stage 8, and Integrated, Stage 9. Descriptions of these stages are provided in an earlier chapter of this volume, and can be found elsewhere (e.g., Hauser, 1976).

As the title of this chapter suggests, there is an assumption that the stage sequence itself may represent qualitative differences in adaptive functioning, with the higher stages representing greater adaptation. The Loevinger stages, similar to Kohlberg's and Piaget's, often are regarded as an invariant, hierarchical stage sequence, with each progressive stage reflecting greater flexibility of thought, increases in cognitive complexity, and greater recognition and toleration of individual differences. It must be noted, however, that Loevinger maintained that ego development is orthogonal to mental health (Loevinger, 1976, 1979), meaning at any ego stage individuals may experience mental health symptoms; and in fact there is no clear evidence that any particular type of psychopathology is more or less prevalent at any given stage. However, when examining the descriptions of the stages and the concomitant transitions from stage to stage, one clearly sees that there are qualitative changes occurring in thought, impulse control, and interpersonal style that would seem to have some implications for overall adaptive functioning. For example, the transition from Conformist, Stage 4, to Conscientious, Stage 6, involves an increased appreciation and recognition of one's own inner states, and greater adherence to self- (vs. other-) evaluated standards of behavior. Thus, the Conscientious person may feel a great deal of responsibility for his or her own actions.

Moreover, as one moves into the postconventional levels, the increases in cognitive complexity and toleration of ambiguity become even more marked. This leaves open the question of whether individuals at the highest levels do show indicators of more adaptive functioning, at least in some aspects of life. In other words, does postconventional functioning afford the individual any benefit? And, if it does, what specific strands (e.g., conscious preoccupation, interpersonal style) of ego development might be involved? That is, do the different strands of ego development differentially relate to various outcomes? Although there are numerous studies examining the relation of ego level to various forms of functioning, one problem with focusing on postconventional development is that most studies report very few participants above Stage 6. This is not necessarily unexpected, given that the modal level in the U.S. population is most likely the Self-aware level, which is Stage 5 (Holt, 1980; Loevinger et al., 1985; Redmore & Loevinger, 1979). Consequently, it becomes problematic trying to analyze correlates of *postconventional* functioning in studies with restricted ego-development ranges. Similarly, most studies use correlational analyses, such that, for example, a certain variable may show a positive correlation with ego-development stage. The only possible interpretation of these findings is that as a certain variable increases in magnitude, then so does ego-development level, however, this type of analysis, is not necessarily informative of the correlates specifically of postconventional ego development. For the purposes of this chapter the review of the literature is limited to those studies that report an acceptable range of ego-development scores and that contain an adequate number of participants scoring at the postconventional levels.

First, however, it is necessary to clarify what functioning means and to specify in what *domain* functioning is addressed. *Functioning*, in the simplest terms, is operationally defined as any criterion variable that is related to increased effectiveness, or the potential for increased effectiveness, in one's environment. The domain of functioning refers to the particular environment or setting in which the behavior occurs. Specifically, this chapter focuses on correlates of postconventional ego development among individuals working in the helping professions, and ego development as it relates to the broader domain of coping and mental health. The guiding question of this literature review is: What aspects of postconventional functioning are related to effectiveness in each of these domains?

Postconventional Functioning and the Helping Professions

Several studies have examined the extent to which ego level correlates with or predicts behaviors and traits associated with individuals working in the helping professions. In a sample of 163 female nurse practitioner trainees, M. White (1985) found that ego level was positively associated with personal adjustment and the specific personality trait "nurturance." Additionally, ego level was correlated with increased tolerance of individual differences, capacity for leadership, and lack of aggression. A finding that seems particularly salient for nurse practitioners is that ego level was significantly related to what was termed *responsible caring* in interpersonal relationships. Responsible caring is the notion that one not only genuinely cares about another's well-being, but also that one is committed to fostering another's well-being.

A handful of studies have investigated ego development and its correlates among samples of counselors and counselor trainees. In an early study, Carlozzi, Gaa, and Liberman (1983) found among a sample of counseling psychology practicum students that those at the higher levels of ego functioning demonstrated greater empathy toward their clients. Similarly, related research found that counselor interns at higher ego levels had more awareness of their clients' needs, were more cognizant of countertransference issues, and demonstrated greater objectivity with their clients (Borders & Fong, 1989; Borders, Fong, & Neimeyer, 1986; McIntyre, 1985).

An interesting study by Borders (1989) examined the influence of ego level on practicum students' recall of their own cognitions during videotaped counseling sessions. Participants' recall of cognitions were postcoded for content using a standardized method for coding in-session cognitions (i.e., a "think-aloud" technique; Dole, 1982). This method produced six mutually exclusive categories of thoughts (e.g., thought mode: neutral, planning, positive, or negative; orientation: professional or personal). Frequency analysis of each of the cognition categories by ego-development level revealed that participants at the postconventional level, in this case, the Individualistic stage, Stage 7, reported fewer negative thoughts about their clients, and tended to use more objective processing of information during the session than trainees at lower levels of ego development. They also seemed to have greater awareness of their own feelings triggered by clients' responses, which they then were able to process and use to increase their own effectiveness with clients. Borders (1989) noted that one supervisee "wondered whether her own strong verbal response was 'coming from my need or [the client's] need' " (p. 167). Conversely, individuals at the conventional levels Self-aware, Stage 5 and Conscientious, Stage 6 reported more judgmental thoughts about clients, and tended to think about client issues in black-and-white terms—a trend more pronounced at Stage 5 than at Stage 6.

The evidence is fairly compelling that ego development is related to traits and behaviors that are important for effective performance in the helping professions. But might ego development also serve as a kind of protective factor against risks that are inherent to the helping professions? For example, might ego development contribute to protection against burnout? Burnout is a well-documented and pervasive phenomenon among mental health practitioners working in all types of settings, including schools (Ackerley, Burnell, Holder, & Kurdek, 1988; Fishbach & Tidwell, 1994; Kottler & Hazler, 1996; Skaggs, 1999). Burnout results in significantly reduced quality of care for clients and is also associated with myriad mental and physical health problems in practitioners, including depression and substance abuse (Maslach, 2003; Pines & Maslach, 1978).

Although burnout has been extensively investigated from a variety of perspectives, to date only one study has examined the relation of ego development to burnout. Lambie (2007) examined this association in a large sample of school counseling professionals. Burnout was measured by the Maslach Burnout Inventory–Human Service Survey (Maslach & Jackson, 1996), which provides three subscales (Personal Accomplishment, Emotional Exhaustion, and Depersonalization) that assess various aspects of burnout. Ego development and burnout scores were subject to model testing via path analysis in order to determine if higher levels of ego development contributed to lower levels of burnout. Although path analysis did not support the hypothesized model, subsequent multiple regression analyses revealed that the subscale Personal Accomplishment was significantly predictive of ego level. This subscale assesses an individual's sense of competence in dealing with other people, and it also taps into their overall feelings about the work they do. Lambie (2007) maintains that these results indicate that counselors at higher levels of ego maturity are able to engage in behaviors that "enable them to accept their occupational limitations and maintain affirmative feelings about their work" (p. 86).

The guiding question of this chapter—What aspects of postconventional ego development might be involved in effective functioning in different domains?—would seem to imply that one could separately analyze the various aspects or strands of ego development (i.e., cognitive style, character development, personal and interpersonal awareness, and conscious concerns) as they relate to various criterion measures, such as empathy. In other words, what aspect is contributing the most variance to the observed relation between ego development and the criterion variable? Of relevance, however, is that Loevinger (1976, 1993a) maintained that ego development is the underlying master trait in personality and that the various strands of ego are inextricably inseparable from the whole; thus, it would be pointless to attempt to distill ego development down into its various aspects as, for example, what might occur in a factor analysis of the SCT. That being said, there is some evidence that ego development as operationalized by the ego-stage score may not be the underlying master trait in personality; rather, it is possible that ego development *in combination with* the four strands are aspects of a single unitary dimension of personality (Novy et al., 1994).

An interesting implication of this is that future research could investigate the specific components of ego development as they relate to different dependent measures. For example, what aspect of ego development is contributing to the finding that counselors at higher ego-development levels have increased awareness of countertransference processes? A likely contributor might be cognitive complexity, intrapersonal awareness, or even a combination of both. As another example, what aspect of ego development is involved in the finding that those at higher stages tend to view themselves as more interpersonally competent than those at lower stages? Again, it could be one strand of ego development, or many. The point is that these are empirical questions from which the answers can both broaden and deepen our understanding of the ego-development process, and may suggest mechanisms by which ego development could be fostered, or alternatively, arrested. Additionally, this line of research also would be useful from a psychometric standpoint in that predictive and construct validity of the model and measure of ego development can be further ascertained.

Postconventional Functioning, Coping, and Mental Health

Despite Loevinger's admonishment that ego development and adjustment are separate constructs, there is an ample body of literature that shows that ego development and mental health are interrelated in some important ways (e.g., Noam, 1998; Noam, Copeland, & Jilnina 2006). For example, there is some, albeit mixed, evidence that certain psychiatric diagnoses are associated with different ego-development levels (Noam et al., 2006). For example, schizophrenia is most closely associated with preconformist levels (Noam et al., 2006). There is greater evidence, however, that certain kinds of problems are associated with the ego-development level. A useful way of conceptualizing this relation is offered by Noam (1998) who says that it is important to distinguish between the "development of complexity . . . and [the development of] maturity" (p. 273). He argues:

> Because the ego development model combines complexity and maturity, we end up with two sets of findings: With development there is a decrease in mental health problems, and conversely, delay in ego development puts people at risk . . . But another trend emerges as well: With an increase

of developmental complexity can come an increase in more complex problems. (p. 273)

So, perhaps the most effective way of framing the "riddle" of ego development and mental health is to not look for specific pathologies and their relatedness to ego development, but to examine the types of problems and ways of coping that may be particularly germane to people functioning at different ego levels. This more sophisticated and theoretically informed approach not only provides potentially useful clinical information, but also allows researchers to make specific predictions about the relationships among ego development, problem complexity, and coping style, which, in turn, may provide further evidence of the construct validity of the SCT.

Do individuals at the higher stages cope with various stressors differently than individuals at lower levels? In a sample of adults being treated for chronic pain, Novy, Nelson, Gaa, Blumentritt, and Hetzel (1998) found that ego development was positively correlated with dispositional optimism, and negatively correlated with affective distress, depression, and state anxiety. Although ego level was not related to physical adjustment to pain (such as degree of mobility and bodily self-care), it did significantly predict psychosocial adjustment (e.g., quality of social interactions). Ego development also is related to increased medical compliance and better adjustment to a long-term physical impairment (Hauser, Diplacido, Jacobson, Willett, & Cole, 1993). Finally, studies have shown that higher ego levels are associated with better adjustment to various major life changes, such as adjustment to a chronic medical condition or to divorce (Bursik, 1991; Hauser et al., 1993).

Within a clinical setting, one aspect of coping is the ability to envision, set, and commit to appropriate therapy goals. In a sample of adults with major mental illness (e.g., schizophrenia, bipolar disorder), Stackert and Bursik (2006) investigated the possibility that ego-development level relates to qualitative differences in goals set during the course of therapy. The goal-setting literature is replete with studies showing the positive benefit, therapeutically or otherwise, of setting commitments to appropriate goals (e.g., Hofer & Chasiotis, 2003). From a theoretical standpoint, one should expect to find the type and complexity of goals to be related to ego-development level, with the higher ego stages being associated with more complex, multifaceted, and realistic goals. Indeed, Stackert and Bursik found that individuals at the higher stages reported increasingly more complex therapeutic goals and reported greater commitment to those goals. This study is particularly important to the current discussion because it is one of the few that obtained an adequate number of participants scoring at a postconventional Individualistic level, Stage 7.

Noam et al. (2006) provide the most recent and exhaustive review of the mental health–ego development literature. Although many studies were included, the majority of studies reviewed by Noam et al. included samples with somewhat restricted ego-development ranges, a trend especially true of adolescent samples. However, lack of ego-development variability notwithstanding, two general conclusions can be drawn about mental health and ego development:

1. Ego development levels tend to be lower in clinical compared with nonclinical samples.

2. The types of symptoms expressed are differentially related to the ego-development level.

A research example of the second conclusion is from Borst and Noam (1993) who examined the relations among depressive symptoms, suicide attempts, and ego level. Individuals with depressive symptoms and suicide attempts were more likely to be at the Conformist, Stage 4 (vs. preconformist) levels. However, when further analyzing the motives and characteristics of suicide attemptors, it was found that those who were described as "angry-defiant" were more likely to be preconformist, whereas those characterized as having a more "self-blaming" style were more likely to be at the Conformist stage. A second related study found that self-reported feelings of shame in a clinical sample were related in a curvilinear fashion to ego development: Feelings of shame were lowest at both the pre- and postconventional stages, and highest at the Conformist stage (Einstein & Lanning, 1998). The reasons for feeling less shame at the pre- and postconventional levels changes as well. One feels less shame in the lower stages because standards of behavior are poorly internalized, thus one essentially has nothing to feel shameful about. At the postconventional levels, when self-evaluated inner standards are well developed and one has an increased capacity for self-reflective thought, shame is simply an emotion that is less likely to be experienced. The latter two studies are a good illustration of the importance of going beyond merely looking for correlations between ego level and disorder type, and instead examining specific facets of symptomology and behavior as they relate to ego level.

A related line of research examined the interplay between various aspects of "positive mental health" and ego development. Positive mental health is not merely the conceptual opposite of negative mental health (viz., mental illness); rather, it is the idea that mental health is achieved when individuals are able to psychologically thrive across various life domains (Ryff, 1989). Ryff, who delineated two aspects of positive functioning: environmental mastery and personal growth, proposed an important model of positive mental health. Individuals high in environmental mastery have a strong sense of competence in managing their environment, particularly competence in dealing with the vicissitudes of everyday life; individuals high in personal growth are interested in self-exploration and "see the self as changing in ways that reflect more self-knowledge and effectiveness" (Ryff, 1989, p. 1072).

Using this model, Helson and Srivastava (2001) explored patterns of relationships between positive functioning and various measures of psychological maturity, including ego development and generativity (wisdom). First, they combined the two aspects of functioning to produce four positive mental health dimensions that were based on the four identity statuses. Individuals classified as "Achievers" were high on both environmental mastery and personal growth; "Seekers" were high on personal growth, low on environmental mastery; "Conservers" were low on personal growth, high on environmental mastery; "Depleted" were low on both. Helson and Srivastava found that the Seekers group had the highest scores on both wisdom and ego development. This does not constitute an unexpected finding given that the highest stages of ego development are particularly characterized by increasing inner awareness, self-exploration, and tolerance of ambiguity rather than mastery over the environment. In other words, at the highest levels one is more likely to experience self-mastery, not necessarily environmental mastery.

Finally, several studies have found that ego development is positively related to what is certainly an important aspect of positive functioning, self-esteem (e.g., L. King et al., 2000). Interestingly, however, ego development has not been consistently linked with increased life satisfaction (e.g., Diamond, 1997), or with better maturity as assessed by measures of psychological adjustment and well-being (Young, 1998). What these results suggest is that although one may feel better about one's self at the higher ego levels, one might not necessarily feel more satisfied with life.

Conclusions

To return to the original question, "Is higher better?" the answer seems to be, "it depends." It clearly seems to be beneficial to be at the higher stages if one is working as a helping professional. Counselor trainees at the higher stages (in most cases Stage 6 and above) tend to be more empathic, more accurate and objective in their assessment of their clients' needs, and better able to recognize countertransference issues. Higher ego development also may provide a buffer against burnout in the helping professions.

It also is quite likely that people in the higher stages cope better with major life stressors. Ego development is positively related to dispositional optimism, medical compliance, adjustment to a chronic medical condition, and adjustment to divorce. Moreover, individuals with higher ego development set more realistic, appropriate, and complex therapy goals. They also are more likely to commit to those goals.

The mental health–ego development connection is not quite so clear cut, particularly with respect to mental illness and postconventional functioning. Part of the problem in attempting to draw clear conclusions about the association between mental illness and postconventional functioning is that so few people in clinical samples are postconventional. Of course, one might argue that the relative absence of postconventional individuals with mental illness *is* the main conclusion (i.e., mental illness suppresses ego development or, conversely, individuals at postconventional levels are less likely to develop mental illness).

Although beyond the scope of this chapter, future discussion could focus on the work that has been conducted on the impact of various successful interventions on ego development (e.g., Alexander & Orme-Johnson, 2003). Another relevant and interesting line of future work involves identifying the specific strand (or strands) of ego development that might be connected to different kinds of successful interventions. For example, in using cognitive-behavioral approaches, which strand offers the best avenue for promoting therapeutic change: cognitive complexity, interpersonal style, or impulse control? Finally, the literature on positive mental health offers clear evidence not only of a link between postconventional functioning and various aspects of optimal mental health, but also evidence for the construct validity of the model and measure of ego development. Studies that show that higher ego levels are associated with wisdom, self-esteem, and a personality type characterized by intense interest in personal growth provides additional evidence for what Manners and Durkin (2001) refer to as the "conceptual soundness" of ego development. Clearly, however, there are numerous possibilities for future work in the area of postconventional ego development.

11

The Challenge of Ego Development

Intentional versus Active Development

Laura A. King

> Now, from this peculiar sideway position of the whale's eyes, it is
> plain that he can never see an object which is exactly ahead, no
> more than he can one exactly astern. . . . This peculiarity of the
> whale's eyes is a thing always to be borne in mind in the fishery;
> and to be remembered by the reader.
>
> —Herman Melville (*Moby Dick*, Chapter 74)

In autumn 1991, shortly after the beginning of my first semester as
a new assistant professor, my mother was diagnosed with pancreatic
cancer. She was given six months to live. Exactly as predicted, she died
in early 1992. After her death, I was simply and utterly bereft, in the
midst of intense grief, longing, and what seemed like bottomless sadness. Messages from popular culture and even the scholarly literature
on trauma and loss (with which I was quite familiar) suggested that
I should make meaning out of this experience, perhaps grow, become
better for it, and most importantly, find a way to be happy. I was
profoundly unsatisfied by the notion that the central focus of enduring,
examining, or coping through such a significant negative life experience
should be enhanced happiness. It was clear to me that being happy (or
happier) was not necessarily at the top of the list of the priorities of
grief. Inspired by my personal experience, I embarked on a program of
research dedicated to understanding narratives of traumatic life experi-

ences as signs and portents of personality development. This research interest provoked a search for an outcome that might capture aspects of development that are qualitatively distinct from happiness, a sign of development that might capture what happened to me, and perhaps what happens to people when life challenges their very sense of the meaning of existence.

Certainly, researchers have questioned the central role of happiness in psychological notions of the Good Life (e.g., Ryan & Deci, 2001; Ryff, 1989; Ryff & Singer, 1998, 2008). What perplexed me about these approaches was that very often constructs that were promulgated as something other than happiness (e.g., Self-Determination Theory's organismic needs, Ryan & Deci, 2001; or the facets of Ryff's approach to positive functioning, Ryff & Singer, 1998) were themselves very strongly related to happiness (e.g., Kashdan, Biswas-Diener, & King, 2008).

If happiness really isn't everything, then surely there must be something that is good that isn't happiness, that isn't even related to happiness, that is, in fact, centrally irrelevant to happiness. Was there something truly apart from happiness that might be gained from loss?

My search led me to the construct of ego development, the Sentence Completion Test (SCT), and to the work of Jane Loevinger (e.g., 1976; Hy & Loevinger, 1996; Loevinger & Wessler, 1970). Becoming a self-taught scholar of ego development was not the easiest undertaking. However, it quickly became clear that, at the very least, ego development is not (and has not been) related to happiness, subjective well-being, or psychological adjustment (e.g., Helson & Wink, 1992 L. King, 2001; L. King et al., 2000; Noam, 1998), making it an ideal construct for the study of one developmental outcome of difficult life experience. In this chapter, I focus on the challenge ego development presents to the adult developer as well as to psychologists interested in adult development. In particular, I draw a distinction between active and intentional adult development. I believe that, in the context of ego development, the active adult developer is like Melville's whale, heading toward an object that cannot be seen or articulated. Like the whale, the active adult developer sees the process but not the end of development. The stories adults tell about their important life experiences, those experiences that shook them to their very cores, reveal the sights, sounds, thoughts, and feelings they picked up as a result of and along the way to that unseen end, ego development. Essentially, ego development may be understood as an unintended consequence of active engagement in experience: They got there, but they didn't mean to.

Active versus Intentional Development

To explore this central distinction between active and intentional development, it might be helpful to consider the analogy between child and adult development. By *active development*, I refer to the active contribution of the organism in his or her own development. By *intentional development*, I refer to the conscious and effortful seeking out of characteristics, skills, and behavioral patterns. Active development occurs when development depends on the active engagement of the organism with the environment. Intentional development, in my view, involves something more specific: the active, self-conscious pursuit of a developmental end.

Since Piaget, we have recognized the child as an active participant in development. The child's role in development is active, but unintentional. On the way to getting what he or she wants, the child acquires the abilities to reach out and grab, to walk, and to talk, to persuade and cajole. These developmental milestones are, in some sense, happy accidents of the convergence of physical development with fierce determination. The infant is not envisioning "self as walker" to become a toddler. I would suggest that, again with particular focus on ego development, we consider the developing adult as even more like the child than we might initially believe. Just as the child does not consciously set the goal of walking or talking, the adult is very unlikely to set the conscious developmental goal of "becoming more ego developed." Why might this be the case?

Foremost, ego development is a difficult construct to grasp. Scholars have difficulty defining it. Once defined, it remains only slightly less inscrutable. Manuscript reviewers have a hard time "getting it." Surely people cannot consciously strive toward a developmental end that is so elusive and potentially baffling. If adult development were limited to intention then we might look to naïve conceptions of maturity to understand what people are striving to become. In a sample of more than 400 non-college adults, my students and I examined the folk concepts of maturity. We asked these adults to complete a checklist of traits and to provide an open-ended description of the most mature person they could think of. Examination of these folk notions of maturity showed that the highest endorsement for characteristics of the mature person was for traits associated with kindness. These endorsements were significantly higher than those for open-mindedness, which was itself significantly higher than agency, and positive affect. Interestingly, the closest trait to ego development was the word "complexity" and this word remained in the factor analysis (as part of open-minded-ness) despite its low communality, based primarily on its conceptual relevance. The open-ended responses were, not surprisingly, devoid of a definition of ego development.

Still, scholars have become increasingly comfortable with blurring the lines between conscious feelings of personal growth and personality development (e.g., Staudinger & Kunzmann, 2005). Ego development stands as a warning that these two processes may or may not have much to do with each other. Personal growth is available to self-report and people who rate themselves high on this tendency tend to be happier. Ryff (e.g., Ryff & Singer, 2008) includes personal growth in her conceptualization of positive well-being. Whether these feelings of growing or commitment to growth are related to ego development remains to be seen. Research has failed to show a relationship between, for instance, self-reported, stress-related growth and ego development in parents of children with Down syndrome (DS; L. King et al., 2000).

Although the capacity for conscious reflection is certainly an important developmental distinction between the child and the adult, it is important to acknowledge the limits of conscious understanding and, therefore, personal intention. In adulthood, we can become too confident in the value and power of intention. Development can happen to us, unwilled. This is not to say that the adult developer is not active. Rather, as is seen here, in narratives of life change, the active struggle to remain engaged with reality is clear. But this struggle plays a role in developmental change in a way that defies articulation.

Thus, when we think about active development in adulthood, we are wise to avoid equating active development with intentional development. Thinking of development as a motivated, intentional process, for instance, Levenson and Crumpler (1996) portray development as a choice that relies on the commitment of the person. That choice, however, may not be a matter of deciding on some fully elaborated set of consciously pursued developmental goals but rather, simply, *to stay in it*, to remain actively engaged with life, like a rodeo cowboy hanging on to life's bucking bronco, or a pugilist taking punches and refusing to hit the mat.

Ego Development, Narratives of Life Transition, and Lost Possible Selves

In our research, my students and I have examined ego development as it is reflected in and predicted by characteristics of narratives of life changing events (e.g., parenting a child with DS, L. King et al., 2000; coming out as gay or lesbian, L. King & Smith, 2004) and narrative reconstructions of lost goals or what we refer to as lost possible selves (e.g., of divorced women, L. King & Raspin, 2004; and gay men and lesbians, L. King & Smith, 2004). This work is reviewed in a variety of places (L. King, 2001; L. King & Hicks, 2006, 2007a, 2007b). Here, instead I share a sense of the lessons that the relatively developed egos in these samples have taught us about the meaning of ego development and its implications for our understanding of personality development in adulthood. My research has generally examined ego development and psychological well-being as independent sides of maturity. In the present context, I reserve consideration of happiness and focus primarily on the side of maturity that is the focus of this volume, ego development.

Looking to narrative constructions of experience as a sign and portent of ego development is certainly in keeping with the notion that the ego is the author of the "me" (McAdams, 1998), and with Loevinger's (1976) declaration that the essence of the ego is "the striving to master, to integrate, and make sense of experience" (p. 59). These stories allow us to see the ego as it reveals itself in the making of sense, a process not an end. We cannot quite grasp this elusive ego—be it a buffer (Hy & Loevinger, 1996) or a lens (L. King & Hicks, 2006)—but we can see the ego in what it does, including the stories it creates out of experience.

In describing "pacers," Loevinger (1976) suggested that only when the environment fails to meet one's expectations can real development occur. Thus, in confronting pacers, previous meanings are stripped away, previous ways of interacting with the world are utterly insufficient, and new approaches to life experience must be entertained. Accommodation refers to the process of modifying existing cognitive structures when life requires a central change in the self. To capture indicators of accommodation in narratives of life transition, we coded narratives on dimensions including being actively engaged in the struggle, experiencing a "paradigmatic shift," and exploration (L. King et al., 2000).

To summarize briefly, samples of parents of children with DS, women who have experienced divorce after long marriages (>20 years), and samples of gay men and lesbians were asked to write narrative descriptions of an important, identity-challenging experience. They also completed measures of ego development, often twice, over 2 years. Overall, the results of these studies show that individuals who tell transition stories that are rich with imagery indicating accommodation score higher on ego development and are more likely to increase in ego development over time (L. King et al., 2000; L. King & Smith,

2005). Additionally, the level of elaboration in narrative descriptions of lost possible selves relates to ego development, both concurrently and over time (e.g., L. King & Raspin, 2004; L. King & Smith, 2004). The postconventional ego has the capacity to look back on a previous version of the self with clear-eyed openness to the vivid life represented by those lost goals.

Narratives of the Postconventional Ego

Drawing now on the narratives shared by participants in our samples who occupy the very highest ego-development levels, we can extract some sense of these developed egos, the ways that they approach challenging life events, and how they make meaning out of potential chaos. Across all samples, among the highest ego levels, we find uniformly vivid, engaged, and emotionally rich stories. In reading these narratives, one quality that is perhaps not surprising is the tendency of the ego/narrator to provide explicit commentary on its own attempts to cope. In gay men and lesbians, this might be conveyed in stories that talk about weighing the potential pitfalls of coming out, explicitly deciding that one must live true to oneself, or even laughing at one's foolish terror. Among the parents of children with DS, the narratives contain a level of psychological language that is notable. In the wake of a profound life experience, these individuals demonstrate a striking sensitivity to their own mental processes. These narrators show a clear-eyed admission of weakness and denial, and talk explicitly about automatic attempts to cope.

In addition to this clear narrative evidence of the psychological mindedness that has been shown to relate to ego development (Helson & Roberts, 1994), three related themes appear to be emblematic of the highest levels of ego development in these diverse samples. These characteristics are

1. Surprise and Confounded Expectations;

2. Awe, Terror, and Surrender; and

3. Comfort of the Physical World.

These three themes are clearly relevant to the distinction between intention and activity, as is discussed in this chapter.

Surprise and Confounded Expectations

These stories convey the tale of "What Happened to Me" and bear witness to the limits of intention. These are stories of the unexpected, the previously unfathomable. Narratives often begin with a statement of utter shock: "I never imagined that I might be a homosexual." "It never occurred to me that someone in my family would have an illness or handicap." "I was shocked." These stories remind us that "the things we think we want" is a category defined by our capacity to imagine. Very often, ego development appears to emerge out of the unexpected. Often in narratives on lost possible self, the developed ego mentions expecting life to be an easier proposition than it turned out to be. The following excerpt was provided by a woman who experienced divorce after a marriage of more than 20 years:

> I imagined a deliriously happy "empty nest" syndrome. Neither of us likes to travel, but sports are a big priority. I figured we would exercise, go to sporting events, theatre, etc., together. I envisioned weddings with lots of family pictures. There would be grandchildren to baby-sit. Life would be calm, easy and sweet. (L. King & Raspin, 2004, p. 616)

And a gay man commented about lost straight possible self: "As a straight person, my life would be much more contented, peaceful, and happy" (L. King & Hicks 2007b, p. 631). Similarly, the mother of a child with DS notes the now poignant effortlessness of her expectations:

> I had visions of my blonde-haired son playing on the beach, being a movie star, or model. . . . I thought my son would ride his bike around the neighborhood with all his friends, play football, baseball, and all the other "boy" sports with the neighborhood children, effortlessly. I thought the developmental milestones would be attained, effortlessly. (L. King & Hicks, 2006, p. 130)

Clearly, these expectations likely are not unique. Indeed, one can well imagine many adults setting a goal to simplify rather than complicate life. The explicit mention of these expectations in these narratives is contrasted with the tendency of some at lower levels of ego development to explicitly deny ever having expectations (L. King & Hicks, 2007a). In defying our intentions, challenging life experiences also bring these previously helpful expectations to the fore, particularly for those with the insight and lack of defensiveness of the postconventional ego.

Awe, Terror, and Surrender

Often in these narratives, the self is perceived as small in the face of a much larger reality, described with remarkable vividness. These descriptions often include an admission of almost unspeakable vulnerability and a sense that the world looms large. The descriptions convey a sense that one is nearly drowned or overtaken by experience, as the following excerpts (L. King et al., 2000) from parents of children with DS illustrate.

> A wave of feelings passed through me—shock, fear and tremendous sadness, and protectiveness toward my son.
>
> I cried some and experienced waves of "Unknown" embracing me . . .
>
> I felt as though the earth had opened up and swallowed me. My world seemed to grow (almost tangibly) darker. In that short instant, my normal, "perfect" life disappeared.

These narratives convey a sense of activity without intention, describing a moment of engagement with reality, in which the power of experience nearly overcomes the ego's capacity for sense-making. Rather than impose meaning on this moment, they simply stay in it, keeping their heads just above the waves. If development is a choice, then these stories convey a sense of what these individuals allowed to happen to them, when they might have turned away, in fact, might have longed to turn away: "There was construction going on at the hospital and there was scaffolding outside my window. I wanted to crawl out on it and keep on going—just escape."

Conveyed in these narratives, then, is the sense of surrender to what life has thrown at the person. Such experiences can also have a positive tone, as in the coming out stories of gay men and lesbians. Indeed, one particularly common thematic line in the coming out stories is surrender. We coded these stories for McAdams' (1992) intimacy motive. One category for that motive is surrender, which involves acknowledging that forces outside of one's control (fate, luck, etc.) may guide a relationship. In the coming out stories, the developed ego often discovered gay identity in the experience of a love that was "bigger" than they had ever experienced. Such stories that vividly describe falling in love, being "crazy in love," or that refer to an "undeniable force" "sealing one's fate" indicate a sense of one's destiny that is outside of one's control and beyond one's intentions.

> I was taking a college course . . . with my lover. I was late one evening and had to sit several rows behind. As she spoke I watched her and felt the most intense love you could have for someone—her intelligence, her looks, the tone in her voice. I finally knew what it meant to be in love. (L. King & Smith, 2005 p. 285)

The Comfort of the Physical World

In these tumultuous experiences in which the world often has taken on an almost personal character, an interesting source of comfort emerges—concrete reality. Even amid the "waves of Unknown," insight provides access to not only the enormity of change but also the small, good things in life. Often, particularly among the parents of children with DS, the developed ego finds enormous comfort in the simplicity of small, real pleasures. *Nearly every one* of these postconventional parents notes the sheer physical beauty of their child. Some examples follow (from L. King & Hicks, 2007b, p. 631):

> He was not the monster I expected, he was beautiful.
> My daughter was flesh and blood and a good nurser and that was the reality I remember dealing with.
> Then I realized that I was mourning as if my child had died yet I still had a nice fat baby in the nursery. I rang for him to be brought to me expecting him to be a monster instead of the cute thing I saw in the delivery room. I tore all of his clothes off of him and just looked at him. He was beautiful.

These narratives of life transition are the ego's story of "what happened to me" or perhaps more courageously, "what I let happen to me." These stories convey the extraordinary paradox of embracing a life experience that is one no one would wish on another. They involve the admission of surprise, vulnerability, of previous foolishness, of surrender, and of finding relics of hope in the midst of torment. Although admitting the longing for a life that was "calm, easy, and sweet," or "contented, peaceful, and happy," or "effortless," these adults stayed with experience when it challenged them to the utmost. Ego development might be considered something we let happen to us, an expression of humility, openness, and receptivity (L. King & Hicks, 2007a).

What is remarkable in these stories is that they explicitly include the period of disruption itself, as part of the narrative. These individuals have managed to live in the "in between" place of not knowing, without automatically imposing meaning on experience. To be sure, at the lower levels of ego development, denial is not discussed, it is embraced: "This experience has not changed my life, except in very, very, small ways" (from a parent of a child with DS; L. King et al., 2000), or "All of these goals are certainly available to me as a gay person" (from a gay man; L. King & Hicks, 2007a). Meanings are imposed, however ill-fitting or premature they might be ("I never had a second thought that this was God's plan for me," from data reported in L. King et al., 2000). Importantly, the level of sheer trauma in the stories does not distinguish the postconventional ego from lower levels. Rather, somehow amidst the breathless shock, the postconventional ego allows itself to be changed, for better or worse, simply by remaining actively engaged in and receptive to experience.

It might be worth noting what is not apparent in these stories are lost possible selves, as well as narrative closure, resolution, and coherence. Indeed, although not particularly common, another feature of some of these narratives is deep ambivalence, insight coupled with bitter recognition of life's limitations. Insight can come at a high price. The dangers of ego development would appear to be the potential for disillusionment, cynicism and an apparently brutal perspective on the self and world (L. King & Hicks, 2007a). Here, I cannot help but note that happiness may play a role in avoiding these negatives and embracing seemingly difficult hope.

The Challenge of Ego Development for the Science of Personality Development

Just as ego development is communicated in tested assumptions for the developer, it tests the assumptions of the science of human development. In Loevinger's (e.g., 1976) writings, we find a level of courage that is truly remarkable. She embraced the richness of this construct and defied expectations. The construct and its measure are, frankly, unapologetically difficult. For instance, she acknowledged that the highly developed ego will sometimes give very low-level answers. She made it explicit that the items would not provide a nice Cronbach's α and that our old friend the "mean" would not provide an appropriate final score.

Furthermore, even a scholar who is willing to sweat the difficult and even arduous experience of coding these protocols, training raters, and so on, must still think hard about the issues of reliability and validity that are always at the heart of good science. This measure is not a self-report questionnaire for good reason.

Indeed, even as the active developer might look around at the world with new "ego-developed eyes" that see conflict where previously there was contentment, or uncertainty where life was once "black and white," researchers must come to live with the imperfections of the measure, itself. We discover that, over time, some people will develop, others regress, and others stay the same. We worry that some items seem antiquated. Or we come to the horrifying realization that some stems might invite responses that no one could have imagined. For instance, when we were collecting data in Dallas, the city was filled with billboards announcing that "Education is . . . PARAMOUNT!" explaining the sudden frequency of this response in our samples. And to be sure, publishing this challenging work can also be difficult.

On occasion, one might even think, "There must be an easier way," for the researcher and for the developer. In describing his straight possible self, one postconventional gay man commented about the difficulties of being a gay person in a homophobic society, "it forced me to do some very difficult work . . . (as a straight person) I don't know that I would ever have felt the need to do all the work I have done." (cited in L. King & Hicks, 2007b, p. 631). Similarly, as a researcher interested in something other than happiness, "I do not know that I would have ever felt the need to do all the work I have done." When I first started coding protocols myself, I experienced a moment of recognition that I have seen repeated regularly in student-coders, a sudden sense that "something" is here, that we're getting at something that we could not otherwise measure. The results that have emerged from this rich data speak against the notion that this is simply cognitive dissonance.

Some Final Thoughts on Active but Unintentional Development

At the end of *Moby Dick*, we see the differing consequences of intentionality versus activity. For Ahab, the ironic triumph of intentionality is found in death. His intention has won, although not in the way he had imagined. The whale never did fully cooperate by gobbling him up. Ishmael, alive, floats on the Queequeg's coffin, an image filled with tantalizing and all-too-obvious meaning. Life often presents us with such tempting solid ground, daring us to plant both feet and settle on an answer, perhaps at long last, The Answer. But as the developed egos I have studied made clear, the sands will always shift. The greatest achievement might be to embrace *today's answer* heroically, nevertheless, despite full knowledge of its tentative, fragile nature. These egos, like Ishmael, serve as attentive, open narrators, perhaps suspecting that, in the end, the story will be the ultimate pay-off. It might be that these stories are the postconventional ego's gift to the person, who might consciously long for a simpler life, and seek out developmental ends that are utterly at odds with this capacity to master, to integrate and make sense.

The gift that Jane Loevinger left scholars of human development is itself a challenge that will likely continue to inspire questions, difficulty, and even ambivalence, like so many of life's most important experiences. Somehow, this difficult, prickly construct provides access to the mystery of adult development. What I have learned from the work of Loevinger, and adults who score high on her measure of ego development can be summarized as follows. Adult development and the science of that development require similar uncomfortable but profound commitments: To know what we can and to admit to not knowing what we cannot know—all the while knowing that not knowing is part of life, learning, change, and development, itself.

Acknowledgments

I would like to thank Aaron Geise for his contributions to a conversation that informed and inspired this chapter. Thanks also to Lisa Jensen for helpful comments on an earlier version.

12

Transcendent Experience and Development of the Postrepresentational Self

Dennis Heaton

Cross-sectional studies have consistently indicated that a majority of adults are not postconventional. Two large surveys reported that only 2% to 3% of adults scored at or above Stage 8, the Autonomous level, on Loevinger's (1976) Washington University Sentence Completion Test (SCT; Cook-Greuter, 1990; Loevinger & Wessler, 1970). Cohn's (1998) exhaustive review of cross-sectional data indicates that development appears to cease for most adults prior to postconventional stages and that mean adult ego development is relatively unchanging across different age groups. Reflecting on this data, Cohn questioned why development stops for most adults and what types of social experiences might act as pacers for continued development. Marko (this volume) also explores the question: "What facilitative agents do trigger vertical growth?"

Research-based evidence suggests that daily practice of the Transcendental Meditation® (TM)[1] technique, alternated with normal activity, is a facilitator of postconventional development. In a longitudinal study of TM practitioners, an unprecedented 38% of the 34 experiment subjects scored at or beyond Loevinger's Autonomous level, Stage 8.

This chapter reviews some of the findings regarding the effects of this technique on holistic development and then presents theory related to these empirical research findings, including a model of an extended range of human development and an analysis of the mechanics of developmental advances. Vedic psychology describes higher states of consciousness in which the higher Self is realized and distinguished from the lower self—mind, intellect, and ego. These higher states of consciousness have been identified as a postrepresentational range of development, in which the Self knows itself as pure consciousness, rather than a conceptually created identity. Systematic cultivation of experiences that transcend thought promote development to the postrepresentational range. These dynamics, as depicted by Vedic psychology, are related to insights of Kegan (1982) and Maslow (1968) in modern developmental psychology.

The TM Technique as a Facilitator of Development

The TM technique is normally practiced for 20 minutes twice daily sitting quietly with the eyes closed. In the TM technique, a specific sound or *mantra*, chosen for its sound value without reference to meaning, is used to shift attention away from its habitual outward direction (Roth, 1994). During meditation the mantra is experienced at progressively deeper and finer levels until thought is completely transcended, and silent inner wakefulness is naturally experienced.

Developmental outcomes of the practice, reviewed in Orme-Johnson (2000), include self-development as measured by Loevinger's (1976) SCT, moral reasoning as measured by the Defining Issues Test (DIT; Rest, 1987), self-actualization as measured by the Personal Orientation Inventory (POI; Shostrom, 1966), among other psychological findings, as well as qualitative and physiological research on practitioners of this meditation technique. One study provided evidence of unprecedented prevalence of postconventional levels of self-development in a sample of college alumni. This 10-year longitudinal study (H. Chandler, 1991; H. Chandler, Alexander, & Heaton, 2005) found that alumni of Maharishi University of Management, who had been practicing the TM program, increased markedly in ego development as measured by the SCT, in contrast to three control groups at traditional universities, individually matched for gender and age over the same time period ($p=.0000004$). At post-test 53% of the 34 experiment subjects scored at or beyond Loevinger's Individualistic level, Stage 7, and 38% at or above the Autonomous level, Stage 8, versus 1% of controls. The highest previous frequency of scores at or above Stage 8 was 10% for alumni of Harvard University ($N=107$, mean age=55, Vaillant & McCullough, 1987). The TM subjects also increased to very high levels of principled moral reasoning and intimacy. In this study, the SCT rater for pre- and post-tests for all groups was an expert who had scored thousands of protocols and has published extensively on the interpretation of higher stage responses on the SCT (Cook-Greuter, 1990, 2000). She was blind to the experimental design and hypotheses, and was not a TM practitioner. Loevinger and Wessler (1970) allow for a single rater when that rater is of "demonstrated competence" (p. xii):

> Another experiment employing the SCT indicated that the practice of the TM technique produced development advances even in an initially low scoring population of maximum security prisoners, who would not necessarily be regarded as predisposed toward developmental change. Alexander, Walton and Goodman (2002/2003) reported that prison inmates practicing the TM technique for 20 months scored a full level higher cross-sectionally on the SCT (Self-Aware, Stage 5, versus Conformist, Stage 4) than did non-meditating inmates interested in learning the TM technique or inmates in other treatment programs. After 17 months, this initial TM group increased another level, to Conscientious, Stage 6, and a new group that learned the TM technique grew one full level from Conformist to Self-aware. No longitudinal increases were found in other treatment groups or demographically similar controls wait-listed to learn the TM technique. Regular meditators also decreased significantly in aggression, schizophrenia, and trait-anxiety, compared to controls. (Alexander & Orme-Johnson, 2003)

Studies have also found that the TM technique produces longitudinal change in self-actualization, as measured by the POI (Shostrom, 1966). Self-actualization, according to Maslow (1968), is associated with various forms of peak or transcendental experiences. Alexander, Rainforth, and Gelderloos (1991) argued that because the TM technique provides a means to systematically and reliably cultivate experiences of transcendence, it provides an operational procedure for experimentally testing the hypothesis that systematic transcendence can have a causal effect on growth of self-actualization. An exhaustive statistical meta-analysis of all existing studies (42 treatment outcomes) on the effects of the TM technique and other forms of meditation and relaxation on self-actualization found that the effect size, in standard deviation units, of TM on overall self-actualization (ES=.78) was approximately three times as large as that of other forms of meditation and relaxation, controlling for duration of treatment, and strength of experimental design (Alexander et al., 1991). These researchers attributed the differential effect size of the TM to its effectiveness in cultivating experiences of transcendence.

A qualitative study by Herriott (2000) employed interviews to explore the inner development of 21 entrepreneurs who were long-term practitioners of the TM technique and the TM-Sidhi program, an advanced meditation practice. These subjects reported subjective states, such as inner fullness, inner silence, and a secure feeling of being anchored to something deeper. From such responses, Herriott identified a common factor that she termed *unshakability*, implying an ability to stay calm inside and unaffected even in the face of chaotic circumstances.

Travis, Tecce, Arenander, and Wallace (2002) researched brainwave patterns that distinguished a select group of long-term (mean=24.5 years) practitioners of the TM program who report experiencing Cosmic Consciousness (witnessing during activity and sleep) from a short-term TM group and a non-TM group. Eyes-open electroencephalograms (EEGs) in the long-term TM group indicated broadband frontal EEG coherence characteristic of TM practice, even during challenging computer tasks. The authors describe this as permanent integration of "consciousness-itself," or Transcendental Consciousness, during waking activity and sleep. Travis, Arenander, and DuBois (2004) then examined further differences between these groups using interviews and psychological tests of inner versus outer orientation, moral reasoning, and emotional stability. They conclude that a combination of psychological and physiological indicators correspond to differences in phenomenological reports of sense-of-self along an Object-referral/Self-referral continuum.

Although the studies just summarized used objective methods to measure constructs in contemporary psychology, the original context of the TM technique is in the Vedic tradition of subjective discoveries concerning human consciousness. The following discussion intends to draw connections between theory from Vedic psychology and concepts in developmental psychology. Specifically, this chapter applies Kegan's (1992) theory of subject–object relations to explain the role of transcendence in cultivating development. It also relates Maslow's (1972) description of self-actualization to what Vedic psychology depicts as a stable stage in which the transcendental Self is awake to its own nature, which is distinct from the contents and activities of the mind.

Higher States of Consciousness as a Postrepresentational Tier of Self-Development

In a previous paper relating Vedic psychology to developmental psychology, Alexander, Heaton, and Chandler (1994) presented a model that categorized stages of development into three tiers, pre-representational (preverbal), representational (including ego stages up to Loevinger's Integrated, Stage 9), and postrepresentational—comprised of higher states of consciousness in which self-identity is not mediated by symbolic thought but grounded in awareness of transcendental Being. This model identifies higher states of consciousness as developmental stages—"stable positions from which an individual habitually processes experience" (Cook-Greuter, 2000, p. 232).

Our primary source on Vedic psychology is the work of His Holiness Maharishi Mahesh Yogi (hereafter referred to as Maharishi), particularly his translation and commentary on the *Bhagavad-Gita* (1969). This chapter also builds on other psychologists, who have been influenced by Maharishi's work (Alexander et al., 1990; Orme-Johnson, 1988; Travis et al., 2004). Maharishi passed away in 2008, having inspired ongoing research on higher states of consciousness through three convergent approaches: personal experience, Vedic literature, and empirical science. The body of work, which Maharishi has left in his books, as well as thousands of hours of recorded lectures and conferences, constitutes a rich resource for expanding understanding and experience of an extended range of postconventional and transpersonal development.

In his commentary on the *Gita*, Maharishi (1969) explained that Vedic psychology differentiates the lower self from the higher Self. The lower self is "that aspect of the personality which deals only with the relative aspect of existence. It comprises the mind that thinks, the intellect that decides, the ego that experiences." The higher Self is "that aspect of the personality which never changes, absolute Being" (Maharishi, 1969, p. 339). The higher Self is consciousness itself, yet most people remain ignorant of it in their ordinary waking experiences: "Since the mind ordinarily remains attuned to the senses, projecting outwards towards the manifested realms of creation, it misses or fails to appreciate its own essential nature, just as the eyes are unable to see themselves" (Maharishi, 1963, p. 30).

The higher Self is realized by the conscious mind when it gains the state of Transcendental Consciousness—"a state of inner wakefulness with no object of thought or perception, just pure consciousness, aware of its own unbounded nature . . . beyond the division of subject and object" (Maharishi, 1976, p. 123). Maharishi (1995) identified this state as an experience of the spiritual essence of life: "eternal silence, which is pure wakefulness, absolute alertness, pure subjectivity, pure spirituality" (p. 271 fn.). Transcendental Consciousness is shown in Table 12.1 as a state in which there is awareness of the higher Self but no awareness of objects.

Table 12.1. Seven States of Consciousness in Vedic Psychology

State of Consciousness	Awareness of Higher Self	Awareness of Object
1. Sleeping	No	No
2. Dreaming	No	Illusory
3. Waking	No	Yes
4. Transcendental	Yes	No
5. Cosmic	Yes	Yes
6. Refined Cosmic	Yes	Yes, finest relative aspect of object
7. Unity	Yes	Yes, infinite Self in object

Note: Based on "The Science of Creative Intelligence," by Maharishi Mahesh Yogi, 1972, Fairfield, IA: Maharishi International University Press.

Vedic psychology explains that repeated experience of Transcendental Consciousness in meditation, alternated with active living, leads over time toward a state in which Transcendental Consciousness, consciousness of the Self, comes to be lived more and more outside of meditation—along with the changing waking, dreaming, and deep-sleep states of consciousness. Transcendental Consciousness has been related to the unified field of theoretical physics, the foundation of the ever-evolving order of the cosmos (Hagelin, 1987). When the higher Self glimpsed in Transcendental Consciousness (*samadhi*) has become permanently awake to itself throughout all the changing experiences of living, that status of life is called Cosmic Consciousness (*nitya samadhi*; Maharishi, 1969, p. 151).

Although the focus of this chapter is on the Cosmic Consciousness, Vedic psychology describes two further higher states of consciousness. In Refined Cosmic Consciousness the relationship of the fully differentiated Self with the object is characterized by greatly enriched appreciation and intimacy. This culminates in Unity Consciousness, in which one experiences the object as being the same Absolute pure consciousness as the Self (see Table 12.1). A Vedic expression of Unity Consciousness in the *Bhagavad Gita* is: "sees the Self in all beings and all beings in the Self" (chapter 6, verse 29 in Maharishi, 1969, p. 441). Such an end point of development has been conjectured by Kegan:

> The ultimate state of development would have to do with some way in which the self has become entirely identified with the world. It would be the recognition essentially of the oneness of the universe, which is something we have heard

over and over again in wisdom literatures of the East and West. (cited in Debold, 2002, p. 2)

In Cosmic Consciousness, the answer to the question "Who am I" is with reference to direct experience of one's inner Being or am-ness, in contrast to identifying oneself with one's roles, values, or thoughts. Alexander et al. coined the phrase "subject permanence," analogous to the cognitive development milestone of "object permanence" in earlier childhood, to identify a radically new level of invariance in Cosmic Consciousness.

Cook-Greuter (2000) depicts rare Unitive levels of development, Stage 10, scores on the SCT as expressions of a "fluid, open-ended self-identity" (p. 236). This bears some resemblance to the notion of "postrepresentational Self." She postulated that while "At the Unitive stage, individuals can integrate and make use of their transcendent experiences more often" (p. 236); yet they are "still mostly grounded in the symbolically-mediated way of knowing" (p. 239). She further proposed "to become permanently established in higher stages of consciousness . . . ordinary people require systematic instruction and careful guidance by qualified teachers as well as regular, long-term practice" (p. 238). Therefore, the postrepresentational Self described in this chapter could possibly be regarded as a developmental position beyond Cook-Greuter's Unitive level, Stage 10. However, in the same article, Cook-Greuter also suggested that the progression from postconventional stages of development to higher states of consciousness is not necessarily a linear sequence. Similarly, Alexander et al (1994) clarify:

We do not mean to imply that experiences of transcendental consciousness and glimpses of higher states of consciousness are not possible before achievement of certain corresponding subperiods of development as conceived in contemporary psychology. . . . Research and experience have shown that during TM, pure consciousness (and subsequent benefits) can sometimes be experienced rather quickly, irrespective of the initial developmental level of the practitioner. (p. 56)

Travis and Brown (this volume), raise the question of whether higher states of consciousness are on the same trajectory as stages of ego development, or whether growth of higher stages of consciousness is a related but different dimension of development than what is measured by the SCT. Travis and Brown present evidence that subjects for whom cosmic consciousness was indicated by physiological and interview data,

SCT scores ranged from Stage 5, Self-aware, to Stage 8, Autonomous, and did not correlate highly with their measure of brain functioning. This suggests that additional empirical research is needed to determine the relationship between higher states of consciousness and advanced stages of postconventional development.

Depictions of the Postrepresentational Self in the *Bhagavad-Gita*

The direction of development implied by the term *postconventional* is that the individual's self-identity and moral compass become increasing independent of outer influences (Loevinger, 1976). Three key verses from Chapter 2 of the *Bhagavad-Gita* can be analyzed as depictions of a mature stage of self-development in which the postrepresentational Self has grown to be fully independent of changing circumstances. Gita passages in the article are from Maharishi's (1969) translation and commentary.

> Be without the three gunas, O Arjuna, freed from duality, ever firm in purity, independent of possessions, possessed for the Self. (verse 45)

> Established in Yoga, O winner of wealth, perform actions having abandoned attachment and having become balanced in success and failure, for balance of mind is called Yoga. (verse 48)

> When a man completely casts off all desires that have gone (deep) into the mind, O Partha, when he is satisfied in the Self through the Self alone, then he is said to be of stable intellect. (verse 55)

Vedic psychology presents these verses as descriptions of development to a state of life in which, by transcending relative experience, one gains the status of being established in self-sufficient satisfaction in the Self. This naturally gives life a profound inner stability that is independent of, and unattached to, the changing relative aspects of life. Herriott's research on long-term practitioners of the TM program identified an "unshakability" factor that resembles depictions of Cosmic Consciousness in Vedic psychology. In Maharishi's commentary he highlights that the mechanics of this development are through transcending ('be without the three gunas," verse 45) and then acting ("perform action," verse 48). The transient state of Transcendental Consciousness is described as "the state of separation from activity" (p. 151). As this experience becomes a stable reality, not only in meditation but throughout daily activity, "a man realizes his Self is different from the mind which is engaged with thoughts and desires. It is now his experience that the mind, which had been identified with desires, is mainly identified with the Self" (pp. 150–151).

Subject–Object Relationship in Cosmic Consciousness

Expressions in the *Bhagavad-Gita*, such as these, can be seen as describing a transformation in subject–object relationships, to use Kegan's language for describing developmental shifts. Here is how Kegan describes subject and object:

> What is mean by "object" are those aspects of our experience that are apparent to us and can be looked at, related to, reflected upon, engaged, controlled, and connected to something else. We can be *objective* about these things, in that we don't see them as "me." But other aspects of our experience we are so identified with, embedded in, fused with, that we just experience them as ourselves. This is what we experience *subjectively*—the "subject" half of the subject-object relationship. (cited in DeBold, 2002, p. 2)

Kegan explains that as one moves to more developed stages, what had been subject at a prior stage becomes object at the next stage. Kegan (1982) explains the evolutionary activity of subject–object relations, which involves creating the object (differentiation) as well as relating to it (integration):

> Subject-object relations emerge out of a lifelong process of development: as succession of qualitative differentiations of the self from the world, with a qualitatively more extensive object with which to be in relation created each time; a natural history of better guarantees to the world of its distinctness; successive triumphs of "relationship to" rather than "embeddedness in." (p. 77)

Like this, Maharishi has described an advanced stage of development in which the desires of the mind, with which the subject had been identified, have become object. The higher Self (new subject) has been differentiated from "the mind which is engaged with thoughts and desires" (old subject). This new stable Self is realized to be a witness to the activity of the mind. Maharishi explains this phenomenon of witnessing, which differentiates lower stages of development in which one is ignorant of the Self, to Self-realization in Cosmic Consciousness:

> The activity assumed by an ignorant man to belong to himself—to the subjective personality that he calls himself—does not belong to his real Self, for this, in its essential nature, is beyond activity. The Self, in its real nature, is only the witness of everything. (Maharishi, 1969, p. 98)

Realization of this transcendental Self can be seen to follow the same general evolutionary dynamics that Kegan observed in prior stages of developing subject–object relations. The very word *object*, Kegan (1982) reasons, comes from the root *ject*, which implies the activity of throwing; it "suggests the motion or consequences of 'thrown from' or "thrown away from." Object speaks to that which some motion has made separate or distinct from, or to the motion itself" (p. 76). It is interesting to note that Maharishi's commentary on verse 55 uses strikingly similar words to describe how the contents of the mind are as if "thrown upward" when the transcendental Self is realized as subject, distinct from mental activity. The phrase *cast off* in verse 55 has a similar meaning to Kegan's expression "throw away from":

> He experiences the desires of the mind as lying outside himself, whereas he used to experience himself as completely involved with them. . . . All the desires which were present in the mind have been thrown upward, as it were—they have gone to the surface, and within the mind the finest intellect gains an unshakable, immovable status. . . . Thus the wavering intellect gains a very stable basis, and as a result the field of activity is managed with great efficiency. . . . This state of life is such that it maintains the freedom of inner Being, keeping It uninvolved in activity, and at the same time deals with all actions most efficiently and most successfully. (pp. 150–151)

Cosmic Consciousness as Stable Self-Actualization

Maharishi's explanation of how action becomes powerful and efficient when consciousness is established in the freedom of inner Being, is reminiscent of observations in Maslow's (1968) *Towards a Psychology of Being* regarding moments of peak performance in the field of activity. In his chapter "Peak Experiences as Acute Identify-Experiences," Maslow noted: "What takes effort, straining and struggling at other times is now done without any sense of striving, of working or laboring, but 'comes of itself.' . . . He is no longer wasting effort fighting and resisting himself; muscles are no longer resisting muscles" (p. 106). Such a person is seen as possessing a stability or calm steadiness, "as if they know exactly what they are doing, and were doing it wholeheartedly, without doubts. . . . The great athletes, artists, creators, leaders and executives exhibit this quality of behavior when they are functioning at their best" (p. 106). This is very similar to Maharishi's commentary on Chapter 2, verse 55 of the *Gita*: "the wavering intellect gains a very stable basis . . . as a result the field of activity is managed with great efficiency." Recent research relating peak performance in leaders and athletes to growth toward Cosmic Consciousness can be found in the work of Harung, Alexander, and Heaton (1995).

Maslow (1976) indicated that the self-actualized personality is relatively "independent of adverse external circumstances, such as ill fortune, hard knocks, tragedy, stress, deprivation" (p. 35). Likewise, this chapter has quoted some of the many verses in which the *Bhagavad-Gita* describes the experience of inner stability, such as "balanced in success and failure," "independent of possessions," "steady intellect." For Maslow, moments of peak experience can transform one's frame of meaning-making from perceptions that are biased by deficiency needs, to what he calls Being-cognition. He mentions that for self-actualizing persons, or in moments of self-actualization, it becomes possible to have "fully disinterested, desireless, objective and holistic perception of another human being" (Maslow, 1968, p. 36). In the language of the *Gita*, when one is possessed by the Self, one can be independent of other possessions. Maslow (1976) uses the word *witnessing* with reference to plateau experiences: "It then becomes a witnessing, an appreciating, what we might call a serene, cognitive blissfulness" (xiv). As quoted previously, Maharishi's (1969) commentary on the *Gita* identifies witnessing as an essential characteristic of Cosmic Consciousness: "The Self, in its real nature, is only the witness of everything" (p. 98).

Maslow found that self-actualizers with peak or plateau experiences of Being were not selfish but altruistic. They tend to be motivated not by deficiency needs but what he called Being-values including: truth, goodness, beauty, wholeness, perfection, justice, self-sufficiency. A comparison can be made to what the *Bhagavad-Gita* says about motivation of "one who is content in the Self" (Chapter 2, verse 17); the *Gita* says, "The wise act, but without any attachment, desiring the welfare of the world" (Chapter 2, verse 25). Maharishi (1969) writes regarding the individual in cosmic consciousness:

> The individual acts in the world, and this action is quite naturally free from the narrowness of petty individuality, from the shortsightedness of selfish attachment. . . . [A]lthough the individual ego continues to function, the action is that of [cosmic] intelligence working through the individual who is living cosmic existence. (p. 172)

From these and other parallels, it appears that the phenomenon of self-actualization, as observed in Maslow's work, entails, in varying relative degrees, features of a higher stage of development that is more fully realized in the state of Cosmic Consciousness, as depicted by Vedic psychology.

The Postrepresentational Self Is a Lived Experience

Developmental psychology recognizes that how one experiences self-identity and makes meaning in the world is a function of one's developmental position. In this light, we can construe expressions in the *Gita* like "balanced in success and failure," "independent of possessions," "casts off all desires" as phenomenological descriptions of how life is experienced at a particular stage of development. Maharishi's (1969) commentary on verse 55 of Chapter 2 of the *Bhagavad-Gita* notes: "It is now his experience that the mind, which had been identified with desires, is mainly identified with the Self" (p. 151). The words *now his experience* highlight that the postrepresentational Self is the reality of life in this higher developmental position. The status of becoming unshadowed by outer influences is not from trying to feel unattached, but from a developmental transformation of subject–object relations. Maharishi explains that commentaries on the *Bhagavad-Gita* that miss this essential point have led to unfortunate misguidance:

Many a commentator upon these verses has introduced the idea that in order to achieve the state of established intellect one should try to be dispassionate and detached. But . . . trying to make a mood of equanimity in pleasure and pain only puts unnatural, undue stress on the mind, resulting in . . . dullness, artificiality and tension to life in the name of spiritual growth. . . . It is a mistake to copy the behavior of a realized man while remaining in the unrealized state . . . the behavior of a man of steady intellect provides no standard for one whose intellect is not steady. (pp. 156–157)

In developmental psychology, the same point can be made with reference to the different ways in which meaning is constructed at different stages of development. For example, for children who have attained the Piagetian stage of concrete operations, the reality of their experience is that volume is invariant as liquid moves to a different-shaped container. But it could be useless and confusing to tell a younger child to try to see this conservation. It is of little value to make a description of meaning-making at a higher stage of development into a prescription of how one should think and feel. Likewise, conservation of an invariant Self is not a mood or concept to be contrived from descriptions of that state, but it is a lived experience for those who developed to that state. The words *living reality* in the following excerpt from Maharishi's (1969) commentary establishes that what the *Gita* is describing is a developmental position, not a prescription for mood-making. What is prescribed is that systematic experience of transcending, daily cycles of meditation and action, lead to developmental transformation. The TM program is presented as a practice through which this stage becomes established: "[through] the practice of Transcendental Meditation supplemented by activity—one begins to live Being together with activity, one experiences It as separate from activity . . . renunciation . . . is a living reality for the realized man in Cosmic Consciousness" (p. 320).

Conclusion

Vedic psychology explains that the individual's sense of self evolves from identification with objects of attention, to identification with the transcendental Self. This has been related to Kegan's (1982) model of personal evolution through successive differentiations of the self from the world, which dis-embed the subject from the object. The TM technique is a procedure of experiencing thought (object) in successively more subtle states until pure consciousness (subject) transcends the subtlest object and becomes aware of itself. Research studies on the TM technique and developmental outcomes support the theoretical analysis that systematically cultivating the experience of transcendence leads toward realization of a fully differentiated postrepresentational Self. The characteristics of this developmental milestone, as depicted in the *Bhagavad-Gita*, appear to include the stable realization of attributes that Maslow had associated with self-actualization

Note

1. ®Transcendental Meditation and TM are registered trademarks licensed to Maharishi Vedic Education Development Corporation and used under sublicense.

13

Believing As If

Postconventional Stages, Cognitive Complexity, and Postformal Religious Constructions

James M. Day

One of the most vexing, and interesting, problems in the psychology of human development concerns the relationship of developmental trajectories across domains, their mechanisms, processes, and privileged end points. One area in which such questions remain at issue concerns the relationship of moral development to religious, or faith, or spiritual development, an area that has attracted considerable attention in recent years. This chapter considers the history of research in this area, compares models of development, looks at longstanding assumptions and debates, and pays particular attention to the broad consensus privileging *postconventional* thought as a characteristic of "higher" development, showing some recent contributions from research in this light. As is seen here, the Model of Hierarchical Complexity (see e.g., Commons & Pekker, 1995) would appear to be a particularly apt conceptual and methodological approach for addressing problems in this area of psychological science, and throughout the chapter it serves as a point of reference. The whole of the chapter suggests the wisdom of early insights in the theoretical and methodological work of Jane Loevinger.

Psychological Development and the Psychology of Religion

In a recent review of the relationship between constructs and models of religious development and moral development (Day, 2007a), we observed that since its inception psychological science has evidenced an interest in religious experience, and its relationship to other domains of human behavior. Both psychoanalytical writers and experimentalists have argued not only about the nature of religious experience and its relationship to other domains of human conduct, but about the relative merits and impact of such experience on the individual, the group, and on social welfare (Wulff, 1997). Work continues in the psychology of religion, with an exponential growth in numbers of members in related scientific societies (e.g., American Psychological Association, the International Association for the Psychology of Religion, American Counseling Association), and scientific publications, with excellent and highly selective peer-reviewed journals (*International Journal for the Psychology of Religion, Archiv fur Religionspsychologie, Journal of Religion and Mental Health*, etc.) providing a forum for some of the work.

Religious development has been studied in at least three ways in psychological science: (a) as a distinct phenomenon unto itself; (b) in conjunction with other aspects of being a developing human; and (c) in close relation to moral development (see also Day, 2007a, 2007b; 2008a, 2008b, 2008c).

Religious Development

In the field of developmental psychology, Jean Piaget made observations and posed questions about the relationship between religious thinking and scientific thinking. He wondered whether observable relationships could be made between advances in the capacity to conceptualize scientific procedures and concepts, and ways of conceiving religious concepts and practices.

Piaget's stage conceptions have continued to guide the field of developmental psychology and the psychology of religious development, as they have been foundational for ensuing work in the notion of postconventional operations, and for 40 years psychologists have appropriated Piagetian paradigms in order to study related questions. Reviews of the field identify Goldmann's work (e.g., 1964) as an important contribution in examining whether conceptual abilities and stage structures characteristic of reasoning in domains other than religious ones would apply to the descriptions and interpretation of religious images. Goldmann did not observe differences between the logic employed by elementary and secondary school pupils in the Piagetian experiments and the description and interpretation of religious images. These findings were supported by the research of other scholars (Degelmann, Mullen,

& Mullen, 1984; Peatling & Laabs, 1975; Tamminen & Nurmi, 1995).
These researchers replicated, with some variation, the basic, transversal
methods and conceptual models in Goldmann's research, with larger,
cross-cultural samples in a variety of educational settings.

Spilka, Hood, Hunsberger, and Gorsuch (2003) observed, along
with other researchers, that in the samples used, Goldmann's efforts
did not pay adequate attention to the variables of context, including
frequency and depth of exposure to religious material, religious concepts,
and religious education, and subjects' elaboration and sophistication
of interpretation of religious images, stories, and questions. Hoge and
Petrillo (1978) showed that such elaboration was at least in part a function of the familiarity subjects had with religious concepts and themes,
as a function of their education in protestant and catholic schools, in
contrast with students from non-church-related schools. As has been
observed (Day, 2007a, 2008a, 2008b), Batson, Schoenrade, and Ventis
(1993) showed something similar, but argued that the concept of a "performance gap" could help explain such differences. At least 10 groups
of researchers have demonstrated what they have called a *liberal bias* in
the stage interpretations offered by Goldmann, with pupils from families
with more "liberal" political affiliations and attitudes doing better (i.e.,
scoring higher) on Goldmann's interpretative scales. In a meta-analytic
study of research investigating the predictive power of Piagetian stage
on interpretation of religious content, Pierce and Cox (1995) found no
relation between the two, arguing that there were distinctive features
of experience related to religious content that made for a considerable
variety of logical postures regarding its interpretation.

Religious Development: Psychological Models

Reviews of the theoretical, empirical, and applied literature, such as
theological education, religious education in schools, pastoral counseling,
nursing and medicine, (Day, 2007a; 2008a, 2008b) observed that the
dominant models in the psychology of religious development are those of
James Fowler (1981), Fritz Oser and Paul Gmunder (1991), and Helmut
Reich (Oser, Scarlett, & Bucher1999). Their work focused on efforts to
describe a developmental trajectory specific to religious development;
in Fowler's case, a model of what he calls "faith development," and in
Oser's case "religious judgment development." Reich has used Oser's
model in order to understand relationships across domains of religious
thought, critical thinking, and intellectual development. All have based
their schemes of religious development on Kohlberg's (1969) model of

moral judgment development, and employed variants of Piaget's, and later, Kohlberg's uses of hypothetical dilemmas in clinical interview formats, in order to invite subjects to produce "resolutions" that are then interpreted in terms of a framework of supposedly universal, and hierarchical, stages.

Fowler, and critical appraisers of Fowler's work (see Day, 2001, 2007a, 2008a; Day & Youngman, 2003; Fowler, 1981, 1996, 2001; Tamminen & Nurmi, 1995) have observed that his is a multifactorial model, given that its construct of "faith" is sufficiently broad to include dimensions associated with Piaget's notions of intellectual development, Kohlberg's (1969) model of moral development, Erikson's stage model of identity construction, Loevinger's and Levinson's concepts of ego development, Selman's model of role-taking, and Kegan's concepts of self. For Fowler, this development involves "a dynamic pattern of personal trust in and loyalty to a center or centers of value" whose orientation can be understood in relationship to the person's trust in and loyalty to a core set of "images and realities of power" and "to a shared master story or core story" (Fowler 1981, 1996, p. 82). Fowler's model reflects notions derived from liberal Protestant theology (Niebuhr and Tillich), and the field of religious studies, especially Wilfred Cantwell Smith and Lawrence Kohlberg.

The work of Oser and colleagues formulates a more narrow and precise sense of religious development as "religious judgment development," in which an individual's formulations of the relationship between the person and the Ultimate Being are charted on a stage scheme that ranges from states of relative simplicity, ego-centrism, and cognitive dualism, toward more differentiated, elaborated, and complex appreciations of self, relationship, context, perspective-taking, and person–God interaction. Oser and his colleagues use Piagetian terms to argue that there is a universal deep structure of religious cognition. "Religious judgment" reflects the cognitive patterns that characterize an individual's ways of thinking about her or his relationship to the Ultimate, and the rules that govern that relationship. Like Fowler, Oser et al. argued that this deep structure is a universal feature of religious cognition across the life span, regardless of culture or religious affiliation. Indeed, both avowed atheists and agnostics are held by Oser, Gmunder, Reich, Kamminger, Rollett, to be concerned with fundamentally religious questions of relationship to ultimate being and purposes in their lives and in the life of the world, and to think about such questions in ways that fit the stage scheme they lay out (Kamminger & Rollett, 1996; Oser et al., 2006; Oser & Reich, 1996). The problem just suggested is that there are fuzzy boundaries between religious and other domains of reasoning, and these need either sharper discrimination or a basis for removing any discrimination among them (Day, 2008a).

The literature in both developmental psychology and the psychology of religion has been marked by debates as to whether Fowler's and Oser's stages constitute "hard stages" in the Piagetian sense, or more flexible, malleable, and interpenetrating "soft stages," as Power (1991) aptly argued, at least with regard to Fowler's model. Oser and colleagues (Kamminger & Rollett, 1996; Oser & Gmunder, 1991; Oser & Reich, 1996) argued for the soundness of their stages as meeting the criteria of "hard stages" (see also Vandenplas-Holper, 2003). Fowler himself has agreed that his stages may be conceived as more flexible descriptions of ways of constructing and elaborating global meanings in terms of life orientation and commitment, and has observed that Oser's stages are more restrictive in terms of content and movement within the hierarchy of stages contained in their models. However, critical to both models are the notions of stage and sequence as they are known in the work of Piaget and Kohlberg. Whether the models refer to religious or atheistic beliefs, they are rooted in notions of stage and sequence (Day, 2008a).

Religious Development and Moral Development

Fowler's six-stage model of faith development and Oser et al.'s five-stage model of religious judgment development assume a close relationship between moral and religious development. We agree with Fowler and Oser et al. that in light of the fact that religious reasoning includes components of moral reasoning, it would seem logical that stage transition in moral reasoning would precede stage change in religious development. All people must wrangle with and parse through moral dilemmas that confront them throughout life regardless of religious beliefs (Day, 2008a; Day & Naedts, 1996; Day & Youngman, 2003).

Despite this workable internal logic, however, empirical evidence from extensive research with thousands of subjects calls into question the relationship between religious and moral development. "Faith development" and "religious judgment development" theories have made major contributions to the fields of human development and the psychology of religion, and have stimulated debate concerning relationships among structure, content, context, and group belonging and religious affiliation. They relate to notions of human growth, what it means to be "mature," the nature and dynamics of religious belief. They have had a huge influence not only on psychological science but also in the fields of theology, religious education, training for ordained ministry, interreligious dialogue, and debates regarding ecclesiology. They have broadened the scope of neo-Piagetian stage theory to include human religiousness and led us into new critical territory (Day, 2008a).

Religious Development, Postconventional Reasoning, and Postformal Stages

If we intend to meaningfully situate the psychology of religious development in relationship to notions of postconventional ways of thinking and acting, and models for empirical testing of concepts and constructs, it behooves us to consider, at least briefly, the recent literature where psychological science has been instrumental in demonstrating the existence of postconventional cognitive stages. This has best been done in the demonstrations of the existence of postformal stages, which have been described and empirically validated as involving structures, which require greater cognitive sophistication in complexity and problem-solving. Relations are not only functional, but also are transformational, and nonlinear conceptions of causality require a degree of complexity more complex than those outlined by Piaget (Commons & Richards, 2003). The most extensive review of the literature to date, involving a meta-analysis of postformal theories and stage conceptions, involving 17 different bodies of research, showed that across the models proposed, there is a consensus that postformal stages can be identified in human perceiving, reasoning, knowing, judging, caring, feeling, and communicating that are "more complex or more all-encompassing than formal operations" (Commons & Richards, 2003, p. 202).

Four postformal stages, as outlined in Commons and Richards (2003) seem to us the best formulation, on conceptual grounds, and most rigorously examined, on empirical grounds, in the literature involving both human reasoning, and the resolution of problems, across a variety of domains, including tasks issuing from algebra, geometry, physics, moral decision making, legal judgments, and informed consent. We have investigated additional aspects, such as the resolution of problems involving the presence and uses of religious authority, as well as uses of religious tradition and teaching (dogmas, doctrines, received wisdom), religious texts (e.g., the Bible, Koran, rabbinical commentaries), institutional authorities (the Vatican, bishops, priests, pastors, rabbis, imams), group consensus (what obtains in a particular religious community), and personal religious experience. Commons and Richards (2003, pp. 206–208) describe these postformal stages as follow:

Systemic Order: At this stage subjects are able to discriminate the frameworks for relationships between variables within an integrated system of tendencies and relationships. The objects of the relationships are formal operational relationships among variables. Probably only 20% of the U.S. population is able to function at this level.

Meta-Systemic Order: Subjects act on systems, and systems become the objects of meta-systemic actions. The systems are made up of formal-operational relationships, and meta-systemic actions compare, contrast, transform, and synthesize systems. Commons and Richards point out that research professors at top universities are for the most part able to operate in this way.

Paradigmatic Order: Subjects create new fields out of multiple meta-systems. It follows logically that meta-systems are the objects of paradigmatic actions, sometimes in ways that orchestrate new paradigms out of improvements made across meta-systems that are themselves "incomplete" from a paradigmatic point of view. Commons and Richards show how Maxwell's equations, developed in 1817 and showing that electricity and magnetism were united, operated in this way and paved the way for further paradigmatic moves, including Einstein's development of "curved space" to describe space–time relations. In so doing, it replaced Euclidean geometry with a new paradigm.

Cross-Paradigmatic Order: Subjects operate on paradigms as objects of thought, creating a new field of thought, or radically transforming a previous one. Thinkers operating at this order of complexity are extremely rare, but ready examples from the history of science demonstrate its existence and its mechanisms and processes. Commons and Richards provide several persuasive examples in this vein, and also have shown through research studies that some subjects operate in this way when faced with problems designed for research in cognitive complexity, and that Rasch Analysis can validate both the order of complexity of items and possible responses to them, on the orders of complexity represented in the four postformal stages, including this one, outlined here.

Until very recently, little work had been done using the Model of Hierarchical Complexity, and the validation of the existence of four postformal, and thus, clearly postconventional, stages, in the domains of the psychology of religious development. Inferences can be made in comparing stages of faith, and of religious judgment, development, with stages in the Kohlbergian paradigm of moral judgment, allowing the conclusion that stages in the psychology of religious development empirically shown to be parallel to Kohlberg's Stages 4 to 6 (i.e., Stages 4–6 in Fowler's model, and Stages 4 and 5 in Oser's) would qualify for inclusion as stages requiring the management of complexity and solving of problems at orders higher than those in Piaget's descriptions and proofs of formal operational reasoning. Thus, moral judgment stages and faith and religious judgment parallel to moral judgment at Stage 4, would fall under the *systemic stage*, and those parallel at Stages 5 and 6, would fall under the *meta-systemic stage*. Kohlberg (1969) himself argued that morality cannot explain itself; that theories of moral reasoning and its development cannot, in the end, account for why one would decide to act on behalf of the good, of the moral principle and its translation into potential forms of action one knows, cognitively, how to describe, justify, propose, and so on. For this reason, he imagined a *paradigmatic stage*, which he placed seventh in his hierarchy of stages of moral judgment. This stage would find the subject constructing a paradigm able to operate on systems of moral reasoning, including hierarchies such as his own model proposed, which in his view would include an explicitation of cosmological order, and a frankly "spiritual" conception of an underlying order inclining action toward the good, thus making a clear link between moral reasoning and religious concepts and systems, and in the terms Commons and Richards, and we, have outlined, a move from metasystemic to paradigmatic reasoning.

In our own research (Bett, Ost, Day, & Robinett, 2008; Commons et al., 2007; Day, 2008a, 2008b, 2008c), and as we elaborate further in the paragraphs that follow, we have demonstrated with increasing precision that it is possible to identify stages of cognitive operations involving religious questions and problem solving where religious authority is at issue using the Model of Hierarchical Complexity, and to identify subjects operating at systemic, metasystemic, and paradigmatic, levels of reasoning, parallel to the uppermost stages in moral reasoning in Kohlberg's model, and in religious judgment in Oser's model.

A Case for the Model of Hierarchical Complexity

Of the longstanding problems associated with Piaget's theory and subsequent research in domains of Piagetian-influenced developmental psychology, all are characteristic of theory and research regarding faith and religious judgment development (Day, 2007a, 2008a, 2008b). Commons and Pekker (2005) described these problems in Piaget's model, and demonstrated, at least in part, how the Model of Hierarchical Complexity addresses them. Their critique is that the Model of Hierarchical Complexity introduces such improvement within it, that it stands, more than any other approach, to offer useful insights as to how the structuralist paradigm fares in relationship to other paradigms. With Commons and Pekker, we summarize some problems within the Piagetian paradigm, their relationship to the psychology of religious development as conceived in the work of Fowler and Oser et al., and some reasons why the Model of Hierarchical Complexity offers a useful complement to other ways of working within a cognitive-developmental approach, and in relationship to other approaches. Commons and Pekker assert that Piaget's definition of a *stage* "was based on analyzing behaviors and attempting to impose different structures on them. There is no underlying logical or mathematical definition to help in this process." The mathematically-based formal theory of the Model of Hierarchical Complexity eliminates this issue (see also Day, 2002, 2008a; Day & Tappan, 1996, Day & Youngman, 2003). Another problem emerged during attempts by others to verify Piaget's theory empirically and systematically.

The same individual's performances on different tasks often were not found to be at the same stage; that is, performances were only weakly correlated across tasks (Commons & Pekker, 2005). An additional problem concerned the difficulty in replicating the results predicted by Piaget. "The performances on tasks by younger children would be inexplicably competent, while those by older individuals could be inexplicably incompetent: the theory was unable to account for either the difficulty in replication or the unpredictable results."

A fourth problem is that in Piaget's logical model of thought, all people from approximately age 16 through adulthood were assumed able to solve all formal-stage tasks as defined by that logic (Commons & Pekker, 2005; Day, 2007b, 2008a). That was not upheld by research.

Related to the foregoing, a fifth problem with Piaget's theory was its assumption that the formal operations stage was the most complex level with which people could operate—an assumption limited by his observations and the forementioned logical model. The theory provided no method to generate or explain generation of postformal stages. Commons and Richards (2003; Commons, Richards, & Kuhn, 1982), Fischer (1980), Riegel (1973), and others all have shown one or more stages beyond formal operations (Commons & Pekker, 2005). Commons and Richards (1984a) state:

> The problem underlying these and other limitations of Piaget's theory is that the theory was a description of the inferred underlying logic that was to be seen in empirical results, with some post-hoc explanations. It did not, however, have a model that would explain why those discrepant behaviors described above were observed. That is, based on the

performance of an individual, an underlying mental structure was inferred. (p. 184)

An additional problem has to do with the proliferation of stage models in a variety of domains, such as ego development, role-taking development, identity development, and intellectual development, with no clear explication of how the models were related across domains, or with assumptions articulated that have not been substantiated by empirical evidence, for example, between religious and moral development (Day, 2001, 2002, 2007a, 2008a; also see Commons & Pekker, 2005). The case of the supposed relationship between stages of faith and stages of moral reasoning in Fowler's model, and between religious judgment and moral judgment, in Oser et al.'s, is illustrative of this problem. As we have demonstrated, this supposed relationship cannot be empirically verified.

What may account for a theory of such major, decades-long influence, as Piaget's, and the vast bodies of research it has inspired, to be weighted with substantive problems such as those enumerated here? The answer seems to lie in the use, or non-use, of scientific methods and the discrimination of stimuli and tasks. The theories and methods considered here did not adhere to basic scientific premises. "Piaget's stage theory (and other stage theories) did not pay any attention to the stimuli in problem-solving situations and, most particularly, did not pay attention to the tasks. Their account, therefore, is at best incomplete" (Commons & Pekker, 2005, p. 8). We conclude that, allied with Rasch Analysis, the Model of Hierarchical Complexity, as a theoretical model, and as a method, provides the most adequate responses to vexing questions regarding the veracity of claims in Piagetian and neo-Piagetian models of human development, and provides the best bases for comparing those models with other ones.

Religious Development and the Model of Hierarchical Complexity

In order to study whether something akin to religious judgment (the more precise of the two definitions of religious cognition in developmental theory and research) could be studied using the Model of Hierarchical Complexity, we have launched a collaborative research project involving resources in cognitive science, mathematics, and developmental psychology at Harvard, and the Laboratory for Human Development and Psychology of Religion Research Center at Louvain, aimed at construct validation and testing, instrument development, and interdomain analysis, with cross-cultural, and religiously diverse (including atheist and agnostic) samples in North America and Europe.

To date, this research has resulted in two instruments that allow for an empirical appreciation of development in reasoning about religious issues, or where religious categories are at issue. The first is a questionnaire that introduces religious language into a moral dilemma involving a specific case and reasons for and against the death penalty with varying degrees of complexity, demonstrating that it is indeed possible to construct a measure with religious content related to moral reasoning. This results in a valid, reliable measure of hierarchical complexity that can meaningfully be compared to other measures of hierarchical complexity in the domain of moral reasoning (Commons et al., 2007). In keeping with our hypothesis that scores would *not* be the same on our measure and other measures using the Model of Hierarchical Complexity to measure *moral* reasoning, we found that the introduction of *religious* language in relationship to a moral dilemma comparable to dilemmas found in other measures produced different stage scores. This demonstrated that religious variables proved distinct and significant, in varying how people thought about moral problems.

In a second wave of this research aimed at developing a measure that would offer a more precise way of assessing the distinctiveness of religious cognition, we have devised a questionnaire devoted to a more detailed and elaborate use of religious language. In it, we have operationalized a religious cognition construct but made its distinctiveness from moral reasoning more pronounced. We have shown that this construct can be validated in terms of the hierarchy of complexity of tasks (Day, 2008c, 2008d), and that research can be conducted that usefully teases out relationships amongst moral reasoning and religious reasoning that can address longstanding questions both within developmental psychology and beyond it. In our view, this work demonstrates that, although still in nascent form, the psychology of religious development can profit from working with, and within, the Model of Hierarchical Complexity. The fruits of doing so include moving toward a more precise construct of religious cognition, and better understanding the relationship between religious cognition, moral reasoning, and other domains of human development.

Critical and Complementary Approaches, and the Postconventional Consensus

Researchers in cognitive science, developmental psychology, psychology of religion, pastoral psychology, theology, and mathematics have demonstrated an interest in questions pertaining to the fine-tuning, or modification of Piagetian, and Kohlbergian conceptions of stage, structure, and sequence in moral development (which, as we have seen, is intimately related to religious development in the reigning models of it) and/or religious development. In some cases, alternative models have been proposed (see Day & Naedts, 1997; Day & Tappan, 1996; Day & Youngman, 2003; Ganzevoort, 1998, 2006; Gergen, 1994; Streib, 1991, 1997; Streib, Keller, & Csoff, 2007; Tappan, 1989, 1992). Elsewhere, the suggestion is made that *development* is not a useful term for describing structural transformation in reasoning about religious issues in adolescence and adulthood (see Duriez & Soenens, 2006; Hutsebaut, 1995, 1996, 1997a, 1997b). Other researchers, most notably Commons and colleagues (e.g., Commons & Richards, 2003; Commons & Richards, 1984; Commons, Richards, & Kuhn, 1982; Commons, Trudeau, Stein, Richards, & Krause, 1998) argued that the problem of Piagetian stage formulation is not stage itself, but the need for more rigorous definitions and criteria for establishing stage hierarchy and understanding stage transition. As this chapter suggests, we continue to labor within the neo-Piagetian field and to work at the interface of structuralist stage theories and sociocultural models. Commons' Model of Hierarchical Complexity offers, in our view, the most promising post-Piagetian prospects for thinking about development in terms of stage and structure. Initial research shows that instruments related to the measurement of hierarchical complexity can help tease out (a) the relationship between moral judgment and religious reasoning; and (b) the question whether the two are meaningfully distinct constructs, or, instead, variants on a common structure of reasoning, itself; and (c) its relative complexity as applied across domains (see Commons et al., 2007; Day, 2008a, 2008c).

Postconventional Benefits Across Models and Critical Approaches

One of the most striking features of a comparative view to models across the Piagetian tradition in the domain of moral and religious development, *and* in the models proposed by those most critical of it, is the existence of what we would call, for the purposes of this chapter, a *postconventional consensus*. That is, from Piaget onward, in the neo-Piagetian framework, *and* in the models of development most critical of Piaget's notions of stage and structure, and of the notion of development

itself as a unilinear, hierarchical process, there is a common valuing of
postconventional goods; that is, patterns of cognition associated with
dispositions in attitudes and behavior that first appear in psychological
science in delineations of *postconventional* thought and action.

These include, but are not limited to, field independence, a capacity to consider and accurately appraise the impact of one's behavior on
another, the ability to accurately read and appreciate the meaning of
another's thoughts and feelings, the capacity to take, enter into, and
weigh the impact of another's perspective and role and functions in
relationships, interactions, and group dynamics, the ability to convert
conflict into contrast, and the capacity to view any given problem in
human action from a variety of perspectives; movement from dichotomous models of truth toward multiperspectival descriptions of reality;
and a capacity to act on behalf of deeply held notions of what is right,
good, and just, even while holding in tension one's commitments with
a vital humility borne of the knowledge that one is acting from limited
understanding and perspective, and that there are alternative views that
may be reasonably held by others. Thus, for example, Ganzevoort (1998),
Streib (1997), and Tappan (1981), all demonstrate a valued appreciation
in their narrative models, a capacity to tell a story of moral decision
making from more than one actor's perspective, and argued for the
importance of a capacity to consider multiple points of view in coming to a decision. In describing religious development Gergen's (1991)
commented on work in social construction and religious belief, commitment, and behavior. Hutsebaut (1996), Duriez and Soenens (2006),
and others who have charted a model showing relationships among
religious and nonreligious literal and symbolic thinking. Ganzevoort and
Streib showed a clear preference for the human subject who has been
confronted with the limits of dichotomous thinking, taken relativism
and diversity of opinion seriously, and is capable of affirming religious
truth in a postliteral vein. Those individuals are emphasizing symbol
and metaphor, irony and paradox, as elements that are richly present
in religious traditions, and consistent with religious commitment. The
authors move the subject toward a "universalizing tendancy," similar
to subjects in the postconventional stages, certainly the highest ones,
in neo-Piagetian models such as those of Kohlberg, Fowler, and Oser.
These qualities resemble those best delineated, in our view, in the four
postformal stages empirically demonstrated and described by Commons
and Richards (2003), and validated using the Model of Hierarchical
Complexity, in recent research looking carefully at relationships between
moral and religious cognition (Day, 2008a, 2008b, 2008c, 2008d).

Postconventional Religiosity: Complexity and Commitment and Believing *as* If/Though "It Were True"

In a series of recent studies, we compared stage scores of subjects using definitions and instruments rooted in the work of Kohlberg, Oser, and the Model of Hierarchical Complexity, to tease out relationships between moral and religious reasoning, and better understand how *postconventional* subjects operate on measures of religious cognition, that is, at the highest stages of moral judgment, religious judgment, and at meta-systemic and paradigmatic stages of religious reasoning in the Model of Hierarchical Complexity. Subjects from a variety of religious backgrounds, including Roman Catholic, Anglican, Protestant, Muslim, and Hindu traditions, in Belgium and England, responded to standardized questionnaires of reasoning about moral issues, and all who described themselves as religiously active (involved in religious activity at least once per week), and committed (identifying themselves as 'believers'), were asked to define their understanding of religious belief and commitment, and say how it affected their decisions. Subjects at postconventional levels were then asked to meet with trained interviewers for a follow-up, semistructured, interview, in order to better understand how postconventional reasoning and religious commitment "work out." Although it lies beyond the scope of this chapter to go into further detail, it is nonetheless striking that across the religious traditions represented in the study, the subjects who obtained postconventional stage scores in moral and religious cognition, spoke of religion both in terms of *depth of commitment* drawing on what they deemed to be proven truths in life experience, and, especially at the highest stages of religious cognition, used *tentative language* to describe religious truth. Thus they spoke, as one subject did, of religious commitment as:

> My way of remaining engaged with the resources of my religious tradition, and through it, with God, not because I think things are or have to be literally true, or because religion provides a ready answer to every life problem, but because the central truths it conveys have proven right and good, sane, and wise, in living, both for me and for people across the generations.

The words of another subject poignantly describe a move toward paradigmatic operations at work in religious belief and commitment:

> In the end I think religion is as much about poetry, and poetics, and thus, about imagination, as it is about "belief."

It has to do with the conjuring of possible worlds, and the close attention to the data that might support such a conception of the cosmos, and of human action, and finally, ultimately, to the kinds of commitments one makes in the hope of bringing such imaginary constructions to bear, and to fruition, in the world of everyday life. One holds belief and doubt in creative tension, and acts as if, or as though, the imagined world one hears of, feels drawn to, dwells in more and more over time.

Conclusion

The models of faith development and religious judgment development described in this chapter have made considerable contribution to the field of developmental psychology and related domains of inquiry and practice, including our understanding of postconventional development. They are, however, problematic, in terms of (a) internal consistency, (b) relationship to other domains within developmental psychology, and, (c) on theoretical and practical grounds, their ability to describe religious features of human development. Assumptions contained in both models about the relationship between religious and moral development have been supported by research. At the same time, empirical research calls into question on these grounds, and others, the very utility of some features of concepts basic to the models. It is here, as we tried to show, that the Model of Hierarchical Complexity may prove especially useful, both in clarifying what it means to speak of development, and in terms of research methods that may help tease out the relationship of religious elements to other features of human development, including the broad postconventional consensus across developmental models, and the delineation of postconventional religious operations, attitudes, dispositions, and behaviors (see also Day, 2008a, 2008c, 2008d).

14

A Dynamical View of the Personality in Evolution

Allan Combs
Stanley Krippner

The mind proceeds, in the pre-logical period, by the motives of memory, imagery, play, and action, achieving in its own way the use of general and abstract contents which become "notions" and "concepts," the essential instruments of reasoning.

—Baldwin (1930, p. 12)

The Nature of Experience

We owe Jane Loevinger a great debt for her work in exploring the nature of personal growth and development. The fact that she built her theory on actual psychometric research findings adds to her stature, and places her name beside similar students of human development such as Sigmund and Anna Freud, Alfred Adler, Eric Erikson, Karen Horney, Abraham Maslow, and Henry Murray. Some of these pioneers created psychodynamic theories of one form or another, and most placed emphasis on the maturation of the social construct referred to in English as the "self." Modern theory and research on the developmental dimension of the personality (the social aspects of the hypothetical "self"), however, rests almost entirely on Loevinger's contributions. This chapter offers an alternative to Loevinger's approach to the development of the personality, based here on modern ideas from the sciences of complexity. These are not offered as alternatives to Loevinger's own conclusions, but rather to illustrate an alternative logic concerning the nature of personality development that supports her findings from an entirely different direction.

Our basic suggestion is that the personality can be understood as a dynamical flow of events that, taken as a whole, create a kaleidoscopic *onflow* (Pred, 2005) of our moment-to-moment experience. These events are familiar to us all. They are, in William James' (1890/1981) words, the " 'ideas,' faint or vivid [which] by their cohesions, repulsions, and forms of succession, such things as reminiscences, perceptions, emotions, volitions, passions, theories, and all the other furnishings of an individual's mind" (p. 1) are formed. Together they create an "endless carpet of themselves" (p. 2) that is our conscious experience.

Philosophers since Aristotle, Hume, and Mills, and some psychologists who antedated James have, with varying degrees of success, attempted to catalog the rules of interaction between these elements of experience (Hothersall, 2003). Viewing all this from a systems theory perspective we might consider these psychological processes as components of an interactive "component system." Kampis (1991) and Kauffman (1995) have shown that such systems in interaction produce new and novel components that, reacting back on the original components, move the system forward in what is best thought of as an evolutionary progression. In this way the mind (i.e., the brain's repository of information and memories) is in a constant state of creative onflow. Thanks to the contributions of theorists such as Kampis and Kauffman, as well as other scientists of complexity, this onflow can be understood better today than at the time William James originally wrote about it.

One important feature of the onflow is that in several essential ways it exhibits the characteristics of a *chaotic attractor*. Strictly speaking, chaotic attractors are mathematical creations that display a high degree of determination. Although the behaviors of biological as well as cognitive systems rarely exhibit the precision of mathematics, they nevertheless display chaotic-like features that allow them to be understood in significant detail (e.g., Freeman, 1991). The onflow of ordinary human experience is a case in point. To better understand it, let us review some of the features of chaotic attractors.

Mathematically speaking, all attractors represent the course of some "dynamical" system through time, while any system is considered dynamical if it evolves or changes according to a rule of transformation. Such a rule may be a mathematical equation. A simple example is the motion of a pendulum on its cyclic round. The pattern of the pendulum's activity is completely described by a relatively straightforward mathematical expression, which, aside from the influence of friction, predicts the course of the pendulum completely. Such repeated patterns of activity often are referred to as *cyclic* or *fixed-cycle attractors*, meaning that they recur in exactly the same fashion indefinitely. The term *attractor* suggests the fact that the pendulum is drawn into this pattern of action by the laws of physics that constrain it. From a theoretical point of view, however, it indicates that the pendulum is attracted back into this characteristic pattern even if it is pushed out of its orbit, say, by a slight thrust of the hand that slows or quickens its motion. This "attraction" back to the fixed cycle is what makes it useful as a clock.

On first appearance many systems in nature seem to represent fixed-cycle attractors. Examples include the motion of the moon as it orbits the Earth and the beating of the human heart. On closer examination, however, most such systems do not follow the same course precisely through each cycle, and thus do not meet the strict definition of a cyclic attractor. The human heart, for example, shows considerable variation from beat to beat. Lock-step regularity indicates serious pathology, and suggests that the individual does not have long to live (Solé & Goodwin, 2000). When mathematicians first discovered equations that produced such patterns, similar in each iteration but never exactly the same, they humorously referred to them as "strange." In time, these became known as *strange* or *chaotic* attractors. Further study indicated that they have certain features in common that are of interest to our examination of onflow.

Important among these is the already mentioned fact that they appear to repeat themselves in a cyclic fashion, but each repetition is slightly different than those that precede it. The fact that the system described by the attractor is never in exactly the same state twice is reflected in W. James' (1890/1981) observation of the same characteristic of onflow:

> For there it is obvious and palpable that our state of mind is never precisely the same. . . . Every thought we have of a given fact is, strictly speaking, unique, and only bears a resemblance of kind with our other thoughts of the same fact. When the identical fact recurs, we must think of it in a fresh manner, see it under a somewhat different angle, apprehend it in different relations from those in which it last appeared. (p. 233)

To cinch this point, James noted that it is impossible to think that the brain and its many processes would be exactly the same at

two different times. Studies of the quality of the onflow of experience support the observation of this general cyclic feature. Moods,
thoughts, memories, and feelings recur in a recognizable and more
or less cyclical fashion, for example, over the course of a day, but
like the weather they do not repeat themselves precisely (e.g., Hanna,
1991; Winkler et al., 1991). Moreover, the pattern seems unique for
each individual, and in James' thinking this distinctiveness defined the
essence of the person.

A richly heuristic conceptual model is obtained when the ideas
just presented are applied to a particular class of systems identified
by Ilia Prigogine (Prigogine & Stengers, 1984) and his associates as
"dissipative structures." These systems have a special capacity to take
in energy from the environment and use it to create within themselves
greater complex and often hierarchical organization. Living organisms are
"dissipative systems," ingesting energy in the form of food or sunlight
and dissipating less-organized byproducts back into the environment.
Such systems are also said to be "self-organizing" because of their
tendency to grow toward increasing complexity.

Living organisms are not only self-organizing, they are also self-
creating or *autopoietic*. An autopoietic system is one whose first order
of business is the production of a network of processes that, taken as
a whole, comprise that very system. The most important product of
the metabolic activities of a living cell, for instance, is nothing less
than that very cell (e.g., Kauffman, 1995; Maturana, Varela, & Uribe,
1974). From this point of view we come to conceive of the cell as a
network of processes sustaining themselves through time, although the
material substances that constitute the cell change continuously. In fact,
all living organisms are autopoietic systems, as are ecologies and the
intricate web of the life processes that form the entire Earth system
itself (Lovelock, 1988; Lovelock & Margulis, 1974).

Previously, we have argued that the constituents of onflow—James'
"reminiscences, perceptions, emotions, volitions, passions" and so
on—comprise nothing less than a component autopoietic system (Combs,
2002; Combs & Krippner, 1998, 1999a, 1999b, 2003). To take a brief
example of how this process works, consider the tendency of moods
to recreate themselves in a continuous cycle of thought, memory, and
feeling. A particular state of mind such as anger, sadness, or joy promotes the recollection of state-specific memories that arise from events
experienced during previous instances of that particular state (Bower,
1981; Eich, 1980) and in turn perpetuates its continuation.

Let us take another example, in this instance dealing with the
development of intelligence. From the Piagetian (Flavell, 1963; Piaget,
1977a, 1977b) perspective, a particular kind of experience of reality

is made possible by the formal operations intellect with its conservation schemata, sequential linear processing, and so on. This experience in turn constitutes a context that supports and confirms the formal operations mode of mentation itself, and within that mode various operations conspire to co-create each other. The schema of conservation, for instance, is in part the result of an ability to reverse mental operations, running them backwards like a film to re-examine initial conditions. It also is the result of the ability to examine an object such as a piece of clay from more than one perspective at once, taking into account both its width and height. Simultaneously, however, the schema of conservation provides both the context for, and a confirmation of, reversibility and multidimensional perception.

The Evolution of the Psychological Processes

> Passage into the logical or discursive period brings with it three very striking and fruitful gains. First, language develops pari passu with generalization, and gives to all the cognitive and emotional processes the adequate instrument of expression and of personal intercourse. Secondly, the sense of self passes, along with other contents, through various phases of growth, and becomes the "ego" over against the social "alter." . . . And, thirdly, the rise of judgment brings in reflection, the turning-in of the thinker upon his own mental processes. With reflection, the thinker and agent becomes the judge, the critic, the interpreter, the philosopher.
>
> —Baldwin (1930, p. 13)

The growth of autopoietic regimes typically transitions through a series of "bifurcations" in which basic structures spontaneously reorganize into hierarchical patterns of increasing complexity, flexibility, and resilience (e.g., Csanyi, 1989; Goerner, Dyck, & Lagerroos, 2008; Laszlo, 1987). We see this evolutionary pattern in the hierarchical organization of the human body, where individual living cells conspire in cooperative collaborations to form organs such as the heart, lungs, and brain, which in turn engage in cooperative interactions that form the body as a whole. Any particular level of this overall system may or may not be more complex than the subsystems that comprise it. The brain, for instance, is more complex than the individual neurons of which it is formed, whereas the heart and liver are less complex than the cells of which they are formed.

Individual psychological processes, grounded in onflow, appear to follow the same broad agenda. For instance in Piaget's developmental model, mentioned earlier, each stage rests on the advances of earlier stages. At the same time, each forms the foundations for later stages. The acquisition of an understanding of mathematics, for example, begins with a basic concept of what numbers mean. From there it progresses to an understanding of counting (successive numbering), to addition (successive counting), multiplication (successive addition), and perhaps even to calculus. Besides the more or less linear developmental progressions such as the one just cited, separate schemata at every stage combine to form more complex hierarchical structures at the next level up. During the sensorimotor period of infancy the schema of visual tracking and the schema of grasping combine to form the beginning of eye–hand coordination, a schema that will continue to grow increasingly flexible for several years to come. In similar fashion, Rhonda Kellogg (1969) documented the spontaneous productions of art in children from throughout the world, finding that the freely drawn patterns at one stage of development combine to form the elements of the next stage. The circles, squares, and triangles of an early stage, for instance, join to form the houses, cars, and people of a later stage. Apparently, an analogous process underlies something as abstract and seemingly different as moral maturation, as indicated in research by Kohlberg (1981) and Gilligan (1993).

It is worth noting that although psychological models of development such as those of Piaget (Flavell, 1963; Piaget, 1952, 1954), Cook-Greuter (1999), Fischer and Bidell (2006), Gilligan (1993), Gowan, (1974), Kegan (1982, 1994), Kohlberg (1981), Torbert (1972a, 1972b), and Wade (1996) usually are presented in terms of structures, they are more correctly understood as processes that grow and mature through sequences of bifurcations typical of dynamical growth processes in general (Combs, 2002; Combs & Krippner, 2003).

Taking all this information into consideration, it would seem that each developmental stage of psychological processes can be understood as a pattern of cognitive and emotional operations not unlike computer algorithms. In such a system each operation, or algorithm, is equivalent to one of Kampis' (1991) components. In fact, Kampis has demonstrated rigorously that component systems are logically equivalent to algorithmic systems that can be created and set in motion on a computer (see also Kauffman, 1995).

Advanced Levels of Psychological Growth

In the third stage, the super-logical, the mind seeks to return to immediacy, to solve the dualism and oppositions inherent in the practical life of thought and action. One or another of the great ideals arises and becomes the place of retreat; and the universal categories of thought, the absolute forms of value, and the various panaceas of feeling erect their claims to final authority. [And so in the grand scheme] the leading motives of development [are seen passing] from perception and memory, through the various phases of the reasoning processes, and finding their consummation in the highest and most subtle of the super-logical, rational, and mystic states of mind.

—Baldwin (1930, p. 13)

S. Kelly (1999) has shown how formal operations stage schemata recombine in postformal operations thinking to yield the more advanced *recursive, dialogic* (embracing opposites such as the metaphorical *yin* and *yang*), and *holographic* modes of thought described by French philosopher Edgar Morin (1999). She suggested that the combination yields a new level of cognitive development roughly equivalent to Jean Gebser's (1949/1986) "integral" structure. Our point here, however, is that if the sciences of complexity teach us anything it is that small changes eventually lead to new emergent regimes of organization (the so-called "butterfly" effect). These regimes tend to exhibit novel properties unpredictable from the elements that comprise them. Examples range from the "wetness" of water, not predictable on the basis of a knowledge of the physics of hydrogen and oxygen molecules, to the collective behavior of groups of living organisms such as ant colonies, unforeseeable from the study of individual ants. In every instance the new whole is greater than the sum of its parts and in many instances is surprisingly independent of them. The human brain, for example, is capable of all kinds of actions that represent less than optimal choices for the cells of which it is comprised. When the limits of adaptability are reached at one level of organization there is a tendency for the system to create a richer organization at the next. Morin (1999) observed:

If the situation is logically hopeless, this indicates that we have arrived at a logical threshold at which the need for change and the thrust toward complexification can allow for the transformations that could bring metasystems into being. It is when ... novelty and creativity ... can arise. Thus, it was when the chemical organization of groups of millions of molecules become impossible that a living auto-eco-organization first appeared. (p. 107)

In the present case, each level of psychological development is equivalent to a new organizational regime. With it comes a new experience of the world and of reality itself. Consider, for instance, the experience of the child in comparison with that of the adult. We can hardly doubt that these represent different orders of reality.

Table 14.1 incorporates the insights of many developmental theorists to yield an overview of developmental stages. It is based on an unpublished collaboration between Susanne Cook-Greuter and Ken Wilber (2000). The stages are labeled with terms drawn from Piaget

Table 14.1. A 10-Point Developmental Scale

Broad Level	Developmental Stage	Subdivisions
Preconventional (Body)	1. Sensorimotor	Matter Sensation Perception Exocept
	2. Phantasmic-emotional (Preoperational)	Impulse/emotion Image Symbol
	3. Representational mind (Early concrete operations)	Endocept concept
Conventional (Mind)	4. Concrete operations	Rule/role early Rule/role late
	5. Formal Operations	Formal early Formal late
Postconventional (Wilber's Centaur)	Transition	Transition
	6. Post-formal (Gebser's "Integral Consciousness")	Vision early Vision middle Vision late
Post-postconventional (Wilber's Soul)	7. Psychic	Early Late
	8. Subtle	Early Late (archetype)
Wilber's Spirit	9. Causal	Early Late (formless)
	10. Nondual	Early Middle Late

Note: Terms are based on a number of developmental systems, e.g., "Integral Psychology," by K. Wilber, 1998a, Boston: Shambhala.

and Wilber and include several levels of postconventional development. We return to these later, but first we note briefly that were we
to move from this large overview to a detailed perspective we would
observe that each person develops in a unique pattern across different
specific content areas. For example, one might be gifted in mathematics,
or music, or moral thinking, but relatively slow to develop in other
areas. Such a distribution or *décalage*, to use Piaget's (1952; Flavell,
1963) term, of development along separate "lines" (Wilber, 1998a) is
recognized in virtually all developmental theories. We recognize it as
well, but to carry its detailed consideration every step along our way
would be impossible in a single chapter.

Psychological Growth as Increasing Complexity

Our view is that psychological growth can be thought of as the evolution
of psychological process moving through increasingly complex regimes.
This can be conceptualized as a series of attractors, each representing a
higher order of complexity than the one before. In fact, these attractors
correspond to the levels of development shown in Table 14.1. Each
level is a new and more complex regime, more flexible and competent
than the one before, but incorporating previous regimes into its own
process. Above, we have tried to give a clear indication of how such
transformative growth processes occur in developmental theories such
as those of Piaget, Kohlberg, and Kegan. Now, we extend this idea
in the direction of postconventional levels of development as well.
According to our view, it is these advanced levels that carry us into
the transpersonal realms where the socially constructed "self" appears
to be transcended.

    What evidence is there to support this view? Unfortunately, when
we come to the transpersonal levels of development we leave most
mainstream psychological research behind, sometimes finding ourselves
relying on the personal reports of putative sages and mystics. Although
there have been many scientific investigations of the correlates and
effects of spiritual practices such as meditation, prayer, Tai Chi, yoga,
and the like, these usually address specific interests of particular groups
of researchers, with questions such as: "Does meditation contribute
to stress reduction?" Findings are rarely framed in a developmental
context by these researchers. There are, however, a few exceptions.
A notable study of postconventional development, for example, was
conducted by Cook-Greuter (1999; and this volume) as a dissertation under the supervision of Robert Kegan. She based her work on

Loevinger's (Loevinger & Wessler, 1970) model of ego development, carefully analyzing more than 1,000 interviews with postconventional individuals of both genders. Cook-Greuter found a spiraling pattern of postconventional growth in which individuals first move toward individuation and autonomy, and then begin to experience a growing sense of unity with others and the universe.

The broad view of postconventional development seen in Cook-Greuter's findings is consistent with that shown in Table 14.1. Moving through postconventional Stage 6, her participants disclosed an upward trend, first toward increasing individuation and autonomy; then, with a growing awareness of their own self-constructs of reality, they shifted toward an increasing sense of unity with others and with the world in general. These findings are in agreement with the pattern of development seen in Table 14.1, and are also in accord with Clair Graves' (2005) finding that growth at all levels tends to oscillate between self-actualization (Maslow, 1971) and identity with the greater community.

Paradoxically, the highest levels of growth seem to carry an inherent simplicity reflected in a more direct experience of reality. Surprisingly, such clarity is in fact obtained through complexity. The basic idea, developed in detail by psychoanalyst Stanley Palombo (1999), is that through the development of complex networks of interactions in the brain, one's sense of self becomes integrated into a single fabric of thoughts, feelings, and motivations. Otherwise they drift as disconnected attractors, manipulating us like puppets without our control or understanding. In other words, wholeness brings clarity. In contrast to this highly desirable state of affairs, the human condition often involves considerable fragmentation. Motivational aspects of the mind are only loosely connected to cognitive belief systems, rational process, perceptions, and emotions. Palombo argues that it is the goal of psychotherapy to connect these disparate elements into more complex, fully interconnected systems in which few psychological processes continue on their own outside of awareness. A similar process has been outlined by Feinstein and Krippner (2006), who have described ways in which individuals can examine their "personal myths" to determine which belief systems are functional and which are dysfunctional, as people move toward developing a complex system that can be described as their "personal mythology."

Seen from the experiential side, simplicity and purity is possible because the individual can stand back from the typical welter of mental and emotional activity to find a place of greater quiet and beauty. Thus, it is through *objectivity* that we gain the ecstatic realms of pure experience (Combs, 2002). This may seem a strange notion, but we find it expressed in virtually every wisdom tradition. Sri Aurobindo's (1971) writings, for instance, remind us again and again that the yogic transformation begins only when we acquire the ability to look down on the buzzing mechanistic mind from a position of dispassionate clarity. All types of insight meditation advise us to learn the skill of quietly observing our thoughts and feelings. In the Taoist masterpiece on meditation, *The Secret of the Golden Flower*, we are instructed to follow our thoughts back to their origins, and thereby dissolve them into clear light (Cleary, 2000). Many other examples could be given, but the point is that to gain the highest forms of experience we must first become masters of dispassionate, unattached objectivity.

States of Consciousness: The Human Growth Potential

So far we have said that the dynamical regimes of the psyche, especially patterns of cognition, play a major role in defining developmental stages. Now we consider how *states of consciousness* might be understood in terms of a similar framework. In a series of papers, we explored the idea that states of consciousness—ordinary wakefulness, sleeping and dreaming states, meditative and drug-elicited states, and so on—occur when elements of our experience such as thoughts, memories, emotions, and perceptions, combine to form unique patterns of activity that characterize each such state (Combs, 2002; Combs & Krippner, 1997, 1998, 1999a, 1999b, 2003). Rock and Krippner (2009) argued that "patterns of phenomenological properties" make a better description than states of consciousness. In any case, we suggest that these patterns are best thought of as *attractors*, that is, regimes of ideas, feelings, memories, and the like, that together form temporary or persistent structures. Such patterns seem to be self-organizing and self-sustaining. In this way, states of consciousness, like their cousins developmental stages, can be understood as self-organizing or autopoietic processes. This view is consistent with Charles Tart's (1972, 1975) early conceptualization of states of consciousness as combined systems of psychological and physiological functions that join together to form coherent patterns or gestalts.

In this view, the complex patterns of activity that constitute a state of consciousness are made of many of the same psychological constituents—patterns of cognition, perceptions, emotions, and so on—that determine one's level of psychological development. With this in mind, a reasonable hypothesis is that states of consciousness can be thought of as inflections on the developmental patterns of consciousness described earlier (Combs, 2002; Combs & Krippner, 1998). In this sense, we might think of a state of consciousness as a platform resting on a larger supporting developmental stage. A more technically precise way of saying this is that the state of consciousness is viewed as a self-organizing, or autopoietic system, nested within a larger developmental autopoietic system. If this hypothesis is valid we might expect that even seemingly resilient states of consciousness, such as those experienced in drug intoxication and dreaming, might differ for individuals who are at different developmental levels. As counterintuitive as the idea may seem at first, there is, for example, considerable evidence that dream experiences are related to developmental level, at least for children (Foulkes, 1999), and informal observation as well as studies of psychedelic drugs (Masters & Houston, 1966) seem consistent with the idea that drug-induced experiences differ with the individual's developmental level as well. This possibility warrants further research.

Certain states of consciousness seem to have a kind of subjective resilience, or perhaps we should say that they carry a strong sense of reality, which other states, such as daydreaming or hypnagogia lack. What is more, descriptions of certain meditative, imaginal, near-death, and even putative postmortem states appear to have a universal coinage such that they have been described by observers in many times and cultures (Brown, 1986; Combs, 2002; Combs, Arcari, & Krippner, 2006; E. Kelly et al., 2007; Wilber, 1998b). In many wisdom traditions, these are said to be more than subjective states, but actual independent realities or *realms of being* (e.g., Chittick, 1994; Corbin, 1966, 1976/1990; Graham, 1990; Grof & Halifax, 1978; Masters, 2002; Thurman, 1994). Each wisdom tradition has its own version of this theme, but many include four primary realms, whereas some include a variety of subdivisions within these. Examples of the latter include the bardo states of the Buddhists (Thurman, 1994) and the "subtle" and imaginal realms of the Sufis (Chittick, 1994; Corbin, 1976/1990). Indian Vedanta philosophy, said to be the outgrowth of the experiences of yogic practitioners over millennia, has one of the simplest and most inclusive versions of this grand vision. It posits the existence of *gross*, *subtle*, and *causal* realms that often are associated with the conscious states of wakefulness, dream sleep, and, paradoxically, dreamless sleep (e.g., Tigunait, 1983). Vedanta also describes a forth state, *turiya*, the transcendental witnessing of all three.

For the sake of speculation let us entertain the possibility that these realms of being represent realities that cannot be reduced to states of consciousness alone (Combs, 2002; Combs et al., 2006; Wilber, 1998a). This would mean that at least some of the reports of such alternative realms of experience found in spiritual and shamanic traditions throughout the world are valid in the same way that travel reports by individuals who have visited other countries are valid. It also would mean that certain dynamical configurations of the mind carry us not only into altered states of consciousness, in the usual sense, but also into other realms of being. This is a radical idea from the point of view of Western science, but in less technical terms is taken for granted by virtually all wisdom traditions throughout the world. It would be foolish for us to argue the physics or metaphysics of such a proposition, although we speculate on this elsewhere (Combs et al., 2006). But in a scientific community that takes seriously such theoretical wonders as black holes, multiple universes, galaxies that travel backward in time, and nonlocal quantum effects, it is hardly defensible to dismiss any serious proposal simply because it does not fit with traditional beliefs.

Returning, however, to states of consciousness and levels of development, several theorists have pointed to a simpatico, if not an actual identity, between advanced postconventional levels of psychological development and certain peak, or mystical states of consciousness (Combs, 2002; Cook-Greuter, 1999; Gowan, 1974; S. Kelly, 1999; Wade 1996; Washburn, 1988; Wilber, 1998b, 2006). Wilber, for instance, has gone so far as to suggest titles for these developmental levels that indicate their affinity with the realms to which they seem most strongly affiliated, as seen in the middle column in Table 14.1 (Levels 7–10). Now, the idea that the dynamical regimes that undergird the highest postconventional levels of development are themselves states of consciousness, and further that these are somehow resonant with realms of being that have been described in traditional wisdom literatures from around the world, may seem a considerable stretch. But perhaps this seems the case because we have arrived at this possibility through such torturous reasoning! If we were simply to say that human growth at its highest levels becomes spiritual, at which point the individual becomes increasingly conscious of subtle realms of being—or more conservatively, is subject to mystical experiences—the whole proposition seems less labored. In accord with this view, virtually all major theoretical models of psychological growth increasingly emphasize selflessness if not explicit spirituality at the highest levels of development (e.g., Cook-Grueter, 1999; Fischer & Bidell, 2006; Gilligan, 1993; Gowan, 1974; Kegan, 1982, 1994; Kohlberg, 1981; Maslow, 1971).

Approaching the problem from another point of view, we find that without making the assumption of equivalence between the most advanced levels of development and certain states of consciousness, and that these may be uniquely allied with particular realms of being, it is difficult to explain why mystical experiences, evidently more common than one might imagine (Greeley & McCready, 1975; Spence, 1992; Wade, 2004), should so clearly prefigure experiences commonly ascribed to persons at later developmental stages (Combs, 2002; Wilber, 1998b, 2002). Or why such peak experiences should have so much in common when reported by individuals at different levels of development (e.g., Maslow, 1971). Thinking about such problems, theologian Randall Studstill (2002) has carefully examined the mystical experiences described in Tibetan Buddhist Dzogchen literature, comparing these with the Rhineland mystic tradition, especially exemplified in the writings of Meister Eckhart. He found the similarities to be striking. However, he also approached this analysis from a point of view similar to the complex systems perspective presented in this chapter. In doing so, he took pains to point out the awkwardness of attempting to explain how temporary peak or mystical experiences reported by ordinary people can prefigure the stable characteristics of later well-established patterns of experience such as those described in these two traditions.

Let us again note, as well, that no matter what state of consciousness, or realm of being, an individual might experience, we can expect that on returning to ordinary waking consciousness he or she will interpret that experience according to his or her own level of development. Let us say, for instance, that someone has a "peak experience" of Vedanta's subtle, or even causal realm. If that person is functioning developmentally at Gebser's (1949/1986) mythic structure (Table 14.1; Stages 3 and 4; *representational mind* and *concrete operations thinking*) he or she will explain their experience in mythic terms—for example, in terms of deities or devils, and perhaps grand mythic motifs involving heavens and hells. If on the other hand, their dominant developmental level were at Gebser's mental structure (Stage 5, *formal operations thinking*), then they would offer logical explanations, perhaps speaking in terms of grand visions of nature and the physical cosmos.

The idea that each person would interpret peak experiences of other realms of being, whether they are independent realities or not, in terms of their own developmental level led both Combs (1995) and Wilber (1998b, 2006) independently to outline a set of possible intersections between such experiences and the development levels to which the person might return, once back to ordinary consciousness. They subsequently named the graphic representation of this idea the "Wilber–Combs Lattice" (Combs, 2002; Wilber, 2005, 2006), a summary of which appears in Table 14.2. Here, each box represents the intersection of a developmental level, shown in the left-hand column,

Table 14.2. Partial Wilber-Combs Lattice

Levels[a]/Realms[b]	Gross	Psychic[c]	Subtle	Causal	Nondual
Nondual[d]	—	—	—	—	—
Causal	—	—	—	—	—
Subtle	—	—	—	—	—
Psychic[c]	—	—	—	—	—
Integral Consciousness, or Vision Logic	—	—	—	—	—
Formal Operations	—	—	—	—	—
Concrete Operations	—	—	—	—	—
Representational mind (Early Concrete Operations)	—	—	—	—	—
Phantasmic-emotional (Preoperational)	—	—	—	—	—
Sensorimotor	—	—	—	—	—

[a] Levels of development. Terms are based on a number of developmental systems.
[b] Realms of being. These may be thought of as actual realms of being, or states of consciousness that carry a strong sense of reality.
[c] Also termed lower subtle.
[d] Ever-present ordinary mind; the direct experience of the nondual ground.

and a realm of being suggested by Vedanta, seen in the row on top. Note that in this table the subtle realm is divided along traditional lines into a lower subtle or "psychic" realm, and a higher or true subtle realm.

The Wilber–Combs Lattice is a potentially useful guide for identifying and studying a vast range of peak or spiritual experiences, and the interpretations of those experiences as reported by individuals at different developmental levels. In doing so, let us keep in mind, as Kohlberg (1981), Torbert (1972a, 1972b; and this volume), Wade (1996), and others have pointed out, that the evaluation of developmental level is not as simple as it may seem. For instance, a person who appears to exhibit postconventional morality may, in fact, simply be mouthing statements heard from others. The way an individual thinks, perceives reality, and approaches the world, must all be examined. For example, a contemporary shaman may make excellent use of magical technologies in some ways sometimes associated with preoperational thought, but think about them from a Stage 6 or even higher developmental perspective (Krippner, 2000). Finally, consider the spiritual experiences of children, presumably near the bottom of the developmental scale. Children sometimes report experiences of "angelic" realms of consciousness ordinarily reserved for saints and sages (e.g., Morse with Perry, 1990; Wilber, 2002). They, of course, interpret these with the mind of a child, but this does not mean that they do not have authentic spiritual experiences. And so, the visions of children, like the illuminations of mystics and the epiphanies of ordinary men and women, all remind us not only that this world is much richer than science once imagined, but that the dimensions of human experience surpass our finest dreams.

Acknowledgments

Completing these thoughts, we dedicate this chapter to honor the pioneering work carried of Jane Loevinger, who more than any other researcher established a scientific foundation for exploring the developmental trajectory of the ego, and thus the person.

Dr. Krippner's participation in the preparation of this chapter was made possible by his position as chair for the Study of Consciousness, Saybrook Graduate School and Research Center. We thank the editors of *The International Journal of Transpersonal Studies* for permission to reproduce parts of the Combs and Krippner (1993) article.

15

The Prism Self Revisited

The Matter of Integrity

Judith Stevens-Long

> One eyed, one eared yellow purple people eater
> Where did that come from? One eared? Yellow purple?
> That can't be right.
> One eyed, one eared yellow
> *Google it.* I don't want to Google it. I want it to stop.
> *Try humming Beethoven. Tom used to say if you . . .*
> TOM WAS A DRUNK.
> *That doesn't mean he was wrong.*
> One eyed, one eared yellow purple people eater
> Dah, dah, dah DUM . . .
> One eyed, one eared yellow purple people eater
> STOP IT!!!
> That's the old cognitive behavior heave ho.
> Heave ho, heave ho, heave ho
> One eyed, one eared yellow purple people eater
> And, above it all is the one who watches the whole mess.
> —JSL

Given the state of the inside of my head it is little wonder that this chapter is devoted to a review of research and theory on the issue of narrative coherence and ego development. In an earlier version of this meditation (Stevens-Long, 2000), I challenged the idea that integrity necessarily represents an ideal of the optimal state of ego development. In this chapter, I reframe integrity in a way that fits the emerging evidence about the complexity of high-stage ego development.

Recently, the debate over ego development has focused on the issue of whether coherence or multiplicity is the better descriptor of narrative identity (McAdams, Josselson, & Lieblich, 2007). By narrative identity, I refer to the stories that people tell about how they got to be who they are. Over the past 8 years, the literature on narrative identity has burgeoned (Adler & McAdams, 2007; L. King & Hicks, 2006; L. King & Smith, 2004; McAdams & Pals, 2006; Pals, 2006a, 2006b; Pasupathi, Mansour, & Brubaker, 2007). Most of this research has focused on how various themes and types of stories might be related to traits like coping and openness (Pals, 2006a, 2006b), personal well-being (L. King & Raspin, 2004; L. King & Smith, 2004), and developmental markers like generativity (McAdams, 2006). Generally, this research has demonstrated that the ability to create a meaningful, coherent story about one's life is associated with high levels of subjective well-being and maturity (Pals, 2006a, 2006b).

In fact, as several of these researchers point out, psychotherapy often is directed at helping clients to construct or reconstruct life stories so they are more coherent and hopeful. In this research, narrative identity often is defined as a story about motivation (L. King & Hicks, 2006). In other words, narrative identity is a story about the goals a person holds or has held or holds up for the future and how events and forces shaped those goals. Coherence of the story means that the person is able to provide causal explanations that make sense both in terms of time and in terms of the ordinary understandings we hold in the culture. Additionally, good life stories are integrative in the sense that the narrator is able to draw lessons about the self and life in general from the events and sequences narrated.

Of course, none of this means that the life stories people tell are simple. In fact, much of this research suggests that the narratives of well-developed adults are quite complex. They often include regret over lost opportunities, conflicted feelings, painful experiences, and suffering, as well as moments of triumph, joy and achievement. As McAdams (2005) points out, "Stories that succumb to single, dominant perspectives, no matter how coherent they may seem to be, are too simplistic to be true; they fail to reflect lived experience" (p. 119).

On the other hand, it is not clear that coherent, hopeful life stories are associated with high levels of ego development. In fact, King and her associates (L. King & Hicks, 2006; L. King & Raspin,

2004; L. King & Smith, 2004) have demonstrated that positive well-being is associated with the elaboration of one's current goals and one's best possible self. Ego development, on the other hand, appears to be predicted by the elaborate depiction of lost possible selves and unlikely future selves. These researchers claim that investment in goals that are not consistent with one's current identity is associated with lower well-being and regret, and also with personality development as measured by Loevinger (L. King & Smith, 2004). In other words, the ability to create a coherent, accurate narrative about who one is and where one is going is to some extent, independent of personality development.

Yet, personality development as measured by Loevinger (1998a, 1998b) is based on the assumption that high levels of ego development reflect an accurate sense of self and some form of ego integrity. How can ego integrity be reflected in an investment in goals that are not consistent with one's current identity, for example, a developed image of how life would have been had one been straight instead of gay or stayed married instead of getting divorced? And this is just one aspect of the problem. Research that focuses on the experience of the self rather than the life story (Montgomery, 1996; Raggatt, 2007) illuminates a vast inner landscape inhabited by multiple versions of the self, including lost selves, possible selves, best selves, nightmare selves, and rejected selves, voices that argue and critique or agree, contradictions and paradoxes of all sorts. Peter Raggatt (2007) writes that focus on the experience of self reveals a deep level of complexity and conflicts among "voices that bubble beneath the surface of the story" (p. 32).

Part of the problem is explained, or at least rationalized by differences in method. When called on to do so, most people can narrate a reasonably coherent story about who they are and how they got to be that way. If need be, people can describe the trunk of the tree. When called on to describe the branches and leaves, the cones and flowers, they can do that as well. The construct of integrity may be more relevant when talking about narrative identity than the experience of self. How can the construct of integrity be applied to this conflicted and multivocal experience of self? McAdams (2005) suggests that only good or healthy stories are coherent, whereas Raggatt (2007) argues that the imposition of coherence on the life story may merely reflect a cultural disposition.

The conflict arises when we shift focus from the "story" of self to the "experience" of self. So, a place to begin might be a quick review of the construct of self itself.

The Self

Richardson, Rogers, and McCarroll (1998) distinguished several broad ways of thinking about the experience of self. In the *traditional* version, the individual plays a small but meaningful role in both the human community and a wider cosmic drama. In the *modern* version, the self becomes a sovereign entity, separate from the community, atomist, free and rational. The modern self is not so much a part of the community, constrained by its cultural practices and meanings, but rather takes culture to be a medium of self-realization or self-actualization.

In the *postmodern* view, the self becomes a construction of the cultural context. For postmodern thinkers like Foucault (1980), this view represents a strong critique of the modern notion of a disengaged, masterful self. The postmodern challenge is captured by D. White and Hellerich (1988), who suggested that contemporary culture engenders a multiform self best understood as a collection of convenient masks, a variety of characters one might play. As Nietzsche (1968) wrote in the *Will to Power*, "The assumption of one single subject is perhaps unnecessary" (p. 490).

Finally, Richardson et al. (1988) proposed the *dialogic* self. This self is an internalized, ongoing conversation or dialogue concerning the "quality of our motivation, the worth of the ends we seek, or the good or right life for us in our time and place" (p. 510). The dialogic self is an argument about values, principles, and goals. It also is an array of discrepant voices each of which makes serious claims on our loyalty and beliefs, integrated only by the desire to make right choices.

Anderson (1997) covered this ground in a slightly different way. He outlined a traditional self, composed of roles—mother, worker, friend, aunt, citizen, and so forth. He also has described a *romantic* view in which the true inner self can be discovered and nurtured through meditation. He referred to the modern self as the *scientific* self, an entity that can be measured, characterized, and studied and, as he pointed out:

> The modern self was—is—one of the noblest achievements of the human mind, and one of the most inspiring achievements of evolution on the planet. It was a construction of thought that freed people from the tyranny of kings, expanded the horizons of life, opened the mind to the best possibilities of science. (p. 31)

The modern self is characterized by a sense of stability and integrity. The measurement of it emphasizes objectivity and individual differences. Survey and interview instruments are developed with an eye to scalability, reliability, and validity. The maturity of the modern self is understood in terms of increasing objectivity and complexity within an integrated ego. Multiplicity or pluralism of the ego is interpreted as a symptom of crisis or pathology.

In Anderson's view, the modern version of the self began to break down in the 1960's, although the roots of that breakdown can certainly be seen in Freud's tripartite construction of personality or James division of the self into "I" and "me." Jung named a collection of subjectivities in *self, persona, shadow, animus, anima,* and *ego,* but the mainstream human development literature ignored this thinking in favor of Piagetian and Eriksonian ideals of unitary, stage-oriented development.

Anderson has identified four types of postmodern theory about the self. The first he called *multiphrenia* characterizing Gergen (1991, 1994) especially. The multiphrenic self is in constant communication, contact, and conflict, producing an internal experience that is not consistent and integrated. The self becomes fragmented, shifting, outward-oriented and accommodating.

Contemporary personality theory abounds with versions of plurality including Berne's (1964) *parent, adult, child;* Sullivan's (1953) *good me, bad me,* and *not me,* and Winnicott's (1971) *false selves* and *true self.* Gergen speaks of the *pastiche self,* a multiverse of culturally derived internal images. Harter and Monsour (1992) claimed that *human natures* are multidimensional and shift across relationships and roles. Breunlin, Schwartz, and MacKune-Karrer (1992) referred to the *interior family,* whereas Rowan (1990) conceived of the self as an internal community of interactors who "come out" in various relational cultures.

In another version, Anderson described the postmodern self as *protean* after the work of Robert Lifton (1993). Unafraid of change and willing to undergo metamorphosis, the protean self is seen in a "multiplicity of varied, even antithetical images and ideas held at one time by the self, each of which may be more or less ready to act" (p. 8). The protean self seeks to be both fluid and grounded.

In a third view, the idea of separate identity disappears altogether (Derrida, 1982; Foucault, 1980, 1982). The self is decentered, an effect of the rules of discourse and power relations that create and constitute culture. The self is at best a ceaselessly created and recreated "work of art" (Foucault, 1982). At worst, it is an impotent delusion.

Finally, Anderson described "feminist relationalism," in which the self is context-dependent, discontinuous, and contingent. In this view, the self is accommodating and fluid like Lifton's protean self, but lacks the ground Lifton imputs. What is this ground? How does the center hold, if there can be said to be a center? How do we reconcile these descriptions of the postmodern self with the growing body of research that highlights coherent narrative identity or a theory of development that valorizes integrity?

The Problem of Integrity

Erikson (1982) defined integrity as the appreciation of the meaningfulness of one's own life cycle. Carol Hoare (2002) reported that Erikson's unpublished papers contain the following elaboration, "perspective, acceptance, and a serenity born of knowing where one stands in ethical space" (p. 192). In a recent longitudinal study of integrity, James and Zarrett (2006) operationalized Erikson's definition as the ability to adapt to triumphs and disappointment, accept one's life and one's place in it, the absence of death anxiety and satisfaction with life. They did not find strong support for the idea that integrity defined this way increased with age nor did they find it was well related to feelings of personal well-being. On the other hand, they found integrity predicted their measure of personal growth.

In the context of studying moral reasoning and personality Connelly, Lilienfeld, and Schmeelk (2006) argued that integrity can be seen as "a tendency to comply with social norms, avoid deviant behaviors, and embrace a sense of justice, truthfulness and fairness" (p. 82). However, they failed to show a correlation between this definition and ego development or moral reasoning.

Suzanne Cook-Greuter (1999) claimed that, at the highest levels of ego development defined by Loevinger, self-experience is fluid and open-ended rather than accurate and objective. Yet, she still claimed that ego development refers to how people form coherent systems of meaning about the self and objects in the world. She argued that, at the highest stages, the ego is trying to create coherence as a "summary of flux." Somehow, through this process of summary, the ego creates a stable self-identity, according to Cook-Greuter. Manners and Durkin (2001) referred to the ability to reconcile inner conflicts and integrate paradox, yet they admitted that the highest levels of ego development are associated with greater experience of phenomenal variation in the self. It's not clear how the ability to resolve and integrate occurs in light of the experience of phenomenal variation.

Jack Bauer (this volume) suggested that people who demonstrate postconventional ego development use the concept of growth to make sense of their own lives, yet he found that only at Stage 9, when people have given up the ideal of growth, do those at postconventional levels report experiencing happiness and well-being. McAdams and Logan (2007) talked about integration in terms of a dialectic. They wrote that integrity may be accomplished by creating unity within opposites. Perhaps, they seem to say, the conflict itself creates a kind of integrity. Here, I think we might all agree with Raggatt (2007) when he pointed out that we need a model of integrity or coherence that deals with complexity better.

Returning to a preference expressed by Erikson (1982) for the everyday words of the "living languages because they express both what is universally human and what is culturally specific," (p. 58), I retrieved this entry from Wikipedia:

> Integrity is the basing of one's actions on an internally consistent framework of principles. Depth of principles and adherence of each level to the next are key factors. One is said to have integrity to the extent that everything one does is derived from the same core set of values. While those values may change, it is their consistency with each other and with the person's actions that determine one's degree of integrity. *Integrity* can be viewed as personal honesty, acting according to one's beliefs and values at all times. It can emphasize the "wholeness" or "intactness" of a moral stance or attitude. Relevant views of wholeness may also emphasize commitment and authenticity.

Merriam-Webster online agrees that integrity may signify firm adherence to a code of values or the quality or state of being completed or undivided. So, there are two dimensions here: values and wholeness, and, I believe that they are intertwined.

Integrity, Values, and Wholeness

One way to understand the problem here is to consider that the literature may reflect a phenomenon that is both fragmented and full of conflict (particle theory) and coherent (wave theory) depending on how you look. I believe that the literature and our common language both support the notion that the self consists not only in a continuous dialogue between voices, images and ideas that make claims on our attention (particles), but also in the existence of a stance or attitude toward those voices (wave).

The literature supports the notion that the goundedness of the self is essentially ethical and evaluative. Listening to our own internalized dialogue, we reject some voices, harmonize with others, and adopt one or another of the many competing perspectives based on our judgments of what produces more penetrating insights, greater satisfaction or more focus. We look for what is good and sensible, for what has meaning—the ground of the protean self. The experience of self is not so much an experience of "thing," as it is an experience of quest, a stance toward the constantly shifting discourse of our consciousness. The interplay between wave and particle, stance and voices, brings to mind the splaying of light through a prism. Values, this quest, constitute the white light behind the prism. Culture, language, experience, circumstance and relationships form the prism that splays light along the spectrum of perceived colors.

No one voice need dominate others within the prism self. Rather self *is* the interplay of positions through which the individual develops a stance with regard to the quality or worth of his or her motivations, behaviors, and emotional reactions. This self is no longer the integrator or synthesizer of experience, but the interpreter. It is the source that judges the rightness of an action, the meaningfulness of personae, the potential in a circumstance. The Self (the white light) is a witness to the family of subselves that represent both the variety and the unity of voices that allow for fluidity or groundedness, depending on the occasion or situation.

John Beebee (2007) has written that beyond the integration of parts into a whole, integrity means "standing for something" (p. 12) and Dan McAdams (2005) pointed out that life stories make moral assumptions and are grounded in ideological convictions regarding how the world should work and how people should behave. High ego development has been associated with self-regulation and principled moral reasoning (Manners & Durkin, 2001), especially the development of judgment based on caring (Skoe & van der Lippe, 2002).

People who exhibit high scores on ego development and also score high on measures of caring are characterized by the ability to cope with conflict and uncertainty, accept responsibility for the choices they have made, balance the needs of the self with those of the other and renounce the unattainable (Skoe & van der Lippe, 2002). For such people, interpersonal relations are intense and involve "a recognition of inevitable mutual interdependence" (Loevinger, 1966, p. 200).

In her dissertation work, Lael Montgomery (1996) demonstrated that "how I am" in these intense interpersonal relationships becomes internalized as a set of subpersonalities or personae. If I begin to experience myself as a changing collection of personae, an interior that has development in various interdependent relationships, I may begin to experience my inner self as more than, greater than or emergent from this collection. Wilber (1995) understood this sense of self in terms of a developmental position that bridges the personal and transpersonal realms. The self is conceived as a collection of personae by a transcendent Self who is doing the conceiving, much like Jung's supra-personal archetypal Self. In this state, there is freedom of identity—for instance I become freed or liberated from a fixed concept of who I am. But there is potentially a lack of individual responsibility or accountability if an integrative stance has not accompanied the development of multiple subjectivities.

On the other hand, the development of multiple subjectivities may, paradoxically, be related to "wholeness," in the Jungian sense. Here wholeness means the ability to see and accept all the parts of the self, including the shadow. Gisela Labouvie-Vief (2000) proposed that Jung's most important contribution to developmental psychology is the idea that rejected aspects of the self continue to express themselves through dissociation and splitting. She argued that the potential of integrating these aspects into one's sense of self is a unique gift of adulthood. Wilber referred to this process as "taking back the projections," and it is, of course, one of the main tasks of psychotherapy in both the Jungian and the object relations traditions.

To take back the projections means to own the rejected and unacceptable parts of the self—to see the anger or fear or grief that we might not recognize. Often, even in the healthiest of us, these are split off and seen in others rather than the self. Split-off feelings and ideas constitute a major explanation for the rejection of the other. People high in ego development describe quite complex transactions both within the self and between the self and others perhaps as a function of integration, or taking back the projections and acknowledging them as a part of the self.

Young-Eisendrath (1997) argued that successful, long-term psychotherapy or psychoanalysis involves a developmental movement from the breakdown of ego defenses to the acknowledgement of a "number of subpersonalities or states of non-ego or not-I that have been disturbing and/or blocking coherence, continuity, agency and affective patterns in a way that has been destructive or overwhelming" (p. 164). She pointed out that many adults in our society, perhaps most, resist taking responsibility for these subpersonalties. She defined wholeness as the capacity to reflect metaphorically on the whole personality within a dialogic space. She conceived of the archetype of Self as the predisposition toward unity within the context of multiplicity or diversity in inner and outer life. Again, we have the construction of the self both as white light, such as stance or predisposition, and spectrum, such as diversity or multiplicity.

Kegan (1994) also spoke about the exploration of the self in the service of diversity. This path requires the observation and acknowledgement of the Self in the Other. If I can experience within me both the oppressor and the oppressed, the angry and the hurt, the rational and the irrational, and so on, I begin to see all Others in Myself. This perception may move me beyond the experience of separation and duality to a feeling of connection to others, eventually to all living beings (Young-Eisendrath, 1997). Or, as Young-Eisendrath noted, "Developing the capacity for complex self-reflection in a clear dialogical space will open the door to empathy and compassion for others and for oneself, and finally to the experience of interdependence" (p. 164). In this way, the development of caring and the experience of wholeness should be intertwined with ego development.

Hermeneutics, the theory of how we interpret and understand, involves a movement back and forth between attending to the object of inquiry—the text, the other, the event—and analyzing its meaning. The hermeneutic inquirer is the subject of change. "We 'dialogue' with the phenomenon to be understood, asking what it means to those who create it, and attempting to integrate that with its meaning to us. . . . Hermeneutics is an exploration that assumes a deep connection to the whole of our culture and tradition" (Bentz & Shapiro, 1988, p. 111).

One of the clear assumptions of the dialogic/hermeneutic view is that human beings are constantly attempting to make sense of what they are doing and becoming; they care about leading a decent or authentic life. Human life takes place within a space of questions about what is worthwhile and these questions are answered in the interplay between "present and past, interpreters and events, readers and texts, one person and another"(Richardson et al., 1998, p. 507). As our attention flows from present to past, from event to interpreter, from self to other, dialogic understanding grows through openness and application.

Hermeneutic interpretation requires engagement with the world. Contemplation is not sufficient. One must engage, reflect on, and interpret actions or events in terms of their meanings for one's own development and the development of others. Transpersonal knowing is hermeneutic and, according to Ferrer (1998), transpersonal knowledge is enactive, participatory, and transformative. It is not an experience. It is a participatory event. It is not a movie. It is a party. Perhaps one of the mistakes we have made about integrity is thinking of it as a noun. The ego does not so much achieve integrity, as it is a process of integrating. Rather than possessing a Self, one may be engaged in the process of selfing.

And what would this look like if it were integrative? It would be more a constant process of acknowledging buried, distorted, or suppressed parts of the self as they arise in relationship. There may even be new parts of the self to discover and add to the collection. As long as we are living, even when we are elderly or ill or dying, there are always new people, new relationships in which new personae may arise. The evolved self is constantly noticing these new relationships, how they are like or not like old ones and the internal responses that accompany them. Some people bring out the best in us, some the worst, but regardless of what is brought out, the job of the evolving ego is to see it and find space for it in the dialogic space of the Self.

In this chapter, I have defined integrity as the process of keeping the self whole through observing and acknowledging the split off or distorted or new aspects of the self that come to consciousness in interpersonal relationships. This process is accompanied by a set of values or a stance about what makes a good person and a good life. As wholeness increases, that stance turns more and more toward caring, toward the ability to identify with and accept the Other. It should certainly be possible to measure each of these attributes and see whether or not they are intertwined. Separate research studies have connected ego development to complexity and internal dialogue and to the development of caring. Clinical observation and measurement should allow us to assess defensive structure.

It also is possible that this formulation has some possibility of standing up to cross-cultural scrutiny. In work on narrative identity, the cross-cultural evidence has suggested that stories vary over cultures in their emphasis on individualism versus collectivism (Cross, Gore, & Morris, 2003; Wang, 2004). If we define integrity as a moral stance and identify high ego development, it may make no difference whether people speak in terms of individualism or collectivism. Other evidence challenges the notion of integrity defined as autonomy and separateness. Braun (1993), for instance, claimed that in India, the ego is answerable to many competing and contradictory forces leading to a self that is experienced as less integrated than the Western ideal. The formulation suggested here provides for what Braun describes when he writes that "The Indian normally has a number of ego nuclei based on conformity to various social rules" (p. 143). Furthermore, Indian tribal groups often exhibit close identification of the self with nature, so that changes in the environment lead to changes in the sense of identity (Vasudev, 1994).

Closer to home, feminist psychologists have long argued that the self is more context-dependent and relational than the modern, autonomous version suggests. Oyama (1993) has gone so far as to imply there is no such thing as individual personality or identity at all. She posits that a person is a moving complex of elements that exist in shifting interpersonal environments, always in dialogic relations to the other. Young-Eisendrath (1997) noted that many interpersonal and feminist theorists have "cautioned us not to universalize the story of a masterful, bounded self as a necessity for everyone." These conceptualizations can be understood in terms of the prism metaphor. What is emphasized in each of these works is the play of light along the spectrum. What I have added here is the possibility that behind this play is a tendency to choose among the possibilities in a way that depends on one's moral stance, or as Guignon (2000) has written, to act "for the sake of being a person of a particular sort" (p. 72).

In a recent work on the uncanny, the sacred and the narcissism of culture, Victor Andrade (2007) related the development of ego to the progress of civilization. Primary narcissism, he explained, perverts object relations and encourages the aversion to what is different. Its examination is crucial to an understanding of civilization's problems. Without the development of the ego, the "different" remains an object of attack. As Andrade argued, "Since attacks are usually directed at something that the subject has projected on to the other, aggressiveness, though aimed at an external target, may destroy the subject himself, or life on this planet. The taming of destructiveness is the most urgent task that lies before civilization, and it involves [the development of the ego]" (p. 1034).

He implored scientists to bring what they know to bear on the subject of ego development. Certainly, this volume and the work of those represented here is an attempt to do so. Meanwhile, I did Google "purple people eater" and discovered the lyric goes "one-eyed, one-horned flying purple people eater," which refers to a being that eats purple people, so it could possibly be yellow. I was 14 when the song hit the top of the charts and, as I recall, quite angry with my mother.

References

Ackerley, G. D., Burnell, J., Holder, D. C., & Kurdek, L. A. (1988). Burnout among licensed psychologists. *Professional Psychology: Research and Practice, 19,* 624–631.

Adler, J., & McAdams, D. (2007). Time, culture, and stories of the self. *Psychological Inquiry, 18*(2), 97–128.

Alexander, C. N., Davies, J. L., Dixon, C., Dillbeck, M. C., Druker, S. M., Oetzel, R., et al. (1990). Growth of higher stages of consciousness: Maharishi's Vedic psychology of human development. In C. N. Alexander & E. J. Langer (Eds.), *Higher stages of human development: Perspectives on adult growth* (pp. 286–341). New York: Oxford University Press.

Alexander, C. N., Heaton, D. P., & Chandler, H. M. (1994). Advanced human development in the Vedic psychology of Maharishi: Theory and research. In M. E. Miller & S. R. Cook-Greuter (Eds.), *Transcendence and mature thought in adulthood* (pp. 39–70). Lanham, MD: Rowman & Littlefield.

Alexander, C. N., & Langer, E. (Eds.). (1990). *Higher stages of human development: Perspectives on adult growth.* New York: Oxford University Press.

Alexander, C. N., & Orme-Johnson, D. W. (2003). Walpole study of the Transcendental Meditation program in maximum security prisoners II: Longitudinal study of development and psychopathology. *Journal of Offender Rehabilitation, 36,* 127–160.

Alexander, C. N., Rainforth, M. V., & Gelderloos, P. (1991). Transcendental meditation, self-actualization, and psychological health: A conceptual overview and statistical meta-analysis. *Journal of Social Behavior and Personality, 6,* 189–247.

Alexander, C. N., Walton, K. G., & Goodman, R. S. (2003). Walpole study of the Transcendental Meditation program in maximum security prisoners I: Cross-sectional differences in development and psychopathology. *Journal of Offender Rehabilitation, 36,* 97–125.

Amritaswarupananda, Swami. (1998). *Awaken children!* IX. San Ramon, CA: Mata Amritanandamayi Center.

Anderson, W. A. (1997). *The future of the self: Inventing the postmodern person.* New York: Jeremy P. Tarcher/Putnam.

Andrade, V. (2007). The "uncanny," the sacred and the narcissism of culture: The development of the ego and the progress of civilization. *International Journal of Psychoanalysis, 88*, 1019–1037.

Aurobindo, S. (1971). *Letters on yoga* (Vols. 1–3). Pondicherry, India: All India Press.

Austin, J. H. (2006). *Zen-brain reflections.* Cambridge, MA: MIT Press.

Baldwin, J. M. (1930). *History of psychology in autobiography.* Worcester, MA: Clark University Press. Retrieved June 1, 2007, from http://psychclassics.yorku.ca/ Baldwin/murchison.htm

Balsekar, R. (1999). *Who cares?* Redondo Beach, CA: Advaita Press.

Baltes, P. B., Staudinger, U. M., & Lindenberger, U. (1999). Lifespan psychology: Theory and application of intellectual functioning. *Annual Review of Psychology, 50*, 471–501.

Basseches, M. A. (1984). *Dialectic thinking and adult development.* Norwood, NJ: Ablex.

Batson, D., Schoenrade, P., & Ventis, L. (1993). *Religion and the individual: A social-psychological perspective.* New York: Oxford University Press.

Bauer, J. J. (2008). How the ego quiets as it grows: Ego development, growth narratives, and eudaimonic personality development. In H. A. Wayment & J. J. Bauer (Eds.), *Transcending self-interest: Psychological perspectives on the quiet ego* (pp. 199–210). Washington, DC: American Psychological Association.

Bauer, J. J. (2009). Growth goals. In S. J. Lopez (Ed.), *Encyclopedia of positive psychology.* London: Blackwell.

Bauer, J. J., & McAdams, D. P. (2004a). Growth goals, maturity, and well-being. *Developmental Psychology, 40*, 114–127.

Bauer, J. J., & McAdams, D. P. (2004b). Personal growth in adults' stories of life transitions. *Journal of Personality, 72*, 573–602.

Bauer, J. J., & McAdams, D. P. (2010). Eudaimonic growth: Narrative growth goals predict increases in ego development and subjective well-being three years later. *Developmental Psychology, 46*, 761–772.

Bauer, J. J., McAdams, D. P., & Pals, J. L. (2008). Narrative identity and eudaimonic well-being. *Journal of Happiness Studies, 9*, 81–104.

Bauer, J. J., McAdams, D. P., & Sakaeda, A. R. (2005). Interpreting the good life: Growth memories in the lives of mature, happy people. *Journal of Personality and Social Psychology, 88*, 203–217.

Beck, D., & Cowan, C. (1995). *Spiral dynamics.* Malden, MA: Blackwell.

Beebee, J. (2007). The place of integrity in spirituality. In M. Miller & P. Young-Eisendrath (Eds.), *The psychology of mature spirituality* (pp. 11–20). London: Routledge.

Bentz, V., & Shapiro, J. (1998). *Mindful inquiry in social research.* Thousand Oaks, CA: Sage.

Berne, E. (1964). *Transactional analysis in psychotherapy.* New York: Grove Press.

Bett, E., Ost, C., Day, J., & Robinett, T. (2008). *The effectiveness of the Model of Hierarchical Complexity in accounting for various moral measures.*

Paper presented at the 38th annual meeting of the Jean Piaget Society Québec City, Canada.

Block, J. (1971). *Lives through time*. Berkeley, CA: Bancroft Books.

Blumtritt, T., Novy, D. M., Gaa, J. P., & Liberman, D. (1996). Effects of maximum performance instructions on the Sentence Completion Test. *Journal of Personality Assessment, 67*(1), 79–89.

Borders, L. D. (1989). Developmental cognitions of first practicum supervisees. *Journal of Counseling Psychology, 36*, 163–169.

Borders, L. D., & Fong, M. L. (1989). Ego development and counseling ability during training. *Counselor Education and Supervision, 29*, 71–83.

Borders, L. D., Fong, M. L., & Neimeyer, G. J. (1986). Counseling students' level of ego development and perceptions of clients. *Counselor Education and Supervision, 26*, 36–49.

Borst, S. R., & Noam, G. (1993). Developmental psychopathology in suicidal and nonsuicidal adolescent girls. *Journal of the American Academy of Child and Adolescent Psychiatry, 32*, 501–508.

Bower, G. H. (1981). Mood and memory. *American Psychologist, 36*, 129–148.

Boyer, T. (2005). A constructive development approach to assessing variations within a community college population. *Community College Journal of Research and Practice, 31*(10), 781–795.

Boyer, T. R. (2005). Using a constructive developmental approach to assess variations within a community college population. *Dissertation Abstracts International, 66*(8), 2814B. Retrieved from ProQuest Dissertations and Theses database. (AAT 3184907)

Bradford, D. L., & Cohen, A. R. (1987). *Managing for excellence: The leadership guide to developing high performance in contemporary organizations*. New York: Wiley.

Bradford, D. L., & Cohen, A. R. (1998). *Power up: Transforming organizations through shared leadership*. New York: Wiley.

Brandtstadter, J., Wentura, D., & Rothermund, K. (1999). Intentional self-development through adulthood and late life: Tenacious pursuit and flexible adjustment of goals. In J. Brandtstadter & R. M. Lerner (Eds.), *Action and self-development: Theory and research through the life span* (pp. 373–400). Thousand Oaks, CA: Sage.

Braun, J. (1993). Some cultural sources of ego development. In J. Braun (Ed.), *Psychological aspects of modernity* (pp. 143–147). Westport, CT: Praeger.

Breunlin, D., Schwartz, R. C., & Mackune-Karrer, B. (1992). *Metaframeworks*. San Francisco: Jossey-Bass.

Brown, D. P. (1986). The stages of meditation in cross-cultural perspective. In K. Wilber, J. Engler & D. P. Brown (Eds.), *Transformations of consciousness* (pp. 191–218). Boston: Shambhala.

Bucke, R. M. (1901). *Cosmic consciousness*. New York: E. P. Dutton.

Bursik, K. (1991). Adaptation to divorce and ego development in adult women. *Journal of Personality and Social Psychology, 60*, 300–306.

Calhoun, L. G., & Tedeschi, R. G. (2001). Posttraumatic growth: The positive lessons of loss. In R. A. Neimeyer (Ed.), *Meaning reconstruction and the experience of loss* (pp. 157–172). Washington, DC: American Psychological Association.

Carlozzi, A. F., Gaa, J. P., & Liberman, D. B. (1983). Empathy and ego development. *Journal of Counseling Psychology, 30,* 113–116.

Chandler, D., & Torbert, W. (2003). Transforming inquiry and action: By interweaving 27 flavors of action research. *Journal of Action Research, 1,* 133–152.

Chandler, H. M. (1991). Transcendental Meditation and awakening wisdom: A longitudinal study of self-development. *Dissertation Abstracts International, 51*(10), 5048B. Retrieved from ProQuest Dissertations and Theses database. (AAT 9107332)

Chandler, H., Alexander, C., & Heaton, D. (2005). The transcendental meditation program and postconventional self-development: A 10-year longitudinal study. *Journal of Social Behavior and Personality, 17*(1), 93–122.

Chittick, W. (1994). *Imaginal worlds: Ibn al-'Arab and the problem of religious diversity.* Albany: State University of New York Press.

Cleary, T. (Ed. & Trans.). (2000). *Taoist meditation: Methods for cultivating a healthy mind and body.* Boston: Shambhala.

Cohen, A., & Desai, A. (2000). Yoga, ego & purification. *What is Enlightenment, 17,* 60–79.

Cohn, L. D. (1998). Age trends in personality development: A quantitative review. In P. M. Westenberg, A. Blasi, & L. D. Cohn (Eds.), *Personality development: Theoretical, empirical and clinical investigations of Loevinger's conception of ego development* (pp. 133–143). Mahwah, NJ: Erlbaum.

Cohn, L. D., & Westenberg, P. M. (2004). Intelligence and maturity: Meta-analytic evidence for the incremental and discriminant validity of Loevinger's measure of ego development. *Journal of Personality and Social Psychology, 86*(5), 760–772.

Colby, A. (2002). Moral understanding, motivation, and identity. *Human Development, 45*(2), 130–135.

Colby, A., & Damon, W. (1992). *Some do care: Contemporary lives of moral commitment.* New York: Free Press.

Colby, A., & Kohlberg, L. (Eds.). (1987). *The measurement of moral judgment.* Cambridge, UK: Cambridge University Press.

Colby, A., Kohlberg, L., Gibbs, J., & Lieberman, M. (1983). A longitudinal study of moral judgment. *Monographs of the Society for Research in Child Development, 48*(1–2, Serial No. 200).

Combs, A. (1995). *The radiance of being: Complexity, chaos, and the evolution of consciousness.* Edinburgh, Scotland: Floris Books.

Combs, A. (2002). *The radiance of being: Understanding the grand integral vision: Living the integral life* (2nd ed.). St Paul, MN: Paragon House.

Combs, A., Arcari, A., & Krippner, S. (2006). All the myriad worlds: Life in the Akashic plenum. *World Futures: The Journal of General Evolution, 62*, 75–85.

Combs, A., & Krippner, S. (1997, June). *A process view of dream states in mind and brain*. Paper presented at the meeting of the Association for the Study of Dreams, 14th International Conference, Asheville, NC.

Combs, A., & Krippner, S. (1998). Dream sleep and waking reality: A dynamical view of two states of consciousness. In S. Hameroff, A. W. Kaszniak, & A. C. Scott (Eds.), *Toward a science of consciousness: The second Tucson discussions and debates* (pp. 487–493). Cambridge, MA: MIT Press.

Combs, A., & Krippner, S. (1999a). Consciousness, evolution, and spiritual growth: A critique and model. *World Futures: The Journal of General Evolution, 53*, 193–212.

Combs, A., & Krippner, S. (1999b). Spiritual growth and the evolution of consciousness: Complexity, evolution, and the farther reaches of human nature. *The International Journal of Transpersonal Studies, 18*, 9–19.

Combs, A., & Krippner, S. (2003). Process, structure, and form: An evolutionary transpersonal psychology of consciousness. *The International Journal of Transpersonal Studies, 22*, 47–60.

Commons, M. L., Ost, C., Lins, M., Day, J., Ross, S., & Crist, J. (2007). *Stage of development in understanding Christ's moral sayings*. Paper presented at the Society for Research in Adult Development Annual Symposium, Boston, MA.

Commons, M. L., & Pekker, A. (2005). *Hierarchical complexity: A formal theory*. Unpublished manuscript, Dare Institute, Cambridge, MA.

Commons, M. L., & Richards, F. A. (1984). A general model of stage theory. In M. L. Commons, F. A. Richards, & C. Armon (Eds.), *Beyond formal operations* (pp. 120–140). New York: Praeger.

Commons, M. L., & Richards, F. A. (2003). Four postformal stages. *In J. Demick & C. Andreoletti (Eds.), Handbook of adult development* (pp. 199–219). New York: Kluwer Academic/Plenum.

Commons, M. L., Richards, F. A., & Kuhn, D. (1982). Systematic and meta-systematic reasoning: A case for levels of reasoning beyond Piaget's stage of formal operations. *Child Development, 53*, 1058–1068.

Commons, M. L., Trudeau, S., Stein, F., Richards, F., & Krause, S. (1998). The existence of developmental stages as shown by the hierarchical complexity of tasks. *Developmental Review 8*(3), 237–278.

Connelly, B. S., Lilienfeld, S. O., & Schmeelk, K. M. (2006). Integrity tests and morality: Associations with ego development, moral reasoning, and psychopathic personality. *International Journal of Selection and Assessment, 14*(1), 82–86.

Cook-Greuter, S. (1990). Maps for living: Ego development theory from symbiosis to conscious universal embeddedness. In M. L. Commons, C. Armon, L. Kohlberg, F. A. Richards, T. A. Grotzer, & J. D. Sinnott. (Eds.),

Adult development: Models and methods in the study of adolescent and adult thought (Vol. 2, pp. 79–104). New York: Praeger.

Cook-Greuter, S. (1999). Postautonomous ego development: A study of its nature and measurement. *Dissertation Abstracts International, 60*(6), 3000B. Retrieved from Proquest Dissertations and Theses database. (AAT 9933122)

Cook-Greuter, S. (2000). Mature ego development: A gateway to ego transcendence? *Journal of Adult Development, 7*(4), 227–240.

Cook-Greuter, S. (2004). Making the case for a developmental perspective. *Industrial and Commercial Training, 36*(7), 275–281.

Cook-Greuter, S. (2005). *A detailed description of the development of nine Action-Logics in the Leadership Development Framework.* Available from http://www.cook-greuter.com/.

Cook-Greuter, S., & Wilber, K. (2000). Unpublished table developed for *The Human Change Project*, Integral Institute, Boulder, CO.

Coomaraswamy, A. (1943). *Hinduism and Buddhism.* New York: Philosophical Library.

Corbin, H. (1966). The visionary dream in Islamic spirituality. In G. E. von Grunebaum & R. Caillois (Eds.), *The dream in human societies* (pp. 381–407). Berkeley: University of California Press.

Corbin, H. (1990). *Spiritual body and celestial earth: From Mazdean Iran to Shi'ite Iran.* London: I.B. Tauris. (Original work published 1976)

Cross, S. E., Gore, J. S., & Morris, M. L. (2003). The relational-interdependent self-construal, self-concept consistency and well-being. *Journal of Personality and Social Psychology, 85*, 933–944.

Csanyi, V. (1989). *Evolutionary systems and society: A general theory of life, mind, and culture.* Durham, NC: Duke University Press.

Damon, W. (1996). The lifelong transformation of moral goals through social influence. In P. B. Baltes & U. M. Staudinger (Eds.), *Interactive minds* (pp. 198–220). Cambridge, UK: Cambridge University Press.

Damon, W., & Hart, D. (1988). *Self-understanding in childhood and adolescence.* Cambridge, UK: Cambridge University Press.

Danner, F. W., & Day, M. C. (1977). Eliciting formal operations. *Child Development, 48*, 1600–1606.

Day, J. (2001). From structuralism to eternity? Re-imagining the psychology of religious development after the cognitive-developmental paradigm. *International Journal for the Psychology of Religion, 11*, 173–183.

Day, J. (2002). Religious development as discursive construction. In C. Hermans, G. Immink, A. de Jong, & J. van der Lans (Eds.), *Social construction and theology* (pp. 63–92). Leiden, Netherlands: Brill.

Day, J. (2007a). Moral reasoning, religious reasoning, and their supposed relationships: Paradigms, problems, and prospects. *Adult Developments: The Bulletin of the* Society *for Research in Adult Development, 10*(1), 6–10.

Day, J. (2007b). Personal development. In F. Watts & E. Gulliford (Eds.), *Jesus and psychology: Approaching the Gospels psychologically* (pp. 123–139). London: Longman, Dartmann, Todd.

Day, J. (2008a, June). *Cognitive complexity, human development, and religious influence in moral problem-solving: Empirical evidence and some implications for human evolution.* Paper presented at the Transdisciplinary Approaches to Personhood Congress, Madrid, Spain.

Day, J. (2008b). Conscience: Does religion matter? Empirical studies of religious elements in pro-social behaviour, prejudice, empathy development, and moral decision-making. In W. Koops, D. Brugman & A. Sander (Eds.), *The structure and development of conscience* (pp. 133–152). London: Psychology Press.

Day, J. (2008c). Human development and the Model of Hierarchical Complexity: Learning from research in the psychology of moral and religious development. *World Futures: The Journal of General Evolution, 64*(5–7), 452–467.

Day, J. (2008d). *Stages of religious belief.* South Bend: IN: Association for Moral Education International Conference, University of Notre Dame.

Day, J., & Naedts, M. (1999). Religious development. In R. Mosher, D. Youngman, & J. Day (Eds.), *Human development across the lifespan: Educational and psychological applications* (pp. 239–264). Westport, CT: Praeger.

Day, J., & Tappan, M. (1996). The narrative approach to moral development: From the epistemic subject to dialogical selves. *Human Development, 39*(2), 67–82.

Day, J., & Youngman, D. (2003). Discursive practices and their interpretation in the psychology of religious development: From constructivist canons to constructionist alternatives. In J. Demick & C. Andreoletti (Eds.), *The handbook of adult development* (pp. 509–532). New York: Plenum.

De Lisi, R., & Staudt, J. (1980). Individual differences in college students' performance on formational operations tasks. *Journal of Applied Developmental Psychology, 28,* 925–932.

de St. Aubin, E., McAdams, D. P., & Kim, T.-C. (Eds.). (2004). *The generative society: Caring for future generations.* Washington, DC: American Psychological Association.

Debold, E. (2002, Fall/Winter). Epistemology, fourth order consciousness, and the subject–object relationship, or . . . how the self evolves with Robert Kegan. *What is Enlightenment, 22.* Retrieved March 12, 2008, from http://www.wie.org/j22/ kegan.asp?page=2

Deci, E. L., & Ryan, R. M. (2008). Hedonia, eudaimonia, and well-being: An introduction. *Journal of Happiness Studies, 9*(1), 1–11.

Degelman, D., Mullen, P., & Mullen, N. (1984). Development of abstract thinking: A comparison of Roman Catholic and Nazarene youth. *Journal of Psychology and Christianity, 3,* 44–49.

Derrida, J. (1982). *Margins of philosophy* (A. Bass, Trans.). Chicago: University of Chicago Press.

Diamond, A. (1997). Portraits of complexity and simplicity: A study of the integrative complexity of life narratives. *Dissertation Abstracts International, 57*(11), 7263B. Retrieved from ProQuest Dissertations and Theses database. (AAT 9714575)

Diener, E., Emmons, R. A., Larson, R. J., & Griffen, S. (1985). The satisfaction with life scale. *Journal of Personality Assessment, 49*, 71–75.

Diener, E., Lucas, R. E., & Scollon, C. N. (2006). Beyond the hedonic treadmill: Revising the adaptation theory of well-being. *American Psychologist, 61*, 305–314.

Dixon, C. A., Dillbeck, M., Travis, F. T., Msemaje, H. I., Clayborne, B. M., Dillbeck, S. L., et al. (2005). Accelerating cognitive and self-development: Longitudinal studies with pre-school and elementary school children. *Journal of Social Behavior and Personality, 17*, 65–92.

Dole, A. A., DiTomasso, R. A., Johnson, M., Sachs, R., Yiung, J., Learner, J., et al. (1981). *Six dimensions of restrospections by therapists and counselors: A manual for research.* Unpublished manuscript.

Drewes, M. J., & Westenberg, P. M. (2001). The impact of modified instructions on ego level scores: A psychometric hazard or indication of optimal ego level. *Journal of Personality Assessment, 76*(2), 229–249.

Durckheim, K. (1990). *The way of transformation: Daily life as spiritual exercise.* London: Unwin.

Duriez, B., & Soenens, B. (2006). Religiosity, moral attitudes and moral competence: A critical investigation of the religiosity-morality relation. *International Journal for Behavioural Development, 31*(1), 75–82.

Dweck, C. S. (1999). *Self-theories: Their role in motivation, personality, and development.* New York: Psychology Press.

Edelstein, W., Keller, M., & Schröder, E. (1990). Child development and social structure: A longitudinal study of individual differences. In P. B. Baltes, D. L. Featherman & R. M. Lerner (Eds.), *Life-span development and behavior* (pp. 152–185). Hillsdale, NJ: Erlbaum.

Edelstein, W., & Krettenauer, T. (2004). Many are called, but few are chosen: Moving beyond the modal levels in normal development. In D. K. Lapsley & D. Narvaez (Eds.), *Moral development, self, and identity* (pp. 213–237). Mahwah, NJ: Erlbaum.

Eich, J. E. (1980). The cue-dependent nature of state-dependent retention. *Memory and Cognition, 8*, 157–173.

Einstein, D., & Lanning, K. (1998). Shame, guilt, ego development, and the five-factor model of personality. *Journal of Personality, 66*, 555–582.

Elbert, T., Pantev, C., Wienbruch, C., Rockstroh, B., & Taub, E. (1995). Increased cortical representation of the fingers of the left hand in string players. *Science, 270*, 305–307.

Engler, J., & Wilber, K. (1986). *Transformations of consciousness: Conventional and contemplative perspectives on development.* Boston: Shambhala.

Epstein, H. T. (1986). Stages in human brain development. *Brain Research, 395*, 114–119.

Epstein, H. T. (1999). Stages of increased cerebral blood flow accompany stages of rapid brain growth. *Brain Development, 21*, 535–539.

Epstein, H. T. (2001). An outline of the role of brain in human cognitive development. *Brain and Cognition, 45*, 44–51.

Erikson, E. H. (1959). Identity and the life cycle. *Psychological Issues, 1.*

Erikson, E. H. (1968). *Identity: Youth and crisis.* New York: Norton.

Erikson, E. H. (1982). *The life cycle completed: Review.* New York: Norton.

Erikson, E. H. (1993). *Childhood and society.* New York: Norton.

Feinstein, D., & Krippner, S. (2006). *The mythic path.* Santa Rosa, CA: Elite Books.

Ferrer, J. (1998). *Revisioning the relationship between transpersonal psychology and the perennial philosophy.* Palo Alto, CA: Panel on multiculturalism and transpersonal psychology at the Institute of Transpersonal Psychology.

Ferrer, J. (2002). *Revisioning transpersonal theory.* Albany: State University of New York.

Ferrer, J. (2003). Integral transformative practice: A participatory perspective. *Journal of Transpersonal Psychology, 35*(1), 21–42.

Fink, A. (Ed.). (1995). *How to measure survey reliability and validity* (Vol. 7). Thousand Oaks, CA: Sage.

Fischer, K. W., & Bidell, T. R. (2006). Dynamic development of psychological structures in action and thought. In W. Damon & R. M. Lerner (Series Eds.) & W. Damon & R. M. Lerner (Vol. Ed.), *Handbook of child psychology: Vol 1. Theoretical models of human development* (6th ed., pp. 313–399). New York: Wiley.

Fishbach, S. M., & Tidwell, R. (1994). Burnout among crisis intervention counselors and its relationship to social support. *California Association of Counseling and Development Journal, 14,* 11–19.

Fisher, D., & Torbert, W. (1991). Transforming managerial practice: Beyond the achiever stage. In R. Woodman & W. Pasmore (Eds.), *Research in organization change and development* (Vol. 5, pp. 143–173). Greenwich, CT: JAI Press.

Fisher, D., & Torbert, W. (1995). *Personal and organizational transformations.* London: McGraw-Hill.

Flanagan, O. (1991). *Varieties of moral personality: Ethics and psychological realism.* Cambridge, MA: Harvard University Press.

Flavell, J. H. (1963). *The developmental psychology of Jean Piaget.* New York: Van Nostrand.

Flor, H., Elbert, T., Knecht, S., Wienbruch, C., Pantev, C., Birbaumer, N., et al. (1995). Phantom-limb pain as a perceptual correlate of cortical reorganization following arm amputation. *Nature, 375,* 482–484.

Foucault, M. (1980). *Power/knowledge: Selected interviews and other writing.* New York: Pantheon.

Foucault, M. (1982). On the genealogy of ethics: An overview of work in progress. In H. Dreyfus & P. Rabinow (Eds.), *Michel Foucault: Beyond structuralism and hermeneutics* (pp. 229–252). Chicago: University of Chicago Press.

Foulkes, D. (1999). *Children's dreaming and the development of consciousness.* Cambridge, MA: Harvard University Press.

Fowler, J. (1981). *Stages of faith. The psychology of human development and the quest for meaning.* San Francisco: Harper & Row.

Fowler, J. (1996). *Faithful change*. San Francisco: Harper & Row.

Freeman, W. J. (1991, February). The physiology of perception. *Scientific American, 264*, 78–85.

Ganzevoort, R. (Ed.). (1998). *De praxis als verhaal: Narrativiteit en pratische theologie*. Kampen, Netherlands: Uitgeverij Kok.

Ganzevoort, R. (2006). *De hand van God en andere verhalen: Over veelkleurige vroomheid en botsende beelden*. Zoetermeer, Netherlands: Meinema.

Gebser, J. (1986). *The ever-present origin* (N. Barstad & A. Mickunas, Trans.). Athens: Ohio University Press. (Original work published 1949)

Gergen, K. (1991). Social understanding and the inscription of self. In J. W. Stigler & A. Richard (Eds.), *Cultural psychology: Essays on comparative human development* (pp. 445–523). Cambridge, UK: Cambridge University Press.

Gergen, K. (1994). *Realities and relationships: Soundings in social construction*. Cambridge, MA: Harvard University Press.

Gibbs, J. C. (1979). Kohlberg's moral stage theory: A Piagetian review. *Human Development, 22*, 89–112.

Gibbs, J. C. (2003). *Moral development and reality*. Thousand Oaks, CA: Sage.

Gilligan, C. (1982). *In a different voice: Women's conceptions of the self and of morality*. Cambridge, MA: Harvard University Press.

Gilligan, C. (1993). *In a different voice: Psychological theory and women's development*. Cambridge, MA: Harvard University Press.

Goerner, S., Dyck, R. G., & Lagerroos, D. (2008). *The new science of sustainability: Building a foundation for great change*. Chapel Hill, NC: Triangle Center for Complex Systems.

Goldmann, R. (1964). *Religious thinking from childhood to adolescence*. New York: Seabury Press.

Goleman, D. (1988). *The meditative mind*. New York: Putnam.

Goleman, D. (1995). *Emotional intelligence: Why it can matter more than IQ*. New York: Bantam Books.

Gowan, J. C. (1974). *Development of the psychedelic individual*. Brooktondale, NY: J. A. Gowan.

Graham, A. C. (1990). *The book of Lieh Tzu: A classic of the Tao*. New York: Columbia University Press.

Graves, C. W. (2005). *The never-ending quest: Dr. Clare W. Graves explores human nature* (with C. C. Cowan & N. Todorovic, Eds.). Santa Barbara: ECLET.

Greeley, A., & McCready, W. (1975). Are we a nation of mystics? In D. Goleman & R. J. Davidson (Eds.), *Consciousness, brain, states of awareness, and mysticism* (pp. 175–183). New York: Harper & Row.

Grof, S., & Halifax, J. (1978). *The human encounter with death*. New York: Dutton.

Groth-Marnat, G., & Summers, R. (1998). Altered beliefs, attitudes, and behaviors following near-death experiences. *The Journal of Humanistic Psychology, 38*(3), 110–125.

Guignon, C. (2000). Authenticity and integrity: A Heideggerian perspective. In M. Miller & P. Young-Eisendrath (Eds.), *The psychology of mature spirituality* (pp. 62–74). London: Routledge.

Hagelin, J. S. (1987). Is consciousness the unified field? A field theorist's perspective. *Modern Science and Vedic Science, 1,* 29–88.

Haidt, J. (2006). *The happiness hypothesis: Finding modern truth in ancient wisdom.* New York: Basic Books

Hanna, T. (1991, August). *Moods and daily stress: The contribution of a dynamical systems approach.* Paper presented at the Inaugural meeting of The Society for Chaos Theory in Psychology, San Francisco.

Hart, D. (2005). The development of moral identity. In G. Carlo & C. P. Edwards (Eds.), *Moral motivation trough the life span* (pp. 165–196). Lincoln: University of Nebraska Press.

Harter, S., & Monsour, A. (1992). Developmental analysis of conflict caused by opposing attributes of the adolescent self-portrait. *Developmental Psychology, 28,* 251–260.

Harung, H., Travis, F., Pensgaard, A. M., Boes, R., Cook-Greuter, S., & Daley, K. (2009). Higher psycho-physiological refinement in world-class Norwegian athletes: Brain measures of performance capacity. *Scandinavian Journal of Medicine and Science in Sports.*

Harung, H. S., Alexander, C. N., & Heaton, D. P. (1995). A unified theory of leadership: Experiences of higher states of consciousness in world-class leaders. *Leadership and Organization Development Journal, 16,* 44–59.

Hauser, S. (1976). Loevinger's model and measure of ego development: A critical review. *Psychological Bulletin, 83,* 928–955.

Hauser, S. T., Diplacido, J., Jacobson, A. M., Willett, J., & Cole, C. (1993). Family coping with an adolescent's chronic illness: An approach and three studies. *Journal of Adolescence, 16,* 305–329.

Helson, R., Mitchell, V., & Hart, B. (1985). Lives of women who became autonomous. *Journal of Personality, 53*(2), 258–285.

Helson, R., & Roberts, B. W. (1994). Ego development and personality change in adulthood. *Journal of Personality and Social Psychology, 66,* 911–920.

Helson, R., & Srivastava, S. (2001). Three paths to adult development: Conservers, seekers, and achievers. *Journal of Personality and Social Psychology, 80*(6), 995–1010.

Helson, R., & Wink, P. (1992). Personality change in women from the early 40s to the early 50s. *Psychology and Aging, 7,* 46–55.

Herriott, E. (2000). Elements of entrepreneurial success: An exploratory study of the links between inner competencies, inner development, and success. *Dissertation Abstracts International, 60*(12), 6398B. Retrieved from ProQuest Dissertations and Theses database. (AAT 9956511)

Hewlett, D. C. (2004). A qualitative study of postautonomous ego development: The bridge between postconventional and transcendent ways of being. *Dissertation Abstracts International, 65*(2), 1050B. Retrieved from ProQuest Dissertations and Theses database. (AAT 3120900)

Hoare, C. (2002). *Erikson on development in adulthood: New insights from the unpublished papers.* New York: Oxford University Press.

Hofer, J., & Chasiotis, A. (2003). Congruence of life goals and implicit motives as predictors of life satisfaction: Cross-cultural implications of a study of Zambian male adolescents. *Motivation and Emotion, 27*(3), 251–272.

Hoge, D., & Petrillo, G. (1978). Development of religious thinking in adolescence: A test of Goldmann's theories. *Journal for the Scientific Study of Religion, 17*, 139–154.

Holt, R. R. (1980). Loevinger's measure of ego development: Reliability and national norms for male and female short forms. *Journal of Personality and Social Psychology, 39*, 909–920.

Hothersall, D. (2003). *History of psychology.* Columbus, OH: McGraw-Hill.

Hutsebaut, D. (1995). *Een zekere onzekerheid: Jongeren en geloof.* Leuven, Belgium: Acco.

Hutsebaut, D. (1996). Post-critical belief: A new approach to the religious attitude problem. *Journal of Empirical Theology, 9*(2), 48–66.

Hutsebaut, D. (1997a). Identity statuses, ego integration, God representation, and religious cognitive styles. *Journal of Empirical Theology, 10*(1), 39–54.

Hutsebaut, D. (1997b). *Structure of religious attitude in function of socialization pattern.* Paper presented at the sixth European Symposium on Psychology and Religion, Barcelona, Spain.

Huxley, A. (1962). *The perennial philosophy.* Cleveland, OH: The World Publishing.

Hy, L., & Loevinger, J. (1996). *Measuring ego development* (2nd ed.). Mahwah, NJ: Erlbaum.

James, J. B., & Zarrett, N. (2006). Ego integrity in the lives of older women. *Journal of Adult Development, 13*(2), 61–75.

James, W. (1961). *The varieties of religious experience.* New York: Macmillan. (Original work published 1902)

James, W. (1981). *The principles of psychology.* Cambridge, MA: Harvard University Press. (Original work published 1890)

John, O. P., Pals, J. L., & Westenberg, P. M. (1998). Personality prototypes and ego development: Conceptual similarities and relations in adult women. *Journal of Personality and Social Psychology, 74*, 1093–1108.

Joiner, B., & Josephs, S. (2007). *Leadership agility: Five levels of mastery for anticipating and initiating change.* San Francisco: Jossey-Bass/Wiley.

Jones, A., & Crandall, R. (1986). Validation of a Short Index of Self-Actualization. *Personality and Social Psychology Bulletin, 12*(1), 63–73.

Jurich, J., & Holt, R. (1987). Effects of modified instructions on the Washington University Sentence Completion Test of Ego Development. *Journal of Personality Assessment, 51*, 186–193.

Kamminger, D., & Rollett, B. (1996). *The Vienna religious judgment coding manual.* Unpublished manuscript, University of Vienna, Austria.

Kampis, G. (1991). *Self-modifying systems in biology and cognitive science.* New York: Pergamon.

Kashdan, T. B., Biswas-Diener, R., & King, L. A. (2008). Reconsidering happiness: The costs of distinguishing between hedonics and eudaimonia. *Journal of Positive Psychology*, 3(4), 219–233.

Kasser, T., & Ryan, R. M. (1993). A dark side of the American dream: Correlates of financial success as a central life aspiration. *Journal of Personality and Social Psychology*, 65, 410–422.

Kauffman, S. (1995). *At home in the universe: The search for the laws of self-organization and complexity*. New York: Oxford University Press.

Kegan, R. (1982). *The evolving self: Problem and process in human development*. Cambridge, MA: Harvard University Press.

Kegan, R. (1994). *In over our heads: The mental demands of modern life*. Cambridge, MA: Harvard University Press.

Keller, M., & Edelstein, W. (1991). The development of socio-moral meaning making: Domains, categories, and perspective-taking. In W. M. Kurtines & J. L. Gewirtz (Eds.), *Handbook of moral behavior and development* (Vol. 2, pp. 89–114). Hillsdale, NJ: Erlbaum.

Kellogg, R. (1969). *Analyzing children's art*. Palo Alto, CA: National Press Books.

Kelly, E. F., Kelly, E. W., Crabtree, A., Gauld, A., Grosso, M., & Greyson, B. (2007). *Irreducible mind: Toward a psychology for the 21st century*. New York: Rowman & Littlfield.

Kelly, S. (1999). The complexity of consciousness and the consciousness of complexity. *Proceedings of the 43rd Annual Conference of the International Society for the Systems Sciences*. Pocklington, York, UK: International Society for the Systems Sciences.

King, L. A. (2001). The hard road to the good life: The happy, mature person [Special issue on Positive Psychology]. *The Journal of Humanistic Psychology*, 41, 51–72.

King, L. A., & Hicks, J. A. (2006). Narrating the self in the past and the future: Implications for maturity. *Research in Human Development*, 3, 121–138.

King, L. A., & Hicks, J. A. (2007a). Lost and found possible selves: Goals, development and well-being. In M. Rossiter (Ed.), *Possible selves and adult learning: Perspectives and potential* (pp. 27–38). San Francisco: Jossey-Bass/Wiley.

King, L. A., & Hicks, J. A. (2007b). Whatever happened to "what might have been"? Regret, happiness, and maturity. *American Psychologist*, 62, 625–636.

King, L. A., & Noelle, S. S. (2005). Happy, mature, and gay: Intimacy, power, and difficult times in coming out stories. *Journal of Research in Personality*, 39, 278–298.

King, L. A., & Raspin, C. (2004). Lost and found possible selves, subjective well-being, and ego development in divorced women. *Journal of Personality*, 72, 603–632.

King, L. A., Scollon, C. K., Ramsey, C. M., & Williams, T. (2000). Stories of life transition: Happy endings, subjective well-being, and ego development in parents of children with Down Syndrome. *Journal of Research in Personality, 34,* 509–536.

King, L. A., & Smith, N. G. (2004). Gay and straight possible selves: Goals, identity, subjective well-being, and personality development. *Journal of Personality, 72,* 967–994.

King, L. A., & Smith, S. N. (2005). Happy, mature, and gay: Intimacy, power, and difficult times in coming out stories. *Journal of Research in Personality, 39,* 278–298.

King, P. M., & Kitchener, K. S. (1994). Developing reflective judgment: Understanding and promoting intellectual growth and critical thinking in adolescents and adults. San Francisco: Jossey-Bass.

Knapp, R. R. (1990). *Handbook for the Personal Orientation Inventory.* San Diego, CA: EdITS. (Original work published 1976)

Kohlberg, L. (1969). Stage and sequence: The cognitive developmental approach to socialization. In D. A. Goslin (Ed.), *Handbook of socialization theory and research* (pp. 348–480). Chicago: Rand McNally.

Kohlberg, L. (1981). *Essays on moral development: Vol. 1. The philosophy of moral development.* San Francisco: Harper San Francisco.

Kohlberg, L., Boyd, D. R., & Levine, C. (1986). Die Wiederkehr der sechsten Stufe: Gerechtigkeit, Wohlwollen und der Standpunkt der Moral. In W. Edelstein & G. Nunner-Winkler (Eds.), *Zur Bestimmung der Moral* (pp. 205–240). Frankfurt/M.: Suhrkamp.

Kohlberg, L., Levine, C., & Hewer, A. (1984). The current formulation of the theory. In L. Kohlberg (Ed.), *The psychology of moral development* (pp. 213–386). San Francisco: Harper & Row.

Kottler, J., & Hazler, R. J. (1996). Impaired counselors: The dark side brought into light. *The Journal of Humanistic Education and Development, 34,* 98–107.

Krettenauer, T. (2004). Metaethical cognition and epistemic reasoning development in adolescence. *International Journal of Behavioral Development, 28,* 461–470.

Krettenauer, T., & Eichler, D. (2006). Adolescents' self-attributed moral emotions following a moral transgression: Relations with delinquency, confidence in moral judgment, and age. *British Journal of Developmental Psychology, 24,* 489–506.

Krettenauer, T., Hofmann, V., Ullrich, M., & Edelstein, W. (2003). Behavioral problems in childhood and adolescence as predictors of ego-level attainment in early adulthood. *Merrill-Palmer Quarterly, 49,* 85–105.

Krettenauer, T., Malti, T., & Sokol, B. W. (2008). The development of moral emotions and the happy-victimizer phenomenon: A critical review of theory and application. *European Journal of Developmental Science, 2,* 221–225.

Krippner, S. (2000). The epistemology and technologies of shamanic states of consciousness. *Journal of Consciousness Studies, 7,* 93–118.

Kroger, J. (2008). *The convergence of self, ego, and identity during late adolescence: A Rasch analysis.* Retrieved from the University of Leiden,

Developmental Psychology, Faculty of Social Sciences Web site: http://www.ontw.psychologie.leidenuniv.nl/personality-development/index.php3?m=16&c=18&garb=0.83595722973511&session=On 5.5.2008

Spike Lee's panoramic view of a culture in a color bind. *Newsweek*, pp. 44–47.

Labouvie-Vief, G. (2000). Affect complexity and views of the transcendent. In M. Miller & P. Young-Eisendrath (Eds.), *The psychology of mature spirituality* (pp. 103–119). London: Routledge.

Labouvie-Vief, G. (2005). Emerging structures of adult thought. In J. J. Arnett & J. L. Tanner (Eds.), *Emerging adults in America: Coming of age in the 21st century*. Washington, DC: American Psychological Association.

Lambie, G.W. (2007). The contribution of ego development level to burnout for school counselors: Implications for professional school counseling. *Journal of Counseling & Development, 85*, 82–88.

Lasker, H. (1978). Ego development and motivation: A cross-cultural cognitive-developmental analysis of achievement. *Dissertation Abstracts International, 39*(4), 2013B. Retrieved from ProQuest Dissertations and Theses database. (AAT T-26888)

Laszlo, E. (1987). *Evolution: The grand synthesis*. Boston: Shambhala.

Lefancois, R., Leclerc, G., Dube, M., Herbert, R., & Gaulin, P. (1997). The development and validation of a short self-report measure of self-actualization. *Social Behavior and Personality, 25*(4), 353–366.

Leonard, G., & Murphy, M. (1995). *The life we are given: A long-term program for realizing the potential of our body, mind, heart, and soul*. New York: Jeremy P. Tarcher/Putnam.

Levenson, M. R., & Crumpler, C. (1996). Three models of adult development. *Human Development, 39*, 135–149.

Lifton, J. L. (1993). *The Protean self: Human resilience in an age of fragmentation*. New York: Basic Books.

Loevinger, J. (1976). *Ego development: Conceptions and theories*. San Francisco: Jossey-Bass.

Loevinger, J. (1979). Construct validity of the Sentence Completion Test of Ego Development. *Applied Psychological Measurement, 3*, 281–311.

Loevinger, J. (1997). Stages of personality development. In R. Hogan, J. Johnson, & S. Briggs (Eds.), *Handbook of personality psychology* (pp. 199–208). Boston: Academic Press.

Loevinger, J. (1998a). Completing a life sentence. In P. M. Westenberg, A. Blasi, & L. Cohn (Eds.), *Personality development: Theoretical, empirical and clinical investigations of Loevinger's conception of ego development* (pp. 347–354). Mahwah, NJ: Erlbaum.

Loevinger, J. (Ed.). (1998b). Reliability and validity of the SCT. In J. Loevinger (Ed.), *Technical foundations for measuring ego development* (pp. 29–41). Mahwah, NJ: Erlbaum.

Loevinger, J. (Ed.). (1998c). *Technical foundations for measuring ego development: The Washington University Sentence Completion Test*. Mahwah, NJ: Erlbaum.

Loevinger, J., Cohn, L. D., Bonneville, L. P., Redmore, C. D., Streich, D. D., & Sargent, M. (1985). Ego development in college. *Journal of Personality and Social Psychology, 48,* 947–962.

Loevinger, J., & Wessler R. (1970). *Measuring ego development: Vol. 1. Construction and use of a Sentence Completion Test.* San Francisco: Jossey-Bass.

Loevinger J., Wessler R., & Redmore, C. (1976). *Measuring ego development: Vol. 2. Scoring manual for women and girls.* San Francisco: Jossey-Bass.

Lourenço, O., & Machado, A. (1996). In defense of Piaget's theory: A reply to 10 common criticism. *Psychological Review, 103,* 143–164.

Lovejoy, A. (1964). *The great chain of being.* Cambridge, MA: Harvard University Press.

Lovelock, J. E. (1988). *Ages of Gaia.* New York: W.W. Norton.

Lovelock, J. E., & Margulis, L. (1974). Biological modulation of the earth's atmosphere. *Icarus, 21,* 471.

Lubinski, D., & Humphreys, L. G. (1997). Incorporating general intelligence into epidemiology and the social sciences. *Intelligence, 24,* 159–201.

Lutz, A., Dunne, J., & Davidson, R. (2007). Meditation and the neuroscience of consciousness. In P. Zelazo, M. Moscovitch, & E. Thompson (Eds.), *Cambridge handbook of consciousness.* Cambridge, MA: Cambridge University Press.

Maguire, E. A., Woollett, K., & Spiers, H. J. (2006). London taxi drivers and bus drivers: A structural MRI and neuropsychological analysis. *Hippocampus, 16,* 1091–1101.

Maharishi Mahesh Yogi. (1963). *Science of being and art of living.* New York: Penguin Books.

Maharishi Mahesh Yogi. (1969). *On the Bhagavad-Gita: A new translation and commentary with Sanskrit text—Chapters 1 to 6.* Baltimore, MD: Penguin/Arkana.

Maharishi Mahesh Yogi. (1976). *Creating an ideal society: A global undertaking.* Rheinweiler, Germany: MERU Press.

Maharishi Mahesh Yogi. (1986). *Thirty years around the world: Dawn of the Age of Enlightenment.* Vlodrop, The Netherlands: Maharishi Vedic University Press.

Maharishi Mahesh Yogi. (1995). *Maharishi University of Management: Wholeness on the move.* Vlodrop, The Netherlands: Maharishi Vedic University Press.

Maharishi Mahesh Yogi. (1999). *Celebrating perfection in education.* Vlodrop, The Netherlands: MERU Press.

Manners, J., & Durkin, K. (2000). Processes involved in adult ego development: A conceptual framework. *Developmental Review, 20,* 475–513.

Manners, J., & Durkin, K. (2001). A critical review of the validity of ego development theory and its measurement. *Journal of Personality Assessment, 77*(3), 541–567.

Manners, J., Durkin, K., & Nesdale, A. (2004). Promoting advanced ego development among adults. *Journal of Adult Development, 11*, 19–27.

Manz, C., & Neck, C. (2003). *Mastering self-leadership: Empowering yourself for personal excellence* (3rd ed.). Upper Saddle River, NJ: Prentice Hall.

Marko, P. W. (2006). Exploring facilitative agents that allow ego development to occur. *Dissertation Abstracts International, 67*(4), 2260B. Retrieved from ProQuest Dissertations and Theses Database. (AAT 3217527)

Maslach, C. (2003). Job burnout: New directions in research and intervention. *Current Directions in Psychological Science, 12*, 189–192.

Maslach, C., & Jackson, S. E. (1996). Maslach Burnout Inventory-Human Service Survey (MBI-HSS). In C. Maslach, S. E. Jackson & M. P. Leiter (Eds.), *Maslach Burnout Inventory manual* (3rd ed., pp. 3–17). Palo Alto, CA: Consulting Psychologists Press.

Maslow, A. H. (1968). *Towards a psychology of being*. New York: Van Nostrand Reinhold.

Maslow, A. H. (1970). *Motivation and personality* (2nd ed.). New York: Harper & Row. (Original work published 1954)

Maslow, A. H. (1971). *The farther reaches of human nature*. New York: Penguin.

Maslow, A. H. (1976). *The farther reaches of human nature* (2nd ed.). New York: Penguin.

Mason, L. I., Alexander, C. N., Travis, F. T., Marsh, G., Orme-Johnson, D. W., Gackenbach, J., et al. (1997). Electrophysiological correlates of higher states of consciousness during sleep in long-term practitioners of the Transcendental Meditation program. *Sleep, 20*(2), 102–110.

Masters, R. E. L. (2002). *Swimming where madmen drown: Travelers tales from inner space*. Maui, HI: Inner Ocean Publishing.

Masters, R. E. L., & Houston, J. (1966). *The varieties of psychedelic experience*. New York: Holt, Rinehart, Winston.

Maturana, H. R., Varela, F. J., & Uribe, R. (1974). Autopoiesis: The organization of living systems, its characterization and model. *Biosystems, 5*, 187–196.

McAdams, D. P. (1985). *Power, intimacy, and the life story: Personological inquiries into identity*. New York: Guilford.

McAdams, D. P. (1998). Ego, trait, identity. In P. M. Westenberg, A. Blasi, & L. Cohn (Eds.), *Personality development: Theoretical, empirical, and clinical investigations of Loevinger's conception of ego development* (pp. 27–38). Mahwah, NJ: Erlbaum.

McAdams, D. P. (2005). The problem of narrative coherence. *Journal of Constructivist Psychology, 19*, 109–125.

McAdams, D. P. (2006). *The redemptive self: Stories Americans live by*. New York: Oxford University Press.

McAdams, D. P. (2008). Personal narratives and the life story. In O. P. John, R. R. Robins, & L. O. Pervin (Eds.), *Handbook of personality* (3rd ed., pp. 241–261). New York: Guilford.

McAdams, D. P., Bauer, J. J., Sakaeda, A. R., Anyidoho, N. A., Machado, M. A., Magrino-Failla, K., et al. (2006). Continuity and change in the life story: A longitudinal study of autobiographical memories in emerging adulthood. *Journal of Personality, 74*, 1372–1400.

McAdams, D. P., & Logan, R. L. (2007). Creative work, love and the dialectic in selected life stories of academics. In D. P. McAdams, R. Josselson, & A. Lieblich (Eds.), *Identity and story: Creating self in narrative* (pp. 89–108). Washington, DC: American Psychological Association.

McAdams, D. P., Josselson, R., & Lieblich, A. (2007). *Introduction.* In D. P. McAdams, R. Josselson, & A. Lieblich (Eds.), *Identity and story: Creating self in narrative* (pp. 3–11). Washington, DC: American Psychological Association.

McAdams, D. P., Reutzel, K., & Foley, J. M. (1986). Complexity and generativity at mid-life: Relations among social motives, ego development, and adults' plans for the future. *Journal of Personality and Social Psychology, 50*, 800–807.

McCallum, D. (2008). Exploring the implications of a hidden diversity in group relations conference training: A developmental perspective. *Dissertation Abstracts International, 69*(8), A. Retrieved from ProQuest Dissertations and Theses database. (AAT 3327080)

McCann, J. E. (2004). Organizational effectiveness: Changing concepts for changing environments. *Human Resource Planning, 3*, 42–50.

McCauley, C., Drath, W., Palus, C., O'Connor, P., & Baker, B. (2006). The use of constructive-developmental theory to advance the understanding of leadership. *The Leadership Quarterly, 17*, 634–653.

McCrae, R. R., & Costa, P. T. (1980). Openness to experience and ego-level in Loevinger's Sentence Completion Test: Dispositional contributions to developmental models of personality. *Journal of Personality and Social Psychology, 39*(6), 1179–1190.

McEwen, B. S. (1998). Stress, adaptation, and disease. Allostasis and allostatic load. *Annals of New York Academy of Science, 840*, 33–44.

McEwen, B. S. (2006). Sleep deprivation as a neurobiologic and physiologic stressor: Allostasis and allostatic load. *Metabolism, 55*, S20–23.

McGuire, J., Palus, C., & Torbert, W (2007). Toward interdependent organizing and researching. In A. Shani, S. Mohrman, W. H. Pasmore, B. Stymne, & N. Adler (Eds.), *Handbook of collaborative management research* (pp. 123–142). Thousand Oak, CA: Sage.

McIntyre, T. J. (1985). Ego development and counseling: The effect of counselors' and clients' ego development levels upon the expressed empathy and preference of counselors (Doctoral dissertation, Michigan State University, 1985). *Dissertation Abstracts International, 46*(5), 1230A.

McLean, K. C. (2005). Late adolescent identity development: Narrative meaning making and memory telling. *Developmental Psychology, 41*, 683–391.

McLean, K. C. (2008). The emergence of narrative identity. *Social and Personality Psychology Compass, 2*(4), 1685–1702.

Melville, H. (1988). *Moby-Dick, or The Whale*. Northwestern-Newberry Edition of the Writings of Herman Melville 6. Evanston, IL: Northwestern University Press.

Meents, J. (2003). *The magic in adult transformation to a construct-aware worldview: Understanding intuition's influence*. Unpublished doctoral dissertation, University of Calgary, Canada.

Mentkowski, M., & Associates. (2000). *Learning that lasts: Integrating learning, development, and performance in college and beyond*. San Francisco: Jossey-Bass.

Merron, K. (1985). The relationship between ego development and managerial effectiveness under conditions of high uncertainty. *Dissertation Abstracts International, 46*(10), 3090A. Retrieved from ProQuest Dissertation and Theses database. (AAT 8523337)

Merron, K., Fisher, D., & Torbert, W. (1987). Meaning making and management action. *Group and Organizational Studies, 12,* 274–286.

Metcalf, M. (2008, March). "Level 5 leadership": Leadership that transforms organizations and creates sustainable results. *Integral Leadership Review, 2, 25–33.*

Mezirow, J. (2000). *Learning as transformation: Critical perspectives on a theory in progress*. San Francisco: Jossey-Bass.

Miller, M., & Cook-Greuter, S. (1994). From postconventional development to transcendence: Visions and theories. In M. Miller & S. Cook-Greuter (Eds.), *Mature thought and transcendence in adulthood: The further reaches of adult development* (pp. xv–xxxii). Lanham, MD: Rowman & Littlefield.

Molloy, E. (1978). *Toward a new paradigm for the study of the person at work: An empirical extension of Loevinger's theory of ego development*. Unpublished doctoral dissertation, University of Dublin, Ireland.

Montgomery, L. (1996). Tracking the inner tribe: Selves evoked in relational worlds across time. *Dissertation Abstracts International, 57*(9), 5948B. Retrieved from ProQuest Dissertations and Theses database. (AAT 9705491)

Morin, E. (1999). *Homeland earth: A manifesto for the new millennium* (S. M. Kelly & R. LaPointe, Trans.). Cresskill, NJ: Hampton Press.

Morse, M. (with Perry, P.). (1970). *Children of the light: Learning from near-death experiences of children*. New York: Villard Books.

Neimark, E. D. (1985). Moderators of competence: Challenges to the universality of Piagetian theory. In E. D. Neimark, R. De Lisi, & J. L. Newman (Eds.), *Moderators of competence* (pp. 1–14). Hillsdale, NJ: Erlbaum.

Nicolaides, A. (2008). *Learning their way through ambiguity: Explorations of how nine developmentally mature adults make sense of ambiguity. Dissertation Abstracts International, 69*(8)A. Retrieved from ProQuest Dissertations and Theses database. (AAT 3327082)

Nietzsche, F. (1968). *Will to power* (W. Kaufmann, Trans.). New York: Vintage Press.

Noam, G. I. (1998). Solving the ego development-mental health riddle. In P. M. Westenberg, A. Blasi, & L. Cohn (Eds.), *Personality development: Theoretical, empirical, and clinical investigations of Loevinger's conception of ego development* (pp. 271–295). Mahwah, NJ: Erlbaum.

Noam, G. G., Copeland, H. Y., & Jilnina, J. (2006). Social cognition, psychological symptoms, and mental health: The model, evidence, and contribution of ego development. In D. Cichetti & D. J. Cohen (Eds.), *Developmental psychopathology: Vol. 1. Theory and method* (2nd ed., pp. 750–794). Hoboken, NJ: Wiley.

Norbu, N. (1996). *Dzogchen: The self-perfected state.* New York: Snow Lion. (Original work published 1989)

Novy, D. M., & Frances, D. J. (1992). Psychometric properties of the Washington University Sentence Completion Test. *Educational and Psychological Measurements, 52*(4), 1029–1040.

Novy, D. M, Nelson, D. V., Gaa, A., Blumentritt, T., & Hetzel, R. D. (1998). The relationship of cognitive processes and ego development with adjustment to chronic pain. *Psychology, Health & Medicine, 3,* 285–298.

Novy, D. M., Frankiewicz, R. G., Francis, D. J., Liberman, D., Overall, J. E., & Vincent, K. R. (1994). An investigation of the structural validity of Loevinger's model and measure of ego development. *Journal of Personality, 62,* 87–118.

Orme-Johnson, D. W. (1988). The cosmic psyche—an introduction to Maharishi's Vedic psychology: The fulfillment of modern psychology. *Modern Science and Vedic Science, 2*(2), 113–163.

Orme-Johnson, D. W. (2000). An overview of Charles Alexander's contribution to psychology: Developing higher states of consciousness in the individual and society. *Journal of Adult Development, 7,* 199–216.

Oser, F., & Gmunder, P. (1991). *Religious judgment: A developmental approach.* Birmingham, AL: Religious Education Press.

Oser, F., & Reich, H. (Eds.). (1996). *Eingebettet ins Menschsein: Beispiel Religion: Aktuelle psychologische Studien zur Entwicklung von Religiosität.* Lengerich, Germany: Pabst Scientific.

Oser, F. K., Scarlett, W. G., & Bucher, A. (2006). Religious and spiritual development throughout the life span. In W. Damon & R. Lerner (Series Eds.), and W. Damon & R. Lerner (Vol. Eds.), *Handbook of child psychology: Vol. 1. Theoretical models of human development* (pp. 942–998). New York: Wiley.

Oyama, S. (1993). How shall I name thee? The construction of natural selves: The future of developmental theory [Special issue]. *Theory and Psychology, 3,* 471–496.

Page, H. (2005). The impact of ego development on spiritual constructs among Hindu, Buddhist, and Christian renunciates. *Dissertation Abstracts International, 66*(5), 2859B. Retrieved from ProQuest Dissertations and Theses database. (AAT 3174545)

Palombo, S. R. (1999). *The emergent ego: Complexity and coevolution in the psychoanalytic process.* Madison, CT: International Universities Press.

Pals, J. L. (2006a). Constructing the "springboard effect": Causal connections, self-making, and growth within the life story. In D. P. McAdams, R. Josselson & A. Leibich (Eds.), *Identity and story: Creating self in narrative* (pp.175–199). Washington, DC: American Psychological Association.

Pals, J. L. (2006b). Narrative identity processing of difficult life experiences: Pathways of personality development and positive self-transformation in adulthood. *Journal of Personality, 74*(4), 1079–1109.

Parks Daloz, L. A. (2000). Transformational learning for the common good. In J. Mezirow & Associates (Eds.), *Learning as transformation: Critical perspectives on a theory in progress* (pp. 103–123). San Francisco: Jossey-Bass.

Pasupathi, M. (2001). The social construction of the personal past and its implications for adult development. *Psychological Bulletin, 127*, 651–672.

Pasupathi, M., & Alderman, K., & Shaw, D. (2007). Talking the talk: Collaborative remembering and self-perceived experience. *Discourse Processes, 43*, 55–77.

Pasupathi, M., & Mansour, E. (2006). Adult age differences in autobiographical reasoning in narratives. *Developmental Psychology, 42*, 798–808.

Pasupathi, M., Mansour, E., & Brubaker, J. R. (2007). Developing a life story: Constructing relations between self and experience in autobiographical narratives. *Human Development, 50*, 85–110.

Pasupathi, M., Staudinger, U. M., & Baltes, P. B. (2001). Seeds of wisdom: Adolescents' knowledge and judgment about difficult life problems. *Developmental Psychology, 37*, 351–361.

Peatling, J., & Labbs, C. (1975). Cognitive development in pupils in grades four through twelve: The incidence of concrete and abstract and religious thinking. *Character Potential: A Record of Research, 7*, 107–115.

Perry, W. G. (1970). *Forms of intellectual and ethical development in the college years.* New York: Holt, Rinehart, & Winston.

Pfaffenberger, A. (2005). Optimal adult development: An inquiry into the dynamics of growth. *Journal of Humanistic Psychology, 45*(3), 279–301.

Pfaffenberger, A. (2007). Optimal adulthood: The need for a reassessment. *Journal of Humanistic Psychology, 47*(4), 501–523.

Piaget, J. (1952). *The origins of intelligence in children.* New York: Basic Books.

Piaget, J. (1954). *The construction of reality in children.* New York: Basic Books.

Piaget, J. (1965). *The moral judgment of the child.* New York: The Free Press.

Piaget, J. (1970a). Piaget's theory. In P. Mussen (Ed.), *Carmichael's manual of child psychology* (pp. 703–732). New York: Wiley.

Piaget, J. (1970b). *Structuralism.* New York: Basic Books.

Piaget, J. (1972). Intellectual evolution from adolescence to adulthood. *Human Development, 15*, 1–12. (Original work published 1970)

Piaget, J. (1978). *The development of thought.* Oxford, UK: Backwell.

Pierce, B., & Cox, W. (1995). Development of faith and religious understanding in children. *Psychological Reports, 76,* 957–958.

Pines, A. M., & Maslach, C. (1978). Characteristics of staff burnout in mental health settings. *Hospitals and Community Psychiatry, 29,* 233–237.

Powell, R. (Ed.). (1996). *The experience of nothingness: Sri Nisargadatta's talks on realizing the infinite.* San Diego, CA: Blue Dove Press.

Power, C. (1991). Hard versus soft stages of faith and religious development. In J. Fowler, K. Nipkow & F. Schweitzer (Eds.), *Stages of faith and religious development: Implications for church, education, and society.* New York: Crossroad.

Pred, R. (2005). *Onflow: Dynamics of consciousness and experience.* Cambridge, MA: MIT Press.

Prigogine, I., & Stengers, I. (1984). *Order out of chaos: Man's new dialogue with nature.* New York: Bantam.

Raggatt, P. T. E. (2007). Multiplicity and conflict in the dialogic self: A life narrative approach. In D. P. McAdams, R. Josselson, & A. Lieblich (Eds.), *Identity and story: Creating self in narrative* (pp. 15–35). Washington, DC: American Psychological Association.

Reason, P., & Bradbury, H. (2007). *The SAGE handbook of action research: Participatory inquiry and practice.* London: Sage.

Redmore, C., & Loevinger, J. (1979). Ego development in adolescence. *Journal of Youth and Adolescence, 8,* 1–20.

Rest, J. R. (1987). *Guide for the Defining Issues Test.* Minneapolis, MN: Center for the Study of Ethical Development.

Rest, J., Narvaez, D., Bebeau, M. J., & Thoma, S. J. (1999). *Postconventional moral thinking.* Mahwah, NJ: Erlbaum.

Richards, F. A., & Commons, M. L. (1984). Systematic, metasystematic, and cross-paradigmatic reasoning. In M. L. Commons, F. A. Richards & C. Armon (Eds.), *Beyond formal operations* (pp. 92–120). New York: Praeger.

Richards, F. A., & Commons, M. L. (1990). Postformal cognitive-developmental theory and research: A review of its current status. In C. Alexander & E. Langer (Eds.), *Higher stages of human development* (pp. 139–161). New York: Oxford University Press.

Richardson, F. C., Rogers, A., & McCarroll, J. (1998). Toward a dialogical self. *American Behavioral Scientist, 41,* 496–515.

Rock, A., & Krippner, S. (2009). Does the concept of "altered states of consciousness" rest on a mistake? *International Journal of Transpersonal Studies, 26,* 33–40.

Rogers, C. R. (1989). A therapist's view of the good life: The fully functioning person. In H. Kirschenbaum & V. L. Henderson (Eds.), *The Carl Rogers Reader* (pp. 409–420). Boston: Houghton Mifflin.

Rogers, G. (2002). Rethinking moral growth in college and beyond. *Journal of Moral Education, 31*(3), 325–338.

Rooke, D., & Torbert, W. (1998). Organizational transformation as a function of CEOs' developmental stage. *Organization Development Journal, 16,* 11–28.

Ross, M. (1989). Relation of implicit theories to the construction of personal histories. *Psychological Review, 96,* 341–357.

Roth, R. (1994). *TM—Transcendental Meditation.* New York: Donald I. Fine.

Rowan, J. (1990). *Subpersonalities.* New York: Routledge.

Ryan, R. M., & Deci, E. L. (2001). On happiness and human potentials: A review of research on hedonic and eudaimonic well-being. *Annual Review of Psychology, 52,* 141–166.

Ryff, C. D. (1989). Happiness is everything, or is it? Explorations on the meaning of psychological well-being. *Journal of Personality and Social Psychology, 57,* 1069–1081.

Ryff, C. D., & Keyes, C. L. M. (1995). The structure of psychological well-being revisited. *Journal of Personality and Social Psychology, 69,* 719–727.

Ryff, C. D., & Singer, B. (1998). The contours of positive human health. *Psychological Inquiry, 9,* 1–28.

Ryff, C. D., & Singer, B. (2008). Know thyself and become what you are: A eudaimonic approach to psychological well-being. *Journal of Happiness Studies, 9,* 13–39.

Selman, R. L., & Schultz, L. H. (1998). *Making a friend in youth: Developmental theory and pair therapy.* Hawthorne, NY: Aldine de Gruyter.

Shani, A., Mohrman, S., Pasmore, W., Stymne, B., & Adler, N. (2007). *Handbook of collaborative management research.* Los Angeles: Sage.

Shayer, M., Demetriou, A., & Pervez, M. (1988). The structure of scaling of concrete operational thought: Three studies in four countries. *Genetic, Social and General Psychological Monographs, 114,* 309–375.

Shear, J. (2006). *The experience of meditation.* St. Paul, MN: Paragon House.

Sheldon, K. M., & Houser-Marko, L. (2001). Self-concordance, goal attainment, and the pursuit of happiness: Can there be an upward spiral? *Journal of Personality and Social Psychology, 80,* 152–165.

Sheldon, K. M., & Kasser, T. (2001). Getting older, getting better? Personal strivings and psychosocial maturity across the life-span. *Developmental Psychology, 34,* 491–501.

Sheldon, K. M., Kasser, T., Smith, K., & Share, T. (2002). Personal goals and psychological growth: Testing an intervention to enhance goal attainment and personality integration. *Journal of Personality, 70,* 5–31.

Sheldon, K. M., & Lyubomirsky, S. (2006). Achieving sustainable gains in happiness: Change your actions, not your circumstances. *Journal of Happiness Studies, 7,* 55–86.

Shostrom, E. L. (1963). *Personal Orientations Inventory.* San Diego, CA: Educational and Industrial Testing Services.

Shostrom, E. L. (1966). *Personal Orientation Inventory Manual: An inventory for the measurement of self-actualization.* San Diego, CA: EdITS.

Skaggs, J. L. (1999). Burnout in relationship to counselor's use of power: Predicting risk with Machiavellianism. *Dissertation Abstracts International, 60*(4), 1030A. Retrieved from ProQuest Dissertations and Theses database. (AAT 9925121)

Skoe, E. A., & von der Lippe, A. (2002). Ego development and the ethics of care and justice: The relations among them revisited, *Journal of Personality, 70*(4), 485–508.

Smetana, J. G. (2006). Social-cognitive domain theory: Consistencies and variations in children's moral and social judgments. In M. Killen & J. G. Smetana (Eds.), *Handbook of moral development* (pp. 119–153). Mahwah, NJ: Erlbaum.

Smith, H. (1991). *The world's religions.* San Francisco: HarperCollins.

Smith, S. (1980). Ego development and the problems of power and agreement in organizations. *Dissertation Abstracts International, 41*(5), 1962B. Retrieved from Proquest Dissertations and Theses database. (AAT 8023872)

Snarey, J. (1986). The relationship of social-moral development with cognitive and ego development: A cross-cultural study. *Cross-Cultural Research, 20,* 132–146.

Snarey, J., & Keljo, K. (1991). In a Gemeinschaft voice: The cross-cultural expansion of moral development theory. In W. M. Kurtines & J. L. Gewirtz (Eds.), *Handbook of moral behavior and development* (Vol. 2, pp. 395–424). Hillsdale, NJ: Erlbaum.

Solé, R., & Goodwin, B. (2000). *Signs of life: How complexity pervades biology.* New York: Basic Books.

Sowell, E. R., Thompson, P. M., Leonard, C. M., Welcome, S. E., Kan, E. & Toga, A. W. (2004). Longitudinal mapping of cortical thickness and brain growth in normal children. *Journal of Neuroscience, 24,* 8223–8231.

Spence, J. (1992). *Hear our voices: A phenomenological study of the transpersonal (spiritual) emergent experienced in American culture, its effects, helps and hindrances, and implications.* Unpublished doctoral dissertation, Union Institute, Cincinnati, Ohio.

Spilka, B., Hood, R., Hunsberger, B., & Gorsuch, R. (2003). *The psychology of religion: An empirical approach.* New York: Guilford.

Stackert, R. A., & Bursik, K. (2006). Ego development and the therapeutic goal-setting capacities of mentally ill adults. *American Journal of Psychotherapy, 60*(4), 357–374.

Staudinger, U. M., & Kunzmann, U. (2005). Positive adult personality development: Adjustment and/or growth? *European Psychologist, 10,* 320–329.

Stevens-Long, J. (2000). The prism self: Multiplicity on the path to transcendence. In M. Miller & P. Young-Eisendrath (Eds.), *The psychology of mature spirituality* (pp. 160–174). London: Routledge.

Stitz, J. (2004). Intimacy and differentiation in couples at postconventional levels of ego development. *Dissertation Abstracts International, 65*(11), 6074B. Retrieved from Proquest Dissertations and Theses database. (AAT 3153925)

Streib, H. (1991). *Hermeneutics of symbol, metaphor, and narrative in faith development theory.* Frankfurt: Peter Lang.

Streib, H. (1997). Religion als Stilfrage: Zur Revision struktureller Differenzi-eurung von Religion im Blick auf die Analyse der pluralistisch-religiösen Lage der Gegenwart. *Archiv für Religionspsychologie, 22*, 48–69.

Streib, H., Keller, B., & Csoff, R.-M. (2007). *The Bielefeld-based cross-cultural research on de-conversion* (Vols. 1 & 2). Bielefeld, Germany: Center for Biographical Studies in Religion, University of Bielefeld.

Studstill, R. (2002). Systems theory and unity of mystical traditions: A com-parative analysis of rDzogs-chen and Rhineland mystics. *Dissertation Abstracts International, 63*(3), 984B. Retrieved from Proquest Disserta-tions and Theses database. (AAT 3047765)

Sumerlin, J. R., & Bunderick, C. M. (1996). Brief Index of Self-Actualization: A measure of Maslow's model. *Journal of Social Behavior and Personal-ity, 11*(2), 253–271.

Sutton, P. M., & Swenson, C. H. (1983). The reliability and concurrent valid-ity of alternative methods of assessing ego development. *Journal of Personality Assessment, 47*(5), 468–475.

Tamminen, K., & Nurmi, K. (1995). Developmental theory and religious experience. In R. Hood Jr. (Ed.), *Handbook of religious experience* (pp. 269–311). Birmingham, AL: Religious Education Press.

Tappan, M. (1989). Stories lived and stories told: The narrative structure of late adolescent moral development. *Human Development, 32*, 300–315.

Tappan, M. (1992). Texts and contexts: Language, culture, and the development of moral functioning. In L. T. Winegar & J. Valsiner (Eds.), *Children's development within social contexts: Metatheoretical, theoretical, and methodological issues* (pp. 93–122). Hillsdale, NJ: Erlbaum.

Tart, C. T. (1972). States of consciousness and state-specific sciences. *Science, 176*, 1203–1210.

Tart, C. T. (1975). *States of consciousness*. New York: E.P. Dutton.

Thatcher, R. W., Krause, P. J., & Hrybyk, M. (1986). Cortico-cortical associa-tions and EEG coherence: A two-compartmental model. *Electroencepha-lography and Clinical Neurophysiology, 64*, 123–143.

Thorne, A. (2000). Personal memory telling and personality development. *Personality and Social Psychology Review, 4*, 45–56.

Thurman, R. A. F. (Trans.). (1994). *The Tibetan book of the dead*. New York: Bantam.

Tigunait, R. (1983). *Seven systems of Indian philosophy*. Honesdale, PA: Himalayan.

Toga, A. W., Thompson, P. M., & Sowell, E. R. (2006). Mapping brain matu-ration. *Trends in Neuroscience, 29*, 148–159.

Torbert, B., & Associates. (2004). *Action inquiry: The secret of timely and transforming leadership*. San Francisco: Berrett-Koehler.

Torbert, W. (1972). *Learning from experience: Toward consciousness*. New York: Columbia University Press.

Torbert, W. (1976). *Creating a community of inquiry*. London: Wiley Inter-science.

Torbert, W. (1987). *Managing the corporate dream*. Homewood, IL: Dow Jones-Irwin.

Torbert, W. (1989). Leading organizational transformation. In R. Woodman & W. Pasmore (Eds), *Research in organizational change and development* (Vol. 3, pp. 83–116). Greenwich, CT: Jai Press.

Torbert, W. (1991). *The power of balance: Transforming self, society, and scientific inquiry.* Thousand Oaks, CA: Sage.

Torbert, W. (1994). Cultivating post-formal development: Higher stages and contrasting interventions. In M. E. Miller & S. Cook-Greuter (Eds), *Transcendence and mature thought in adulthood* (pp. 181–203). Lanham, MD: Rowman & Littlefield.

Torbert, W. (2000a). A developmental approach to social science: A model for analyzing Charles Alexander's scientific contributions. *Journal of Adult Development, 7*, 255–267.

Torbert, W. (2000b). Transforming social science: Integrating quantitative, qualitative, and action research. In F. Sherman & W. Torbert (Eds), *Transforming social inquiry, transforming social action* (pp. 67–92). Boston: Kluwer.

Torbert, W. (2004). *Action inquiry. The secret of timely and transforming leadership*. San Francisco: Berrett-Koehler.

Torbert, W., & D. Fisher (1992). Autobiographical awareness as a catalyst for managerial and organizational development. *Management Education and Development, 23*, 184–198.

Travis, F., Arenander, A., & DuBois, D. (2004). Psychological and physiological characteristics of a proposed object-referral/self-referral continuum of self-awareness. *Consciousness and Cognition, 13*, 401–420.

Travis, F., & Pearson, C. (2000). Pure consciousness: Distinct phenomenological and physiological correlates of "consciousness itself." *The International Journal of Neuroscience, 100*, 1–10.

Travis, F., Tecce, J., Arenander, A., & Wallace, R. K. (2002). Patterns of EEG coherence, power, and contingent negative variation characterize the integration of transcendental and waking states. *Biological Psychology, 61*, 293–319.

Travis, F., Tecce, J. J., & Guttman, J. (2000). Cortical plasticity, contingent negative variation, and transcendent experiences during practice of the Transcendental Meditation technique. *Biological Psychology, 55*(1), 41–55.

Turiel, E. (1998). The development of morality. In W. Damon & R. Lerner (Series Eds.) & W. Damon, R. Lerner & N. Eisenberg (Vol. Eds.), *Handbook of child psychology: Vol. 3. Social, emotional, and personality development* (6th ed., pp. 863–932). New York: Wiley.

Underhill, E. (1929). *The house of the soul*. Minneapolis, MN: Seabury Press.

Vaillant, G. E. (1977). *Adaptation to life*. Cambridge, MA: Harvard University Press.

Vaillant, G. E., & McCullough, L. (1987). The Washington University Sentence Completion Test compared with other measures of adult ego development. *American Journal of Psychiatry, 144*, 1189–1194.

van Lommel, P., van Wees, R., Meyers, V., & Elfferich, I. (2001). Near-death experience in survivors of cardiac arrest: A prospective study in the Netherlands. *The Lancelot, 358*(9298), 2039–2045.

Vandenplas-Holper, C. (2003). *Le développement psychologique à l'age adulte et pendant la viellesse.* Paris: Presses Universitaires de France.

Vasudev, J. (1994). Justice and the unity of life: Postconventional morality from an Indian perspective. In M. E. Miller & S. R. Cook-Greuter (Eds.), *Transcendence and mature thought in adulthood: The further reaches of adult development* (pp. 127–154). Boston: Rowman & Littlefield.

Wade, J. (1996). *Changes of mind: A holonomic theory of the evolution of consciousness.* Albany: State University of New York Press.

Wade, J. (2004). *Transcendent sex: When lovemaking opens the veil.* New York: Paragon.

Walker, L. J., & Hennig, K. (2004). Differing conceptions of moral exemplarity: Just, brave, and caring. *Journal of Personality and Social Psychology, 86,* 629–647.

Walsh, R. (2001). Shamanic experiences. *Journal of Humanistic Psychology, 41*(3), 31–52.

Walsh, R., & Vaughan, F. (Eds.). (1993). *Paths beyond ego.* New York: Jeremy P. Tarcher/Putnam.

Wang, W. (2004). The emergence of cultural self-constructs: Autobiographical memory and self-description in European-American and Chinese children. *Developmental Psychology, 40,* 3–15.

Washburn, M. (1988). *The ego and the dynamic ground.* Albany: State University of New York Press.

Weiss, A. S. (1986). Shostrom's Personal Orientation Inventory: Arguments against its basic validity. *Personality and Individual Differences, 8*(6), 895–903.

Weiss, A. S. (1991). The measurement of self-actualization: The quest for the test may be as challenging as the search for the self. *Journal of Social Behavior and Personality, 6*(5), 265–290.

Welwood, J. (2000). Psychological work in the service of spiritual development. In G. Watson, S. Batchelor, & G. Claxton (Eds.), *The psychology of awakening* (pp. 137–166). York Beach, ME: Samuel Weiser.

Westenberg, P. M., Blasi, A., & Cohn, L. (Eds.). (1998). *Personality development: Theoretical, empirical and clinical investigations of Loevinger's conception of ego development.* Mahwah, NJ: Erlbaum.

Westenberg, P. M., & Block, J. (1993). Ego development and individual differences in personality. *Journal of Personality and Social Psychology, 65,* 792–800.

Westenberg, P. M., & Gjerde, P. F. (1999). Ego development during the transition from adolescence to young adulthood: A 9-year longitudinal study. *Journal of Research in Personality, 33,* 233–252

White, D. R., & Hellerich, G. (1998). *Labyrinths of the mind: The self in the postmodern age.* Albany: State University of New York Press.

White, M. S. (1985). Ego development in adult women. *Journal of Personality, 53,* 561–574.

Whitson, E. R., & Olczal, P. V. (1991). The use of the POI in clinical situations: An evaluation. *Journal of Social Behavior and Personality, 6*(5), 291–310.

Wilber, K. (1980). *The atman project.* Wheaton, IL: Quest.

Wilber, K. (1986). The spectrum of development. In K. Wilber, J. Engler, & D. P. Brown (Eds.), *Transformations of consciousness* (pp. 65–106). Boston: Shambhala.

Wilber, K. (1995). *Sex, ecology and spirituality.* Boston: Shambhala.

Wilber, K. (1996). *A brief history of everything.* Boston: Shambhala.

Wilber, K. (1998a). *Integral psychology.* Boston: Shambhala.

Wilber, K. (1998b). *The marriage of sense and soul.* New York: Random House.

Wilber, K. (1999). Spirituality and developmental lines: Are there stages? *Journal of Transpersonal Psychology, 31*(1), 1–10.

Wilber, K. (2000a). *Integral psychology: Consciousness, spirit, psychology, therapy.* Boston: Shambhala.

Wilber, K. (2000b). *A theory of everything.* Boston: Shambhala.

Wilber, K. (2000c). *Ken Wilber online.* Retrieved March 18, 2008, from http://wilber.shambhala.com/

Wilber, K. (2002). *Childhood spirituality; Sidebar D.* Retrieved August 8, 2009, from http://wilber.shambhala.com/html/books/boomeritis/sidebar_dindex.cfm/

Wilber, K. (2005). *A sociable god: Toward a new understanding of religion.* Boston: Shambhala.

Wilber, K. (2006). *Integral spirituality: A startling new role for religion in the modern and postmodern world.* Boston: Integral Books.

Wilber, K., Engler, J., & Brown, D. (1986). *Transformations of consciousness: Conventional and contemplative perspectives on development.* Boston: Shambhala.

Winkler, M., Combs, A., Dezern, D., Alstott, T., Burnham, J., Rand, B., et al. (1991, August). *Cyclicity in moods: A dynamical systems analysis.* Paper presented at the Inaugural meeting of The Society for Chaos Theory in Psychology, San Francisco.

Winnicott, D. W. (1971). *Playing and reality.* New York: Basic Books.

Woike, B., Lavezzary, E., & Barsky, J. (2001). The influence of implicit motives on memory processes. *Journal of Personality and Social Psychology, 81,* 935–945.

Wulff, D. (1997). *Psychology of religion: Classic and contemporary views.* New York: Wiley.

Young, A. (1998). Psychological maturity in women during later adulthood: Ego development and adjustment. *Dissertation Abstracts International, 59*(7), 3755B. Retrieved from ProQuest Dissertations and Theses database. (AAT 9840678)

Young-Eisendrath, P. (1997). The self in analysis. *Journal of Analytic Psychology, 42,* 157–166.

Zelazo, P., Moscovitch, M., & Thompson, E. (2007). *The Cambridge handbook of consciousness*. Cambridge, MA: Cambridge University Press.

List of Contributors

Jack J. Bauer, PhD, is associate professor of psychology and currently holds the Roesch Chair in the Social Sciences at the University of Dayton. His research explores narrative self-identity, growth motivation, and eudaimonic personality development. His work has been published in the leading journals of both personality and developmental psychology. He is associate editor of the *Journal of Personality and Social Psychology: Personality Processes and Individual Differences* and serves on the editorial board of the *Journal of Research in Personality.* He is the co-editor of *Transcending Self-Interest: Psychological Explorations of the Quiet Ego* (2008, APA Books). Before entering psychology he was editor of a newspaper in northern Michigan.

Tracie L. Blumentritt, PhD, is associate professor of psychology at the University of Wisconsin-La Crosse. Her doctoral dissertation and early published work explored various psychometric properties of Loevinger's Sentence Completion Test (SCT) and the relation of ego development to adjustment. More recently, her work has centered on examining the psychometric equivalence of various measures of personality and psychopathology among ethnic minority groups. She also is interested in the dynamics of prejudice formation and stereotype processing among ethnic minority individuals. However, she continues to maintain an avid interest and, indeed, even fascination with Loevinger's model and measure of ego development.

Sue Brown, PhD, from Australia, earned her master's in educational administration in 1987 at Maharishi University of Management (MUM) in Iowa. She has taught in and helped establish consciousness-based education programs and institutions in many countries, including Vietnam, Cambodia, Russia, and Australia. Currently, she is on faculty at MUM, and is completing doctoral work, which includes analysis of SCT protocols for 150 freshman–senior pairs and growth of higher states of consciousness, from the Vedic perspective of Maharishi Mahesh Yogi. She has trained with Susanne Cook-Greuter and has begun to work as a consultant scoring SCT protocols.

Allan Combs, PhD, is a professor of transformative studies at the California Institute of Integral Studies and professor emeritus of psychology at the University of North Carolina-Asheville. His background is in consciousness studies, neuropsychology, and systems science. He is author of more than 100 articles, chapters, and books on consciousness and the brain. Professor Combs is director of the Center for Consciousness Studies at the Integral University, co-founder of the Integral Foundation and The Society for Chaos Theory in Psychology and the Life Sciences, member of The General Evolution Research Group, the Integral Institute, the Forge Guild and the Club of Budapest. He is co-editor of the *Journal of Conscious Evolution*, associate editor of *Dynamical Psychology*, and serves on the editorial boards of the *Journal of Humanistic Psychology* and *Science & Consciousness Review.*

Susanne R. Cook-Greuter, EdD, is an internationally known authority on mature adult development with a doctorate in human development and psychology from Harvard University. She is a founding member of the Integral Institute, a think tank lead by Ken Wilber and a co-director of the Integral Psychology Center. She leads workshops throughout the world in ego-development theory and its applications. Dr. Cook-Greuter consults to various projects in research design (integrated qualitative and quantitative analyses) and in applying a developmental perspective to individual and organizational learning and change efforts. She is the principal of a woman-led management consulting and coaching firm. Cook-Greuter and Associates offers the SCTi-MAP and feedback to individuals, teams, and organizations.

James Meredith Day, PhD, is a professor of psychology and educational sciences; Human Development Laboratory and Psychology of Religion Research Center, Universite catholique de Louvain, Louvain-la-Neuve, Belgium, and co-editor of the *Archiv fur Religionspsychologie: The Journal of the International Association for the Psychology of Religion.* His work on moral judgment and moral action, the role of religious elements in moral decision making, and the psychology of religious experience and development, have been published in *Human Development, American Psychologist, New Directions for Child Development, World Futures: The Journal of General Evolution, Journal of Counseling* *and Development, The Handbook of Adult Development,* and other scientific publications, including *The Structure and Development of Conscience* (Psychology Press, 2009), and four books of which he is co-editor. He holds degrees in religion (Oberlin), psychology (Harvard & Pennsylvania), and theology (Cambridge), is a licensed psychologist practicing at PsyGroup, Brussels, and Priest in the Church of England, Pro-Cathedral of the Holy Trinity, Brussels.

Dennis Heaton, PhD, studied humanistic psychology at the State University of West Georgia with colleagues of Abraham Maslow, and subsequently trained with His Holiness Maharishi Mahesh Yogi. He is presently co-director of the PhD in management program at MUM. Dr. Heaton collaborated with Charles Alexander, co-editor of the seminal book *Higher Stages of Human Development,* on a chapter "Advanced Human Development in the Vedic Psychology of Maharishi Mahesh Yogi." He is co-author of a 2005 research article presenting unprecedented advances in postconventional development in practitioners of the Transcendental Meditation program. His article relating leadership development to development of consciousness will appear in the *Spirituality in Business: Current Theory and Practice and Future Directions* to be published by Palgrave Macmillan.

Elaine Herdman Barker, MSc, is a senior advisor to Harthill, (UK) and a faculty member of De Baak Management Centre (Netherlands). She has researched, lectured, and coached extensively in the field of action logics. Senior scorer of the Leadership Development Profile and research associate of Bill Torbert and David Rooke, she is developing the Leadership Development Framework to identify and support high-potential leaders across action logics. Much of her work centers on identifying, with individuals and multinationals, the constraints that serve to limit in-action postconventional thinking—and how, where helpful, to remove those obstacles.

Bill Joiner, PhD, is co-author of *Leadership Agility: Five Levels of Mastery for Anticipating and Initiating Change,* winner of the Integral Leadership Review's Readers' Choice Award for best leadership book published in 2007. He is also president of ChangeWise, a consulting firm that assists leaders in developing agile executive teams and leadership cultures, creating breakthrough business and operational strategies, rapidly redesigning business processes, and developing cadres of high-potential leaders. He speaks about leadership agility and has more than

30 years experience working with companies based in the United States, Canada, and Europe as an organizational change consultant, executive meeting designer and facilitator, and leadership coach. In partnership with Cambria Consulting, he designed the Leadership Agility 360, an online tool that assesses a manager's stage of leadership development. He holds a doctorate in organization development from Harvard University, as well as a master's in business administration.

Laura A. King, PhD, received her doctorate in personality psychology from the University of California, Davis in 1991. She began her career at Southern Methodist University, moving to the University of Missouri in 2001, where she is now a professor. Her research has focused on topics relevant to the question of what it is that makes a life a good one. She's published more than 70 articles and chapters, as well as two introductory psychology textbooks. A former associate editor of *Personality and Social Psychology Bulletin* and the *Journal of Personality and Social Psychology,* and section editor for *Social and Personality Psychology Compass*, she served as editor-in-chief of the *Journal of Research in Personality* and is currently editor of the *Journal of Personality and Social Psychology: Personality and Individual Differences.*

Tobias Krettenauer, PhD, is associate professor at the Department of Psychology of Wilfrid Laurier University, Waterloo (Canada). He earned his degrees in psychology at the Berlin Free University and Humboldt University (Germany). His research focuses on the interplay of cognitive, emotional, and personality development as it is related to matters of moral conduct and moral consciousness.

Stanley Krippner, PhD, is Alan Watts Professor of Psychology at Saybrook Graduate University and Research Center in San Francisco, California. He is co-editor of *The Psychological Impact of War Trauma on Civilians: An International Perspective* (Praeger, 2003), and is a recipient of both the Ashley Montagu Peace Award and the American Psychological Association's Award for Distinguished Contributions to International Psychology. He is co-author of *Haunted by Combat: Understanding PTSD in War Veterans* (Praeger Security International, 2007), and is a Fellow of the American Psychological Association, the Society for the Scientific Study of Religion, and the Society for the Scientific Study of Sexuality.

Paul W. Marko, PhD has been engaged for many years as an organizational development psychologist specializing in executive coaching and personal development. With a background in art, education, management, and humanist/transpersonal psychology he has worked in all levels of education and for many large corporations throughout the world. He has performed teaching assignments at St. Petersburg College where he taught humanities, art history, and design, as well as with Allan Combs at the California Institute of Integral Studies teaching a course focused on art and its interplay with evolving consciousness.

Heidi Page, PhD is a licensed clinical psychologist. She presently works with maximum-security inmates at a California state prison. Her principle clinical interest is in the field of trauma with a specific focus on how Mindfulness meditation along with somatic interventions effect measurable changes in neurophysiology. Dr. Page has spent extended periods of time in India at the ashram of her teacher, Mata Amritanandamayi Ma. She specializes in the overlap between psychology and spirituality and has a continuing interest in the connections between ego development and spiritual awakening.

Angela H. Pfaffenberger, PhD, is a personality psychologist with an interest in humanistic psychology and critical theory. Her professional activities focus on how adults progress to optimal outcomes over the life course. Dr. Pfaffenberger has previously presented her research at annual conventions of the American Psychological Association in 2004, 2005, and 2007 and also published repeatedly in the *Journal of Humanistic Psychology*. She currently serves as a part-time faculty member at the Oregon College of Oriental Medicine and maintains a private practice as an acupuncturist and psychotherapist.

Judith Stevens-Long, PhD is currently a professor and coordinator of the Certificate in Integral Studies at Fielding Graduate University. She is author of the textbook *Adult Life* and has published numerous journal articles and recent chapters in *Handbook of Adult Development and Learning* and *Handbook of Online Learning* as well as *Handbook of Adult Development*. She serves as associate editor for the *Journal of Adult Development* and the *Integral Review*. Her current research explores the potential of graduate education for the support of advanced stages of development including the growth of wisdom.

William R. Torbert, PhD, received a BA, *magna cum laude*, in political science and economics and a PhD in administrative sciences from Yale University, holding a Danforth Graduate Fellowship during his graduate years. He founded the Yale Upward Bound (War on Poverty) program and the Theatre of Inquiry, and taught at Yale, Southern Methodist University, and Harvard prior to joining the Boston College faculty in 1978. There he served as graduate dean and director of the PhD Program in Organizational Transformation, retiring in 2008. Author and enactor of the Developmental Action Inquiry approach to leadership and to social science, he has published many books and articles, including *The Power of Balance: Transforming Self, Society and Scientific Inquiry* (1991) and *Action Inquiry: The Secret of Timely, Transforming Leadership* (2004). Currently, he partners with Harthill Consulting UK and Context Management Consulting CA and also serves on the Board of Trillium Asset Management.

Frederick Travis, PhD received his master's and PhD degrees in psychology with a specialization in psychophysiology from MUM in 1988. He had a 2-year postdoctoral position at University of California, Davis exploring brain changes during sleep. At the conclusion of his postdoctoral position in 1990, he returned to MUM to direct research at the Center for Brain, Consciousness and Cognition. Since 1990, he has authored 47 papers and conference presentations that investigate the relation between brain patterns, states of consciousness, and meditation practice. His recent work reports brain patterns and subjective experiences of individuals reporting the experience of enlightenment. He regularly teaches undergraduate and graduate courses, gives seminars, and speaks on brain development in children and across the life span.

Index